Collins

LAKELAND
FELLRANGER

CENTRAL FELLS

MARK RICHARDS

LAKELAND FELLRANGER IS DEDICATED TO
MY FAMILY
Helen, Alison & Daniel
the Fells welcome every generation

First published in 2003 by

HarperCollins*Publishers* Ltd
77-85 Fulham Palace Road
London W6 8JB

Everything clicks at **www.collins.co.uk**

Collins is a registered trademark of
HarperCollins*Publishers* Ltd

Text and photographs © Mark Richards 2003

10 9 8 7 6 5 4 3 2
08 07 06 05 04

A catalogue record for this book is available from the
British Library

ISBN 0 00 711365 X

Reproduction by Colourscan, Singapore
Printed and bound in Great Britain by Scotprint

CONTENTS

Key to maps and diagrams   GRID NORTH IS TOP OF EVERY MAP

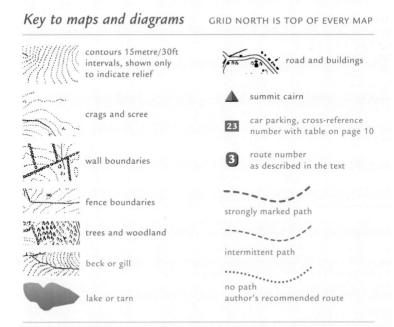

contours 15metre/30ft intervals, shown only to indicate relief

crags and scree

wall boundaries

fence boundaries

trees and woodland

beck or gill

lake or tarn

road and buildings

▲ summit cairn

23 car parking, cross-reference number with table on page 10

3 route number as described in the text

strongly marked path

intermittent path

no path
author's recommended route

The hand-drawn maps and diagrams in this guide are based upon
HARVEY SUPERWALKER: LAKELAND CENTRAL

LAKELAND FELLRANGER

Eight title divisions of the English Lake District

A personal passion

My earliest memories of Lakeland came through studying artistic essays and books of the picturesque that my mother had acquired. They portrayed the romance of a majestic landscape that had formed the backdrop to her youth. Born in north Lancashire she naturally knew of Lakeland as a special place, though she had little opportunity to visit.

At a similar time, through the tales of Black Bob, the Dandy wonder dog, comic strip stories of a shepherd's adventures on the hills about Selkirk, I gained a love of both pen & ink drawing and the hills of the Scottish Borders. All distantly set in a romantic land of my own very youthful dreams, for I was born in rural west Oxfordshire and the magic that my mother clung to was becoming increasingly real to me.

Holidays were always allied to my parents roots. My father's Cornish ancestry gave me early seaside trips to that wonderful coastline and, as my teenage years unfolded, a regular busman's holiday to a fell farm on Lord Shuttleworth's Leck Hall estate gave me the hands-on feel and flavour of rough fell country. My first fragmentary taste of what Lakeland itself was all about came, when I was twelve years old, on a day-trip to Ambleside and Great Langdale, when I remember purchasing The Southern Fells, Book Four of Alfred Wainwright's 'A Pictorial Guide to the Lakeland Fells'. That book was periodically perused as my formative life as a young farmer kept my attention firmly on the needs of a 150-acre farm of cattle and corn. Socially I revelled in the activities of the Young Farmers' movement. I remember an exchange with the Alnwick club gave me a chance to climb The Cheviot in smooth-soled leather shoes, my first real fell climb. After master-minding two ploughing marathons, 100, then 200 acres turned from stubble to tilth in 24 hours, in my early twenties I sought new adventures. I joined the Gloucestershire Mountaineering Club and got to grips with Snowdonia, Scotland and yes, at long last, the Lakeland Fells. Rock climbing and long days in all weathers ridge walking put me in touch with the thrill of high places.

That first Wainwright guide focused my mind on a love of wild places, Lakeland in particular. Quickly I now acquired the remainder of the series and feeling far removed from the beauty of it all, I took to drawing from my own black & white photographs, mimicking AW. Within a year of joining the Mountaineering Club I had become a firm friend of the legend himself, spending regular weekends at Kendal Green joining him on his original exploration of the Coast to Coast Walk, The Outlying Fells *(see page 228 for my one moment of recognition)*, Westmorland Heritage and supplying numerous photographs of Scottish mountains he was unable to reach, for his Scottish Mountain Drawings series. As my walking progressed and his faltered, so my trips to Kendal became fewer. Marriage, a family and farming brought responsibilities so time constraints deflected my attention from AW and the Lakeland I loved.

I remained in farming until almost forty, during which time I had several walking guides published. AW nurtured my first title, a very pictorial map-guide to The Cotswold Way back in 1973. This was followed by guides to the North Cornwall Coast, Offa's Dyke Path, a three-part exploration of the Peak District National Park and Hadrian's Wall. Many small guides and articles later, including a happy sequence of *Out of the Way* pieces for The Countryman, a journal I had known from childhood being published on my doorstep. All along gnawing at the back of my mind was the sense that someday I should prepare my own complete survey of the Lakeland Fells. Having edited a little magazine, *Walking Wales*, for one year, I found I could ignore it no longer and, with the support and encouragement of *HarperCollins*, to whom I will be forever grateful, I moved to Cumbria to begin Lakeland Fellranger.

From fireside to fellside

This land of living dreams we call The Lakes is a cherished blessing to know, love and share. Each and every day we lead our normal lives far removed, we may take a fleeting moment to reflect that someone, some-where, will be tramping up a lonely gill or along an airy ridge, peering from a lofty summit or gazing across a wind-blown tarn taking lingering inspiration from the timeless beauty. The trappings of modern life thrust carpet and concrete under our feet, so how wonderful it is to be restored to the sheep trods and rough trails, to imprint again the fells upon our soles. This guide sets out to give you that impetus and resolve to make time in your life to reclaim the fells.

The regular paths of long tradition deserve consideration. Progressively many super-highways are being re-set with cobbles and pitching, all highly meritorious. But it has to be said in many instances the best consideration we can give them is rest. As lines of desire they came into being, perhaps with the wisdom of our age the green trail-blazer would always desire to tread light on the land by finding new off-beat ways. Hence the underlying message in this guide, to increase sustainability by showing a diversity of route options climbing each and every fell.

The liberty of the Central Fells can be expressed in another way, the chance to leave the car some distance from your walk by using either the

555 'Lakeslink' service Windermere to Keswick via Ambleside and Grasmere, or 79 the 'Borrowdale Rambler' from Keswick to Seatoller. Both of these Stagecoach bus services are as regular as clockwork, run all year round and give genuine flexibility to your walk plans.

For many the Central Fells do not exist. All and sundry know of the Langdale Pikes, in the mind's eye belonging exclusively to Great Langdale; of Loughrigg Fell, Silver How and Helm Crag compatriot heights about Grasmere; the escarpment of Walla Crag above Derwentwater; the exquisite setting of Watendlath and, threading through the Jaws of Borrowdale, Eagle Crag above Stonethwaite. Yet somehow the relationship of these separate parts fails to register as a coherent whole, for all they are wonderful subjects for a day's walk. Perhaps it is because the range is generally of a lower elevation, with few narrow ridges and has no incisive roads that marvelling eyes are averted. But the range does harbour swathes of heather, where the 'go-back, go-back' call of grouse can be heard, solitudinous dales such as Wythburn, Greenburn and Shoulthwaite and to cap it all, superlative view-points at many levels from Loughrigg Terrace to High Raise.

This guide

Each route is identified by a red number which links the diagrams and maps to the adjacent text. The routes themselves recognised in three forms (see preceding key): bold dashes for the principal trails; thin dashes for lesser paths liable to be intermittent or the old green tracks of shepherds' past, and lastly, dots, where there is no path on the ground and represents nothing more than the author's recommended route. Representation of a route, in whatever form, does not infer safe passage for all, at any time, the onus is on each individual to weigh up their own capabilities and the prevailing conditions. In fellwalking, as any mountain travel, retreat is often the greater valour. The author has taken care to follow time honoured routes, and kept within bounds of access, yet cannot attest a right of way.

No two walkers follow the same tread, neither do they explore with the same plot, so what is revealed in this guide is a very personal expression of the potential route structure. Nonetheless, it is fundamentally reliable and for fellwalkers who love to explore, a rich source of entertaining route planning ideas. A good guide should also be a revelation. Hence for each fell summit or better nearby viewpoint, a full panorama is given, which alone should encourage readers to carry the tome to the top!

The guide may be formally structured to cover important matters such as the nature of the summit, safe lines of descent and the linking ridge routes, sprinkled with a few items of interpretation, but underlying it all is a desire to share the pleasure of exploration which is open to each one of us. Let us continue to love Lakeland and care for its future. May its magic remain an inspiration for each new generation.

8

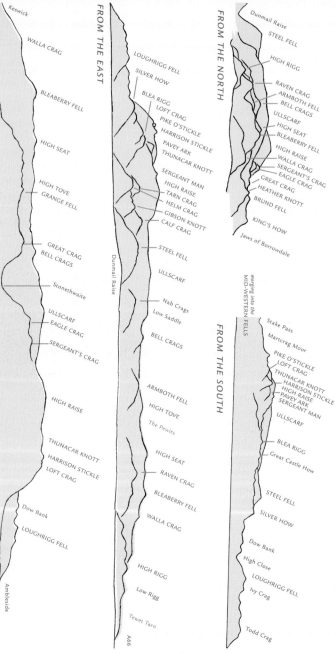

THE CENTRAL FELLS - *four graphic projections of the range*

FROM THE WEST

Keswick
WALLA CRAG
BLEABERRY FELL
HIGH SEAT
HIGH TOVE
GRANGE FELL
GREAT CRAG
BELL CRAGS
Stonethwaite
ULLSCARF
EAGLE CRAG
SERGEANT'S CRAG
HIGH RAISE
THUNACAR KNOTT
HARRISON STICKLE
LOFT CRAG
Dow Bank
LOUGHRIGG FELL
Ambleside

FROM THE EAST

LOUGHRIGG FELL
SILVER HOW
BLEA RIGG
LOFT CRAG
PIKE O'STICKLE
HARRISON STICKLE
PAVEY ARK
THUNACAR KNOTT
SERGEANT MAN
HIGH RAISE
TARN CRAG
HELM CRAG
GIBSON KNOTT
CALF CRAG
STEEL FELL
ULLSCARF
Nab Crags
Low Saddle
BELL CRAGS
ARMBOTH FELL
HIGH TOVE
The Pewits
HIGH SEAT
RAVEN CRAG
BLEABERRY FELL
WALLA CRAG
HIGH RIGG
Low Rigg
Tewet Tarn
A66
Dunmail Raise

FROM THE NORTH

Dunmail Raise
STEEL FELL
HIGH RIGG
RAVEN CRAG
ARMBOTH FELL
BELL CRAGS
ULLSCARF
HIGH SEAT
BLEABERRY FELL
HIGH RAISE
WALLA CRAG
SERGEANT'S CRAG
EAGLE CRAG
GREAT CRAG
HEATHER KNOTT
BRUND FELL
KING'S HOW
Jaws of Borrowdale

FROM THE SOUTH

merging into the
MID-WESTERN FELLS
Stake Pass
Martcrag Moor
PIKE O'STICKLE
LOFT CRAG
THUNACAR KNOTT
HARRISON STICKLE
HIGH RAISE
PAVEY ARK
SERGEANT MAN
ULLSCARF
BLEA RIGG
Great Castle How
STEEL FELL
SILVER HOW
Dow Bank
High Close
LOUGHRIGG FELL
Ivy Crag
Todd Crag

FELL MOSAIC

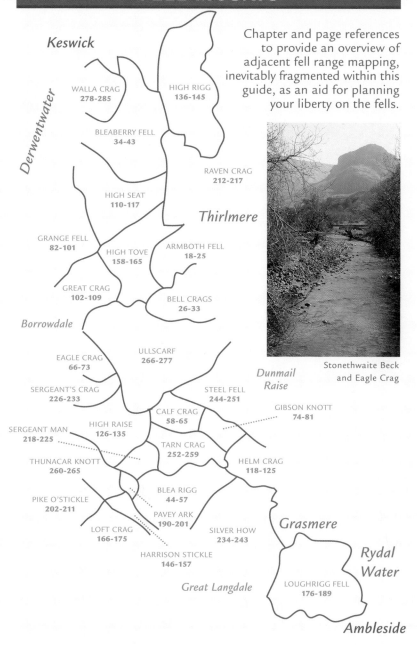

Keswick

Derwentwater

WALLA CRAG
278-285

HIGH RIGG
136-145

BLEABERRY FELL
34-43

Chapter and page references to provide an overview of adjacent fell range mapping, inevitably fragmented within this guide, as an aid for planning your liberty on the fells.

RAVEN CRAG
212-217

HIGH SEAT
110-117

Thirlmere

GRANGE FELL
82-101

HIGH TOVE
158-165

ARMBOTH FELL
18-25

GREAT CRAG
102-109

BELL CRAGS
26-33

Borrowdale

ULLSCARF
266-277

EAGLE CRAG
66-73

*Dunmail
Raise*

Stonethwaite Beck
and Eagle Crag

SERGEANT'S CRAG
226-233

STEEL FELL
244-251

GIBSON KNOTT
74-81

CALF CRAG
58-65

SERGEANT MAN
218-225

HIGH RAISE
126-135

TARN CRAG
252-259

HELM CRAG
118-125

THUNACAR KNOTT
260-265

PIKE O'STICKLE
202-211

BLEA RIGG
44-57

PAVEY ARK
190-201

Grasmere

LOFT CRAG
166-175

SILVER HOW
234-243

*Rydal
Water*

HARRISON STICKLE
146-157

Great Langdale

LOUGHRIGG FELL
176-189

Ambleside

STARTING POINTS

	LOCATION	GRID REFERENCE	PARKING	BUS STOP
1	Stonethwaite	261 139		*
2	Rosthwaite (NT)	257 149	P	*
3	Quayfoot (NT)	254 168	P	*
4	Leathes lay-by	256 177		*
5	Watendlath (NT)	276 163	P	
6	Surprise View	268 189	P	
7	Ashness Bridge	269 196	P	
8	Kettlewell (NT)	267 194	P	*
9	Great Wood (NT)	272 214	P	*
10	Keswick, Lake Road	265 229	P	*
11	Tewet Tarn verge	306 238		
12	St John's-in-the-Vale Church	306 225		
13	Causeyway Foot	293 219	P	
14	Rough How Bridge	300 205	P	*
15	Legburthwaite (NWW)	318 195	P	*
16	Thirlmere Dam (NWW)	306 189	P	
17	Armboth (NWW)	305 172	P	
18	Dob Gill (NWW)	316 142	P	
19	Steel End (NWW)	321 130	P	
20	Dunmail Raise lay-by	329 111		*
21	Mill Bridge	396 092	P	*
22	Grasmere			
	Redbank Road (NP Info. Centre)	335 073	P	*
	Broadgate	338 078	P	*
	Stock Lane	339 073	P	*
	Easedale Road	335 080	P	*
23	White Moss (NT)	350 065	P	*
24	Pelter Bridge, Rydal	336 059	P	*
25	Rydal Road, Ambleside	375 047	P	*
26	Little Loughrigg	345 039	P	
27	Elterwater (NT)	329 052	P	*
28	High Close	337 053	P	
29	Langdale (NP)	295 063	P	*
	Stickle Ghyll (NT)	294 063	P	*
30	Old Dungeon Ghyll (NT)	286 062	P	*

P - formal car parking facilities (some with coin meters)
otherwise informal, limited lay-by parking
* - serviced bus stop close by

Public transport may be a problem elsewhere but here in the heart of Lakeland one may confidently plan a day around a reliable rural service, given a proper study of timetables. The Mountain Goat service is supplemented by regular Stagecoach services throughout the district. Pertinent to this guide the Lakeslink 555 service runs along the A591, from Windermere via Ambleside and Grasmere crossing Dunmail Raise bound for Keswick. Passengers on this service have the benefit of the new 'From A to B to SEE' journey guide - a further creation of the author. For Borrowdale buses leave the Keswick bus terminus (situated beside the Lakes Foodstore): hop aboard either the Honister Rambler 77/77A, a circular service which heads down the shore of Derwentwater bound for Rosthwaite and Seatoller, before crossing the Honister Pass to Buttermere and Lorton, there switching back over the Whinlatter Pass. More specific is the Borrowdale Rambler 79, a shuttle service to Seatoller. The National Trust operate the Watendlath Wanderer from Keswick on summer sundays only. From Ambleside use the Langdale Rambler 526 for Elterwater, Chapel Stile and the Old Dungeon Ghyll Hotel.

For current advice contact : TRAVELINE public transport info 0870 608 2 608

THE CENTRAL FELLS

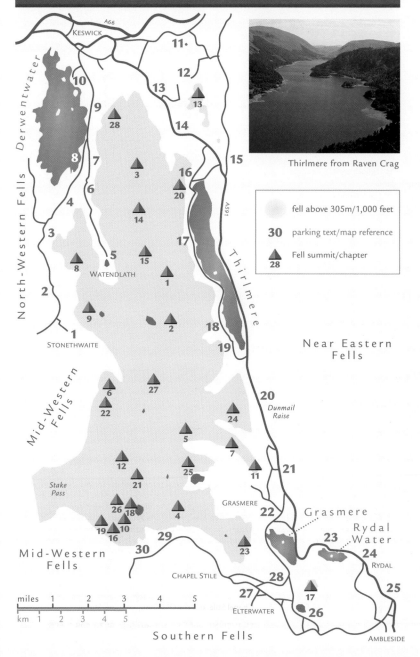

Thirlmere from Raven Crag

fell above 305m/1,000 feet

30 parking text/map reference

▲
28 Fell summit/chapter

A66

KESWICK

Derwentwater

North-Western Fells

Mid-Western Fells

Stake Pass

Mid-Western Fells

WATENDLATH

STONETHWAITE

Thirlmere

A591

Near Eastern Fells

Dunmail Raise

GRASMERE

Grasmere

Rydal Water

RYDAL

CHAPEL STILE

ELTERWATER

Southern Fells

AMBLESIDE

miles 1 2 3 4 5

km 1 2 3 4 5

READER RECKONER *for route planning*

start & route	text reference nos.	ascent *(feet)*	distance *(miles)*
1 Armboth Fell 18-25			
17 ARMBOTH			
via Fisher Gill or Crag	1|2	940	2.0
18 DOB GILL			
via Stone Hause	3	940	2.6
Fisher Crag circuit	4	940	6.0
Launchy Ghyll Trail	5	940	0.3
2 Bell Crags 26-33			
18 DOB GILL			
via Harrop Tarn	1|2|3|4|5	1,960	2.0
via Stone Hause	5|6|7|8	1,960	1.8
9 WATENDLATH			
via Blea Tarn	9	950	2.6
via High Tove	10	990	2.8
3 Bleaberry Fell 34-43			
10 KESWICK			
via Brockle Beck	1	1,680	3.6
9 GREAT WOOD			
via Cat Gill	2	1,670	1.8
7 ASHNESS BRIDGE			
via Falcon Crag	3	1,410	2.0
14 ROUGH HOW BRIDGE			
via Dodd Crag	4|5|6	1,460	1.9
Direct	5|7	1,400	1.5
via Goat Crag	5|8	1,430	1.7
3 Blea Rigg 45-57			
22 GRASMERE			
via Blindtarn Moss	1	1,630	2.7
via Easedale Tarn	2	1,610	3.0
via Belles Knott	3	1,640	4.0
29 NEW DUNGEON GHYLL			
via Stickle Ghyll	4|5	1,550	2.0
via Whitecrag Gill	6	1,530	1.2
via Pye How	7	1,570	2.0
4 Calf Crag 58-65			
21 MILL BRIDGE			
via Greenburn Dale	1	1,450	2.3
via Gibson Knott	2	1,600	2.6
22 GRASMERE			
via Far Easedale	3	1,500	3.6

19 STEEL END

via Wythburn Dale	4	1,250	3.4

6 Eagle Crag 66-73

1 STONETHWAITE

Direct	1	1,400	1.9
via Greenup Gill	2	1,450	2.6

7 Gibson Knott 74-81

21 MILL BRIDGE

via Bracken Hause	1	1,100	1.1
via Greenburn Dale (*mid*)	2	1,150	1.6
via Greenburn Dale (*higher*)	2	1,200	2.0

8 Grange Fell 82-101

3|4 GRANGE-IN-BORROWDALE

via King's How (*north*)	1|2|4	1,200	1.4
via Black Crag & Heather Knott	3	1,150	1.0
via Bowder Stone	4|5	1,280	1.5
via King's How (*south*)	6	1,180	1.2
Direct	7	1,100	1.0

2 ROSTHWAITE

via Puddingstone Bank	8	1,150	1.2

5 WATENDLATH

via Puddingstone Bank	9	510	0.9
Direct	10	510	0.7
via Heather Knott	11	620	1.6

6 SURPRISE VIEW

via Hog's Earth	12|14	620	2.0

8 KETTLEWELL

via High Lodore	13|14	1,200	2.3
via Gowder Crag	14|15|16	1,200	2.3
via Hog's Earth	14|15|17	1,200	2.4

9 Great Crag 102-109

1 STONETHWAITE

via Lingy End	1	1,160	1.2

2 ROSTHWAITE

via Puddingstone Bank	2	1,170	1.8

5 WATENDLATH

Direct	3	640	1.3
via Green Comb	4	750	1.9

10 Harrison Stickle 110-117

29 NEW DUNGEON GHYLL

via Stickle Ghyll	1	2,100	1.4
via Pike How	2	2,100	1.4
via Dungeon Ghyll	3	2,100	1.5

11 Helm Crag 118-125

29 GRASMERE

Direct	1	1,120	1.6
via Bracken Hause	2	1,120	2.3

21 MILL BRIDGE

via Bracken Hause	3	1,040	0.8

12 High Raise 126-135

1 STONETHWAITE

via Greenup Edge	1	2,200	4.0
via Eagle Crag	2	2,250	3.8
via Langstrath	3	2,200	4.7

22 GRASMERE

via Sergeant Man	4	2,200	3.9
via Far Easedale	5	2,200	4.0

19 STEEL END

via Wythburn Dale	6	1,850	4.0

29 NEW DUNGEON GHYLL

via Pike How & Thunacar Knott	7	2,200	2.4
via Stickle Ghyll	8|10	2,200	2.4
via Pavey Ark	8|11	2,200	2.5
via Bright Beck	8|12	2,200	2.5
via Sergeant Man	8|13|14	2,250	2.6
via Whitecrag Gill	9	2,250	2.6

13 High Rigg 136-145

11 TEWET TARN

via Tewet Tarn	1|2	700	1.5

12 ST JOHN'S CHURCH

Direct	2|3	440	0.2

15 LEGBURTHWAITE

Ridge walk	5|6	750	1.7
Dale walk Shoulthwaite & Naddle	7		3.0
Dale walk St John's Vale	8		2.7

14 High Seat 146-157

14/15 DALE BOTTOM/ROUGH HOW BRIDGE

via Mere Gill	1|2|3	1,500	2.1
via Shoulthwaite Gill	2|4	1,500	2.3

7 ASHNESS BRIDGE

Direct	5|6	1,450	2.0

6 SURPRISE VIEW

via Reecastle Crag	7	1,150	2.3

5 WATENDLATH

via High Tove	8	1,200	2.4

15 High Tove 158-165

17 ARMBOTH

Direct	1	1,150	0.9
via Middlesteads Gill	2	1,150	1.1

5 WATENDLATH

Direct	3	870	0.9

16 Loft Crag 166-175

29 NEW DUNGEON GHYLL

via Mark Gate	1	1,970	1.5
via Dungeon Ghyll	2	1,970	1.5

30 OLD DUNGEON GHYLL

via Gimmer Crag	3	1,970	1.3

17 Loughrigg Fell 176-189

25 AMBLESIDE

Direct	1	890	2.0
via Todd Crag	2	900	2.3

26 TARN FOOT

via Ivy Crag	3|4	770	1.3

24 PELTER BRIDGE

via Fox Ghyll	5	890	2.0
via Lanty Scar	6	900	2.0
via Loughrigg Cavern	7|8	900	2.2

23 WHITE MOSS

via Loughrigg Terrace	9|10	900	1.3

22 GRASMERE

via Redbank Road	10	900	1.5

26 HIGH CLOSE

via the west ridge	11	570	0.4
via Intake Wood	12	570	0.6

18 Pavey Ark 190-201

29 NEW DUNGEON GHYLL

via Pike How	1|6	2,000	1.6
via Stickle Ghyll	2|6|7|8	1,990	1.4
via Stickle Ghyll *variants*	3|4|5|7	1,900	1.5

19 Pike o'Stickle 202-211

30 OLD DUNGEON GHYLL

via Troughton Beck	1	2,150	3.2
via Stake Pass	2	2,200	4.2

20 Raven Crag 212-217

16 THIRLMERE DAM

Direct	1	1,000	0.3

17 ARMBOTH

via Middlesteads Gill	2|3	1,050	1.9

15 ROUGH HOW BRIDGE

Direct	4|3	1,100	1.3
Circular	5	1,100	5.0

21 Sergeant Man 218-225

29 NEW DUNGEON GHYLL

via Stickle Ghyll	1	2,150	2.5
via Blea Rigg	2	2,200	2.7
via Whitecrag Gill	3	2,200	2.8

22 GRASMERE

via Easedale Tarn	4	2,250	3.5
via Far Easedale	5	2,250	3.7

22 Sergeant's Crag 226-233

1 STONETHWAITE

via Eagle Crag	1|2	1,580	2.1
via Greenup Gill	1|3	1,570	2.5
via Langstrath	4|5	1,570	3.3

23 Silver How 234-243

28 ELTERWATER

via Pye How	1	1,000	1.2
via Copt How & Megs' Gill	2|3|4	1,000	1.2
via Dow Bank	5|6|7	990	1.1

22 GRASMERE

via Wreay Gill	8	1,090	1.1
via Blindtarn Moss	9	1,190	1.3
via Kelbarrow & Dow Bank	10|11|12|13|14	1,000	1.3

24 Steel Fell 244-251

21 MILL BRIDGE

Direct	1	1,560	1.5

20 DUNMAIL RAISE

via Cotra	2	1,050	1.8
Direct	3	1,000	0.5

19 STEEL END

Direct	4	1,230	1.0
via Rake Crags	5	1,250	1.3
via Wythburn Dale	6	1,280	2.2

25 Tarn Crag 252-259

22 GRASMERE

via Easedale Tarn	1|2	1,400	2.1
via Codale Tarn	3	1,450	2.7
via Stythwaite Steps	4	1,400	2.2
via Deer Bields Crag	5	1,400	2.4

26 Thunacar Knott 260-265

29 NEW DUNGEON GHYLL

via Pike How	**1**	2,140	**1.6**
via Stickle Ghyll	**2**	2,140	**1.6**
1 STONETHWAITE			
via Stake Pass	**1**	2,050	**5.2**

27 Ullscarf 266-277

1 STONETHWAITE			
via Greenhow Gill	**1|2**	2,060	**3.0**
via Lining Crag	**1|3**	2,060	**3.2**
via Lingy End	**4**	2,080	**3.0**
5 WATENDLATH			
via Blea Tarn	**5**	1,540	**3.2**
18 DOB GILL			
via Harrop Tarn	**6|7**	1,800	**2.3**
via Tarn Crag *& variants*	**8|9|10**	1,800	**2.5**
19 STEEL END			
via Wythburn Dale	**12**	1,850	**4.6**

28 Walla Crag 278-285

10 KESWICK			
via Springs Wood	**1**	990	**2.0**
via Friar's Crag approach	**2**	990	**1.9**
9 GREAT WOOD			
via Cat Gill	**3**	980	**0.6**
undercliff path & forest tracks	**4|5**	980	**0.7**
7 ASHNESS BRIDGE			
via Falcon Crag	**6**	530	**1.0**

Hog hole, foxgloves and the omni-present bracken in an outgang lane above Grasmere

ARMBOTH FELL

Fells do not get more pudding-like. Indeed, to add to the analogy, and indignity, Armboth is a squidgy, squodgy fell that looks as if some local monster has set his considerable ungainly posterior down precisely on top – by neat co-incidence Thirlmere actually translates as 'lake of the giant'. Thankfully there are a few outcrops to interrupt from its otherwise nondescript demeanour. Summit-baggers are the more likely visitors to this outpost, its only other claim may be that it is the most centrally placed in the district. Evidence of Celtic rock art has been spotted on rocks west of the summit, but my own searches have been in vain. You are never far from water when strolling about this moor, the ageing heather has a hard time keeping its feet dry and the same may be said of any fell-walker timorous enough to venture anywhere near the peaty sphagnum-encroached hollow where Launchy and Fisher Gills have a common sluggish birth. The stretch of plateau to the south has a small erratic which may be inspected while surveying the shapely profile of Bell Crags to the south. You may be lucky enough to spot the small herd of shy red deer that roam this quiet area. Fisher Crag, the best viewpoint and most characterful feature on the fell is not strictly accessible. Overlooking Thirlmere, Fisher Crag rivals Raven Crag as a brink from which to survey the great fell wall of the Helvellyn range and the more distant Blencathra. As a picturesque subject it must have featured in many a casual photograph taken from Station Coppice car park, across the dark waters of the reservoir.

479 metres   1,572 feet

one kilometre   *one mile*

The
Pewits

17 Armboth
car park

*old summer
house*

folds

Cockrigg
Crags

path to <
WATENDLATH

HIGH TOVE

Thirlmere

Fisher
Crag

Deergarth
How

*raptor
trap*

Wood
Bank

Launchy Ghyll
Nature Trail

Middle
Crags

erratic

Hawes
How

Thackmell
Crags

Hawes
Point

Rough
Crag

Shivery
Man

4

Launchy Gill

Launchy
Tarn

*erratic
& cairn*

Brown
Rigg

folds   *folds*

bridle-path to <
WATENDLATH

Stone
Hause

BELL CRAGS

18 Dobgill
car park

Summer traffic
along the scenic
western shore road
can be completely
ignored by
walkers who may
follow the lovely
······ winding trail
along the
wooded shore
between
Armboth,
Dob Gill and
Steel End car
parks.

ASCENT *from Armboth*

Two options begin from the NWW car park (toilets) situated one mile
south of the dam on the road running down the western shore of
Thirlmere.

1 Facing out from the point of entry, go right and first left at the
kissing-gate, to the start of the fell path destined for Watendlath, which
traverses the intervening ridge via High Tove. A clear path crosses a stout
little bridge spanning Middlesteads Gill. Passing through a wall gap, and
the hurdles in a wooden sheep pen, ascend by a group of large rocks on
a partly repaired and stepped path rising beside the forestry fence
shielding Fisher Gill. The path switches right and enjoys a fine view across
the reservoir to the Helvellyn range. Passing under a sycamore and
skirting juniper, climb to a wall gap beside the plantation fence. Keep to
the footpath for a matter of 200 yards, then fork half-left just after enter-

Armboth Fell may be plain, but to paraphrase Robert Burns... a fell is a fell for all that!

BELL CRAGS

3

Middle Crag

Fisher Crag

here be bogs!

18

5

2

Fisher Gill

cross ridge path to Watendlath *via* HIGH TOVE

1

Launchy Ghyll Forest Trail

Thirlmere

The water tone in this graphic, to be authentic, should reflect the sombre dark-grey hue the conifers confer!

17

Middlesteads Gill

EASTERN APPROACHES

ing bracken, on a strong sheep trod, to ford a feeder gill. Accompany the right-hand rim of the shallow upper ravine of Fisher Gill, shaded by birch and rowan. As the gill winds on with ever decreasing gradient, aim half-left through sickly-looking heather towards the prominent outcropping and if you are lucky you might find the one path which leads to that very evident summit outcrop. Only the latter stages of the route can be said to be free of excitement, that is unless you set yourself the challenge of finding the rock art!

2 Go left along the reservoir's west shore road to the forestry parking area and gate/stile entry right, just before the road crossing of Fisher Gill. A forest track winds uphill crossing Fisher Gill. Note, to the left, the old Armboth Hall summer-house perched among the trees on a knoll – finding contemporary use as a lunch shelter by forest workers. The track continues more steeply, drifting away from the gill at a left-hand bend with young plantation fencing right. Climb to a ladder-stile with a stone sheepfold and bothy ruin close at hand. The path wends up beside the old wall and fence to crest the moor. Carefully cross the locked gate in the fence and climb (no path) onto the immediate top of Fisher Crag, a cairn nestles among the heather. Is its view an improvement on Raven Crag?

Fisher Crag from Middlesteads Gill

Raptor trap near Fisher Crag

Well perhaps not, its mildly 'illicit' nature does add something! Return to the gate and head basically south-westward, initially over marshy ground to work a way up the rocky fell to the summit.

ASCENT *from Dob Gill*

3 The NWW Dob Gill car park (*toilets*) situated 3 miles south of the dam. Exit and follow the road left (north) to where a path commences at a stile left, leading through a wall gateway and up the northern edge of the plantation, passing a curious empty metal tree cage, to reach the open track as it exits the forestry. Go right, then quickly left, to a hand-gate in the wall corner. An old shepherds' path winds steeply up the bracken-dogged fellside, as eventually the ground eases on Brown Rigg pass a couple of old folds tucked into outcrop nooks. Deer management quad vehicles exit at the top forest gate and have provided a line to follow by Stone Hause, out across the bowl-shaped gathering grounds of Launchy Gill to a ford above Launchy Tarn, actually rather a shallow lazy meander. Beyond, the tracks are lost en route to cross the wire fence and climb the rough, though gently angled slope to the summit.

4 Fell-walkers with a wanderlust may make a swiping route that ignores the summit altogether. Having forded the upper course of Launchy Gill, amble downstream by Launchy Tarn and the old wall beside the cascaded section, find a fence stile at the resumption of the wall approaching the forest edge. Hereon follow the forest top wall gradually rising to Fisher Crag. Turn this excursion into a round trip using the lakeside road and include the Launchy Ghyll Trail. Should this circuit begin from the Armboth car park then the forest track below Brown Rigg will be found useful in reducing the extent of road walking.

The upper falls of Launchy Ghyll, aptly secretive and utterly luxuriant!

5 Launchy Ghyll Trail The best series of cataracts falling east into Thirlmere tumbles through the forestry issuing from the lonely wastes between Bell Crags and Armboth Fell, this is Launchy Ghyll. The gill-name contains the Old Norse word laun which means 'secret', while the use of the 'ghyll' spelling is a persistence of Victorian affectation, exclusive to the lower tourist accessible section.

Situated midway between the Armboth and Dob Gill car parks the way-marked forest trail gives a relaxing stroll for casual visitors climbing from lay-bys either side of the road bridge situated midway between the Armboth and Dob Gill car parks. At half-height a footbridge crosses the ravine. Above this point the gorge narrows and steepens, not surprisingly the secure trail smartly turns-tail switching back down to the road. As you may suspect the best of the falls lie out of sight higher up. From the top of the steps on the southern side, half-a-dozen steps intimate the beginning of an old unsecured path up through the conifers to two impromptu viewing points. The top fall is supremely elegant and luxuriant. There is no access to the open fell above, the forest-bounding fence is walker-tight!

The Summit

A slender rib of ice-worn rock, like the inverted hull of a boat, forms the summit. A small cairn precariously perched on the very top. The only evidence of visitation is a narrow trod approaching from the direction of Fisher Gill. Perhaps this lack of obvious human 'damage' is one of the fell's understated virtues. A damp plateau extends south, a solitary erratic acting as a target for otherwise aimless strolls. The southern slopes of the fell, approaching the wide hollow of Launchy Gill, are defined by a tight, fortunately barbless fence, erected in a bid to restrict red deer.

Safe Descent

The simplest course is north across a largely pathless moor. Fording Fisher Gill join the footpath, coming down from High Tove, this leads by the forest fence to the security of the Thirlmere shore road at Armboth. The nearest habitation being left, beyond the dam at Bridgend Farm (camp site) 1.5 miles and the nearest phone kiosk at Legburthwaite a further half-mile.

Ridge Routes to...

HIGH TOVE   DESCENT 150ft   ASCENT 250ft   0.8 mile

Beelines are fine for bees, here enhancing their honey with nectar from the heather, they don't have to set foot in the bogs and twist their delicate ankles in the rough moor grass. To minimise much binding in the marsh follow suit with the safe descent. Head north, descending to ford Fisher Gill and join the old footpath linking Armboth with Watendlath. The westward trending path is never very convincing and even has the temerity to almost 'dissolve' on the wet rise to the summit cairn on the skyline. However, this is far better than following the habits of crows or bees!

Peat hag at the birth-place of Fisher and Launchy Gills

BELL CRAGS   DESCENT 200ft   ASCENT 450ft   1 mile

No path from start to finish, but far sweeter than the spinal ridge trod beside the fence from High Tove to Bell Crags! Walk south to the lone erratic boulder, then descend with the shapely peak of Bell Crags ahead. Carefully cross the plain wire fence and ford Launchy Gill passing another solitary erratic boulder before mounting above the actual Bell Crags outcrop climbing past the large sheepfold to the peaked summit.

Erratic on the southern edge, looking to Bell Crags

PANORAMA

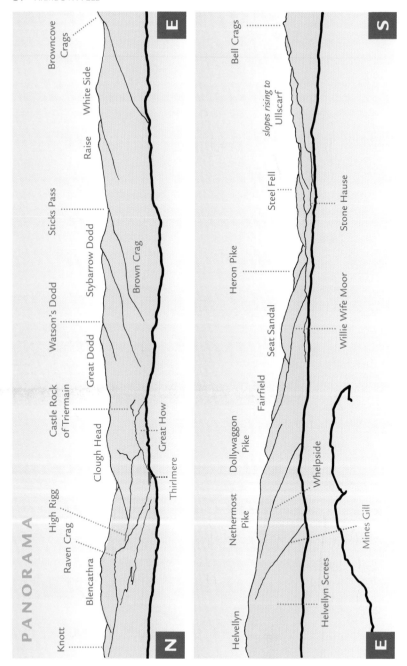

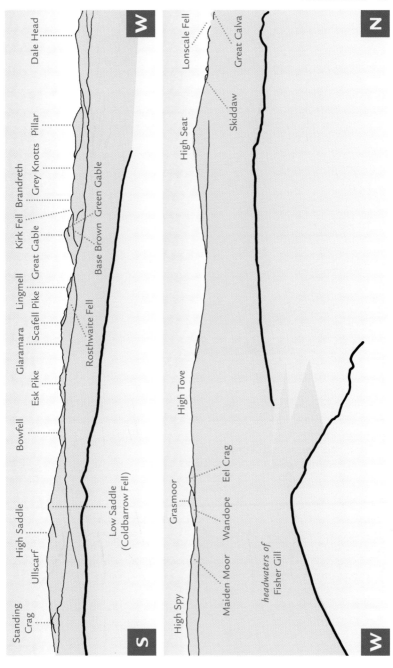

W

Dale Head
Pillar
Grey Knotts
Brandreth
Kirk Fell
Green Gable
Great Gable
Base Brown
Lingmell
Scafell Pike
Rosthwaite Fell
Glaramara
Esk Pike
Bowfell
High Saddle
Ullscarf
Standing Crag
Low Saddle (Coldbarrow Fell)

S

N

Lonscale Fell
Great Calva
Skiddaw
High Seat
High Tove
Eel Crag
Grasmoor
Wandope
Maiden Moor
High Spy
headwaters of Fisher Gill

W

BELL CRAGS

By curious convention Bell Crags is not recognised as a separate fell. Sandwiched between Launchy and Dob Gills, the wedge of rough country rising west from the shores of Thirlmere, initially as craggy afforestation but in fruition wonderfully wild fell, has been cold-shouldered by those who claim to know a fell when they see one.

There's no doubting the merits of Bleaberry Fell and High Seat, but as the ridge trends south towards Ullscarf, the grounds for separate fell status weakens. This low slung ridge has two recognised intermediate tops, High Tove and Armboth Fell, both beset with soggy peat and grouse crying 'go back, go back' as they frantically beat their wings in low flight across the rank, sickly-looking heather. Such fells are poor fish beside the far more striking height of Bell Crags. The fell stands smartly to attention above Launchy Gill, master of all it surveys, hardly a quality one can bestow upon its northern neighbours. The old bridle-path from Wythburn to Watendlath, via Harrop and Blea Tarns might be said to prove the point, effectively annexing the fell from the greater mass of Ullscarf. The fell top can be reached via the long tendril path acutely south-eastward from Watendlath, but more efficiently and scenically from the south-western shores of Thirlmere at Dob Gill.

558 metres   1,831 feet

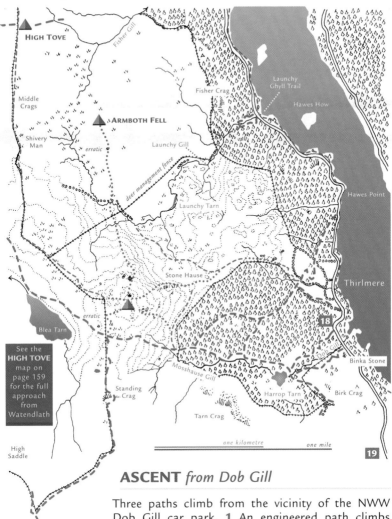

ASCENT *from Dob Gill*

Three paths climb from the vicinity of the NWW Dob Gill car park. **1** An engineered path climbs directly from the signboard winding up the mature forestry to the outflow of Harrop Tarn.

2 While the old bridle route begins from the road (modified start) on the south side of the beck, a signpost and hand-gate give access. Note the Binka Stone a distinctive ice-smoothed outcrop to the left - a 'bink' being a doorstep, alluding to its stepped appearance. Rise via a second hand-gate after 40 yards, the stony stair climbs through dense juniper to a ladder-stile crossing the tall deer fence. The path leads through the forest over a section of duckboards to the footbridge and

EASTERN APPROACHES

ford at the outflow of Harrop Tarn. The tarn forms an attractive scene surrounded by conifers, backed by craggy fellside, the north-eastern slopes of Ullscarf, it can shine like a jewel, though it is much diminished by encroaching marsh. **3** A somewhat circuitous route can be followed climbing the eastern slope through further juniper beyond the Binka Stone, to the cairn on top of Birk Crag, before descending north-west to this point via a deer gate.

4 The old bridle route follows the clear forest track by a small grove of beech. Crossing a footbridge at a shallow feeder gill, the track swings right but the path heads straight on to quickly link up with a further forest track. As this track bears right again a signpost indicates the bridle-path leading straight on up to a double deer door gate by an old fold. Exiting the forestry, the bridle-path winds purposefully on up the open slope to the broad damp depression. With Standing Crag the noble feature to the south and Blea Tarn in view westward. Do not go through the hand-gate at the ridge-top fence, instead tip-toe, as best you can, across an uncomfortable marsh right (north) to firm ground on course for the summit.

5 Alternatively, follow the forest fence immediately right, branching off at will to climb the fell finding your own way, there being no hindrance bar small outcrops, to an easy pathless ascent. The summit lying at the northern tip of the slightly undulating ridge.

6 Leave the road a few yards north of the car park at a stile, a path leads up through a wall gateway and the northern edge of the forest to a track. **7** Pass through the hand-gate into the plantation, at the first fork in the forest track either go straight ahead or bear up right. Both tracks achieve union with the bridle-path waymarking guiding right up to a double deer door gate by an old fold to leave the forestry as per route **4**.

8 Go right, then quickly left, to a hand-gate in the wall corner. An old shepherds' path winds steeply up the grooved fellside with fine views back over the head of Thirlmere giving scope for a breather or two. As the ground eases, pass a couple of old folds tucked into outcrop nooks. Bell Crags comes into view once the forestry corner is passed. Evade bracken patches crossing Stone Hause, mount the ramped slope of the upper fell to the prominent summit with alacrity.

ASCENT *from Watendlath*

The five miles from the shores of Derwentwater to Bell Crags, via Watendlath, is split equally between road and fell path. The alternative approach, which may used during the course of a bus link walk between the regular Borrowdale bus out of Keswick, alighting at Rosthwaite, the traverse picking up the half-hourly 555 service at Wythburn road-end. This uses the Puddingstone Bank bridle-path and makes a four-mile off-road fell walk to the summit. Both routes coalesce at Watendlath.

9 Most walkers will start from the National Trust car park (pay *&* display). Exit, either over the ladder-stile or go right from the point of entry to a gate. The waymarked footpath fords Raise Beck, soon commencing the zig zag ascent of the steep bank, etched by centuries-old sled trails conveying peat from High Tove for domestic heating. The point of departure from the Armboth path is marked on a slate 'to Wythburn' at the wall corner. The green path contouring, initially with an intake wall for company, replaced by strategic cairns as guides on the long gradual south-eastward rise. The path clips the brow missing the fence corner, dipping to the outflow of Blea Tarn, a wind-whipped sheet of water; the term blea means 'coarse or rough ground', explanatory of the immediate environs. The damp path proceeds up the tough tussocky herbage to the watershed fence and hand-gate. Pass through the gate, bearing left negotiate the marsh to reach firm ground rising to the short north/south summit ridge.

10 An option when the ground is either bone dry or gripped in frost is to complete the ascent to High Tove by turning south to follow the east side of the ridge fence. Not an activity upon which one can heap much praise, being reminiscent of a Pennine bog-hopping yomp, the presence of red grouse adding fuel to the notion!

The Summit

Well yes, it's true, the summit is innominate on all maps. I bestowed the name elevating it from an outcrop set low down the northern slope. A small cairn rests on the southern top while a larger outcrop makes a more convincing summit at the northern tip of the ridge. The panorama over the page is taken from this outcrop. On the high shelf, directly beneath of the summit to the north, stands possibly the neatest sheep-fold in Lakeland. It certainly deserves close inspection, the small compartment appears to have had a roof. Nearby is a further small roof-less bothy next to modest evidence of quarrying in the flaky rock. West of the summit find the old metal fence corner strainer post, in front of the present fence. The fell offers the most marvellous northern prospect - as may be judged from the image on page 6, looking to Blencathra.

Safe Descents

Join the old bridle-path traversing the depression immediately south of the summit. The easiest option is east, the improving path leading down into the plantation surrounding Harrop Tarn; though Thirlmere at Dob Gill is bereft of services for the wet and weary. Better then the westward line to Watendlath and Borrowdale beyond, for one's pains facing the prevailing wind and no doubt the worst the elements can throw at you!

Sheepfold below the summit to the north looking to Raven Crag, Blencathra, Clough Head and Great Dodd

Ridge Routes to...

ARMBOTH FELL   DESCENT 540ft   ASCENT 250ft   1 mile

Descend via the grand sheepfold due north, watching for outcropping. As the slope levels, pass an old cairn and an erratic before fording the feeder gill to Launchy Gill, cross the wire fence. Pass through the old wall proceed up the rough, easier angled slope to the prominent erratic on the brow, the summit outcrop lies across marshy ground ahead.

HIGH TOVE   DESCENT 300ft   ASCENT 200ft   1.7 miles

The many energetic souls who innocently set their store on an end to end ridge walk from Great Langdale to Keswick, should be under no illusion, the going north of Bell Crags is as wet as it gets on any ridge walk in Lakeland. The only saving grace is the presence of the fence, to which one either clings or bounces. The final rise to High Tove is at least on improving ground, though affairs degenerate again beyond towards High Seat.

ULLSCARF   DESCENT 100 ft   ASCENT 690ft   1.8 miles

Aim south-west to the fence. Ignore the hand-gate on a clear path which passes a large pool, sliced through by the fence, head directly for the foot of Standing Crag. The path takes a leftward slant in climbing up through a weakness to the top of the crag. The fence resumes from the very top, a spot worth visiting for the fine view. The path keeps close company with the fence to the acute corner, now bear south on the grassy plateau following the line of old fence stumps to the summit cairn.

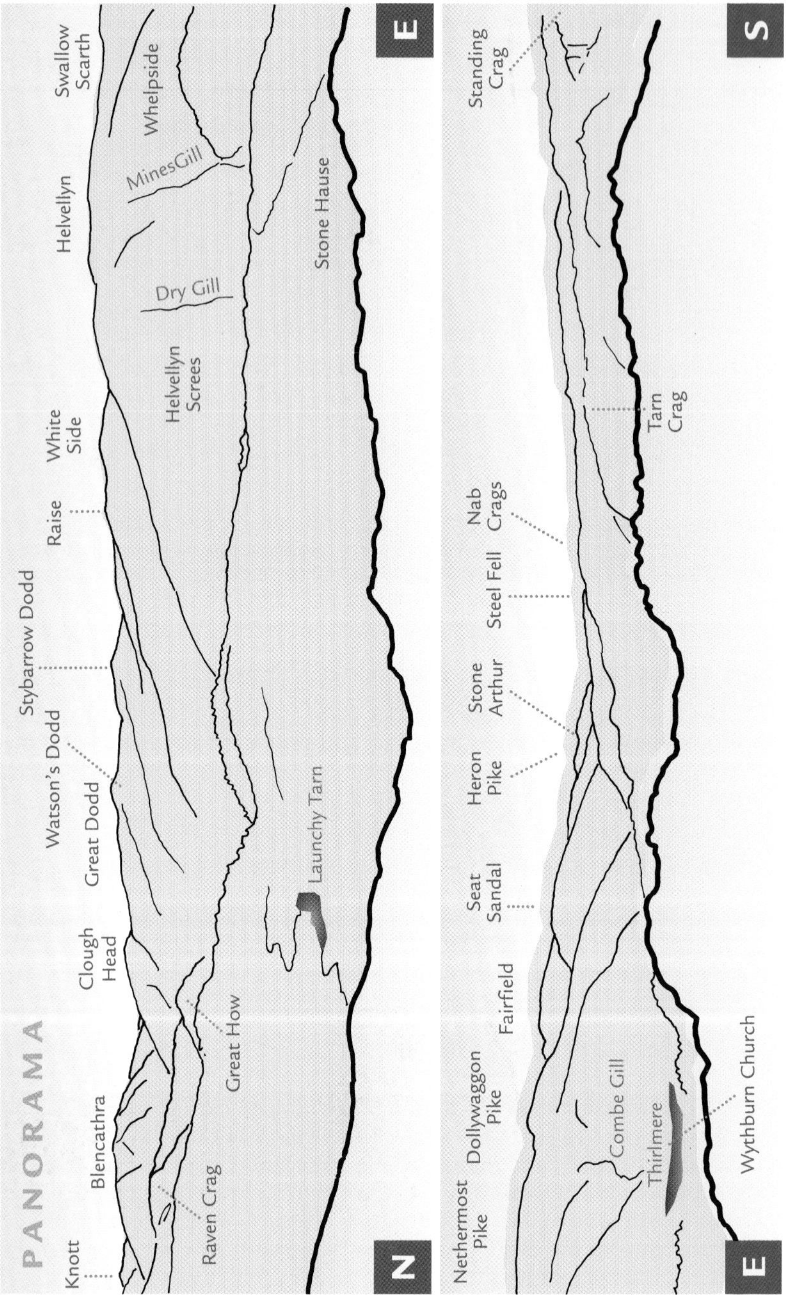

PANORAMA

N panel (top):
Knott
Blencathra
Raven Crag
Clough Head
Great How
Great Dodd
Watson's Dodd
Stybarrow Dodd
Raise
White Side
Helvellyn
MinesGill
Dry Gill
Helvellyn Screes
Whelpside
Swallow Scarth
Stone Hause
Launchy Tarn

E panel (bottom):
Nethermost Pike
Dollywaggon Pike
Fairfield
Seat Sandal
Heron Pike
Stone Arthur
Steel Fell
Nab Crags
Standing Crag
Tarn Crag
Combe Gill
Thirlmere
Wythburn Church

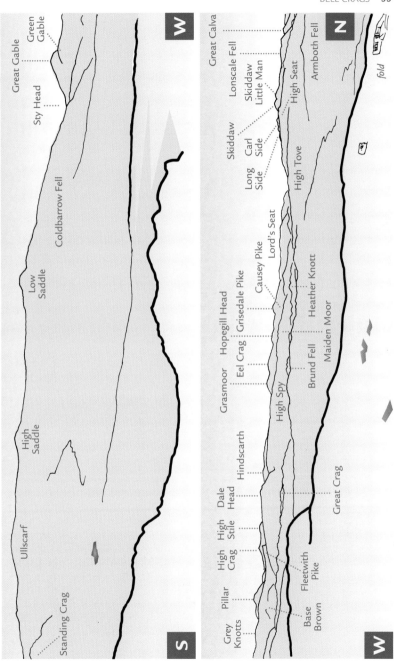

BLEABERRY FELL

The fell forms a convincing northern culmination to a chain of, admittedly modest and greatly be-marshed, tops stemming from the central plateau of High Raise. To east and west stirring crags command valley views. When seen from across the Naddle valley or Castlerigg Stone Circle it projects a striking headland, strengthened by Dodd Crag and the shy cliffs of Shoulthwaite Gill. Walkers lured to explore this eastern aspect are seldom disappointed, especially as the climb to the summit is rewarded with a rapturous panorama of famous fells.

It bears little physical likeness to the adjacent Clough Head, though they both offer dry-shod ascents to major range-end viewpoints. When viewed from Brandelhow (see title view above), or from aboard the Derwentwater orbiting launch, the domed heather-darkened summit stands proudly aloft. Hereon the Central Fell range falters in graceful stages into the Greta gap, forking either side of Brockle Beck, westward to Walla Crag and eastward over Dodd and Pike. The two-tiered competitive climbing walls of Falcon Crag, facing over Derwentwater and warmed by late afternoon sunshine, have long attracted climbers. While to the east the inevitably shaded and seldom tried cliffs of Dodd, Goat and Iron Crags bear down on the little visited wilds of the Shoulthwaite valley, a backdoor to the fell to be treasured.

589 metres   1,932 feet

The fell fits neatly in expeditions from
Keswick travelling out either upon the
Borrowdale Rambler bus, or for greater
novelty, disembarking at the Ashness Gate
landing stage from the lake launch.

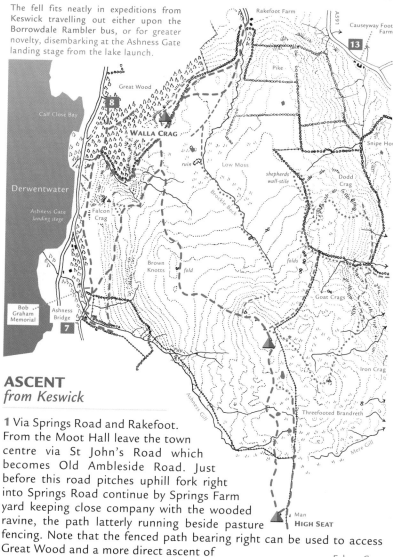

ASCENT
from Keswick

1 Via Springs Road and Rakefoot.
From the Moot Hall leave the town
centre via St John's Road which
becomes Old Ambleside Road. Just
before this road pitches uphill fork right
into Springs Road continue by Springs Farm
yard keeping close company with the wooded
ravine, the path latterly running beside pasture
fencing. Note that the fenced path bearing right can be used to access
Great Wood and a more direct ascent of
Walla Crag. The easier course continues
uphill passing through a kissing-gate,
dipping into the dell again, crosses a
footbridge to join the minor road at a
hand-gate. Go right, forking right at the
approach to Rakefoot Farm. Cross the
footbridge and rise to a stile (and pad-

Falcon Crag

Dodd Crag from Piper House across the Naddle Valley

locked field-gate). A clear track ascends and forks, that by the wall being the direct way to Walla Crag. However, for the purist intent on Bleaberry Fell, keep to the less-well trod track leading straight on and, as this bears up right again, continue on the grass path, little more than a sheep trod, which advances to the fenced sheepfold and ruined shepherd's dwelling - wrecked when targeted for heavy tank firing practice in the Second World War. From this damp hollow on Low Moss traipse through quite dense heather tracing the diminishing Brockle Beck, 'stream associated with badgers'. With increasing vagueness the path leads on by a fold into a shallow combe, angle up right onto the natural scarp shelf, now with evidence of a path to reach the large cairn at the top of the steep section of the popular path from Walla Crag, the worn trail trends up left, via an intermediate cairn, to the summit.

2 Walkers frequently choose to include Walla Crag in their adventure, the reasoning is flawless, two exceptional viewpoints, one rising tide of visual delight. Two main routes are available to Great Wood. Either include Castle Head, a wooded thimble of a hill fashioned from the core of a volcano, following the segregated path beside the valley road or eminently better, join the lakeside path via Friar's Crag, The Ings alder carr and Calf Close (consult Walla Crag page 280 for all the options). From the National Trust car park (pay & display) follow the woodland path south to the footbridge spanning Cat Gill. However, do not cross, instead pass up through the hand-gate and climb steeply beside the confined gill, a further hand-gate

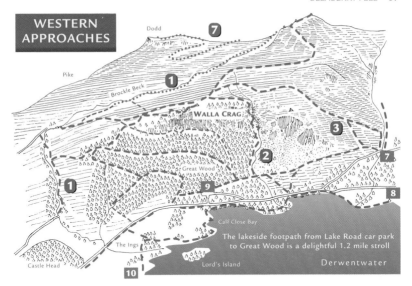

WESTERN
APPROACHES

Dodd

7

Pike

Brockle Beck

1

WALLA CRAG

3

Great Wood

2

7

1

9

8

Calf Close Bay

The lakeside footpath from Lake Road car park
to Great Wood is a delightful 1.2 mile stroll

The Ings

Lord's Island

Derwentwater

Castle Head

10

is encountered on the beautifully engineered and stepped path climbing to the scarp-top. One may cross the first wall-stile left into the wooded scarp-edge enclosure, or continue more easily upon the green sward to a stile much closer to the top. The summit cairn stands back from the edge on a bare rock plinth, from the brink enjoy quite the best view of Derwentwater, backed by Keswick and Skiddaw. Backtrack over the stile, now joining the obvious path shaping to contour above Cat Gill. Being sure to take the left fork, ford two headstreams on course to round the shoulder of Brown Knotts, skirting a marsh climb the eroded slope onto the bluff. **3** The top of Cat Gill can be reached on converging paths climbing from Ashness Bridge. Either follow Ashness Gill's north bank path traversing to the hand-gate left or take the lower path directly from the bridge, branch right after the stile climbing via the higher fence stile to join the upper path, which rises above Falcon Crag; a spur diversion left giving scope to visit the handsomely sited cairn on top of the crag with its fine view of Walla Crag in profile, and across the island dotted lake towards Bassenthwaite and the distant Solway Firth. The continuing path, above the deep re-entrant of Cat Gill, provides another notable scenic moment, before combining with paths from Walla Crag and Cat Gill, in turning right bound for the summit.

Fold by the infant Brockle Beck

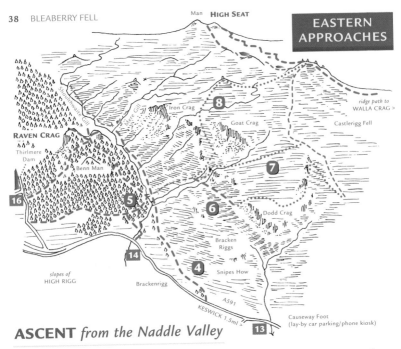

Man   **HIGH SEAT**

Iron Crag

8

Goat Crag

ridge path to
WALLA CRAG >

Castlerigg Fell

RAVEN CRAG

Thirlmere
Dam

Benn Man

7

5

6

Dodd Crag

16

Bracken
Riggs

14

slopes of
HIGH RIGG

4

Snipes How

Brackenrigg

A591

KESWICK 1.5ml >

Causeway Foot
(lay-by car parking/phone kiosk)

13

ASCENT *from the Naddle Valley*

Travellers speeding south from Keswick along the A591 are certain to
catch a periferal glimpse of the craggy edges bearing down upon the
Shoulthwaite Gill valley. Walkers looking for new adventures are encouraged to take a closer look, a trio of intriguing routes climb above the
stern façade, attaining the summit the panorama arrives all the more
rapturous. This secretive backstairs approach may begin from the lay-by
at Dale Bottom, opposite Causeway Foot Farm, **4** though this means a
roadside out-leg passing beyond the old Vicarage to the ladder-stile

Iron Crag

Skiddaw from the nick south of Dodd

right, joining the contouring footpath behind Brackenriggs connecting into the valley. **5** Perhaps the easier start from the Rough How Bridge lay-by will appeal more. Follow the approach lane (footpath) to Shoulthwaite Farm (Caravan Club site beside the yard). Shoulthwaite is thought to mean 'circular enclosure' perhaps even a now lost 'round-house'? Pass through to the kissing-gate entry into the woodland. Branch immediately right up by the internal forest fence to join the forest track, go right. As the track forks go right to the tall deer-balking kissing-gate, cross the Shoulthwaite Gill bridge with an old weir on the upstream side. Follow the winding path up the facing fellside with the wall right, crossing a gill. Coming level with the large erratic, over the wall, the three routes fan their separate ways. **6** Go through the hand-gate and follow the drove way, which contrives to beat back the bracken. It fords then starts to climb, reaching the brow leave the obvious path, climbing the steep slope to the skyline left, short of outcropping. On the face of it an apparent folly, but one the author found essential, as the primary path disappears under Dodd Crag and the way beyond is rough and confused. Steep though the climb may appear it is only hampered by bracken. The grassy fell-top a blessed relief, wander right to the leading edge of Dodd Crag, a superb viewpoint over High Rigg to Clough Head and Blencathra *(see right)*. Follow the scarp edge south-west towards Bleaberry Fell, but as the working wall (it still serves to pen sheep) has only one wall-stile, this must be sought and climbed. To locate it

descend and follow the wall north, as the slope levels encounter the rushy headstream of a gill, look intently for the through-stones in the wall. Cross this old shepherds' stile with due diligence. Turn back south following the wall up and over the ridge to the junction with a fence. Now go right, all the way to the summit, not attractive in itself, but the resultant summit view definitely compensates. **7** The most direct and actually the easiest route from the Shoulthwaite valley. Go straight up the open bracken-inhibited gill, skirting to the left of the outcropping, weaving up and through a ravine, keeping the rising wall to the right to the junction with a fence. Pass to the west side stile/gate and follow the fence left (south) to the summit. **8** On the face of it the more interesting option bears up half-left, climb with several guiding cairns onto the high shelf under Goat Crags via an easy cleft. The rocky edge angles up to pass above a waterfall, better appreciated from the valley floor, though if you already know it from below this moment is all the more impressive. The route turns up the gill, by choice wandering onto the prominent cairned knoll to the south, before traversing north-westward across the damp hollow to the fence corner and stile immediately below the summit.

The Summit

The highest ground is clothed with a ragged mix of heather, bilberry and tough fell grass. Various cairns confirm viewpoints on the rise to the wind shelter and tumbled heap at the top. There is no doubt about its merits as a major viewpoint, combined with Walla Crag, a peerless pair for the greater Derwentwater arena of fells and lakes.

Safe Descents

Follow the main path descending north-westward from the summit, this is the assured way. The fell is lined at a lower level with serious crags making the course of Brockle Beck to Rakefoot a sure release from potential woes, though it is better to keep to the popular turf trail the whole way.

Ridge Routes to...

HIGH SEAT   DESCENT 140ft   ASCENT   200ft   1.1 miles

The ridge path is dubious, dreary and damp - boggy going in 3D! The fence gives some guidance, but is actually better ignored altogether. The usual route leaves the summit passing a cairn and weaves a course due south, well to the west of the fence avoiding excessively wet hollows as best it may. Cross a stile where raw peat gives dry boots their final challenge short of the climb to the summit knoll and old Ordnance Survey pillar.

WALLA CRAG   DESCENT 840 ft   ASCENT 150ft   1.3 mile

Follow the popular path north-west, the steep slope is loose, so take your time, skirt around a marsh and pass a sheepfold sheltering on the eastern slope of Brown Knotts. The clear path runs downhill, fording two gills above the deep combe of Cat Gill to reach a stile entry into the wooded scarp enclosure.

Clough Head from the summit

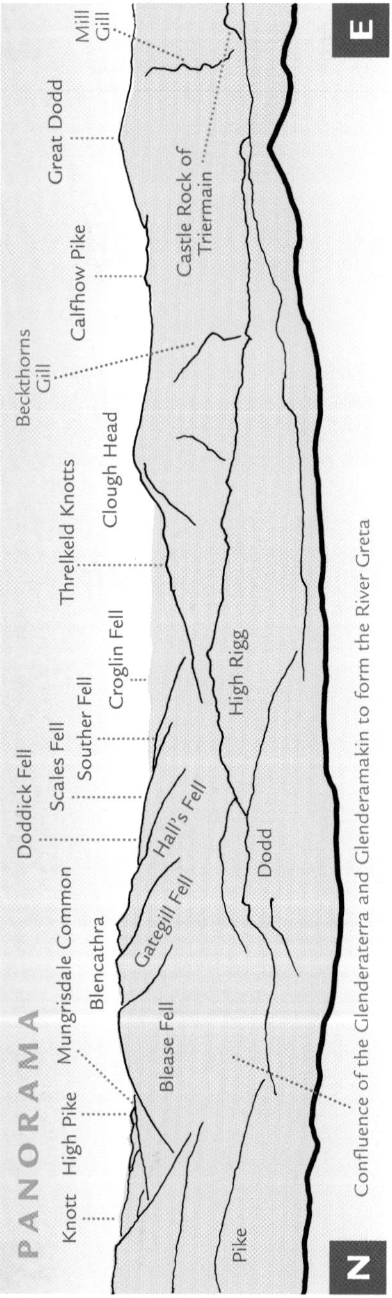

PANORAMA

N Knott · High Pike · Mungrisdale Common · Blencathra · Doddick Fell · Scales Fell · Souther Fell · Threlkeld Knotts · Clough Head · Beckhorns Gill · Calfhow Pike · Great Dodd · Mill Gill **E**

Blease Fell · Gategill Fell · Hall's Fell · Croglin Fell · High Rigg · Castle Rock of Triermain

Pike · Dodd

Confluence of the Glenderaterra and Glenderamakin to form the River Greta

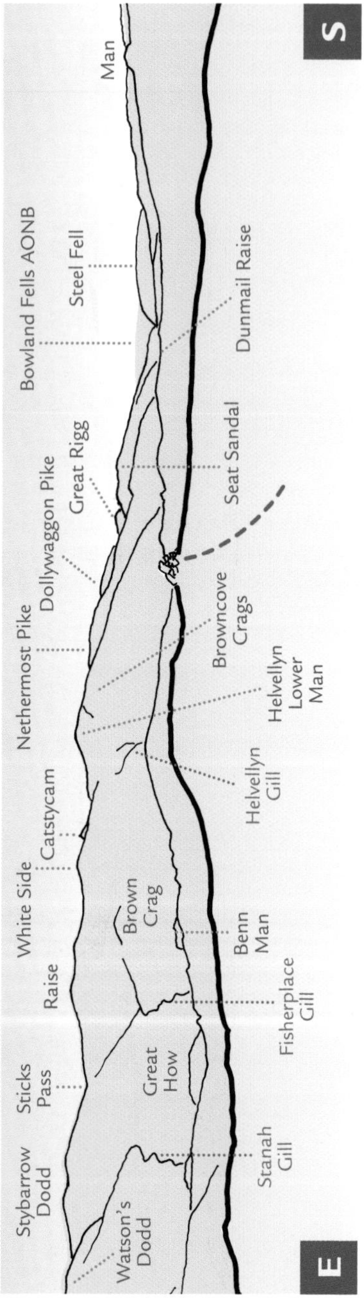

E Stybarrow Dodd · Sticks Pass · Raise · White Side · Catstycam · Nethermost Pike · Dollywaggon Pike · Great Rigg · Bowland Fells AONB · Steel Fell · Man **S**

Watson's Dodd · Great How · Brown Crag · Helvellyn Gill · Helvellyn Lower Man · Browncove Crags · Seat Sandal · Dunmail Raise

Stanah Gill · Fisherplace Gill · Benn Man

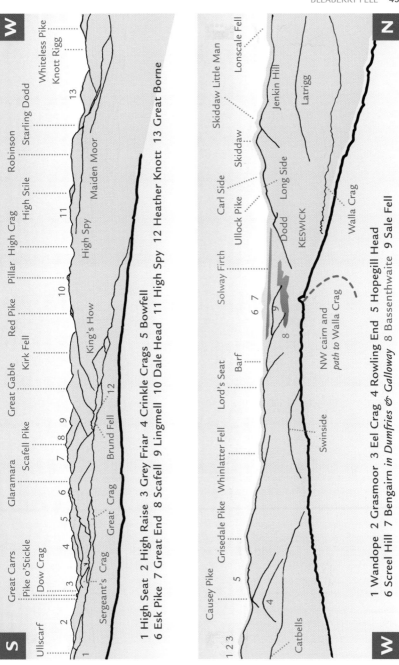

W

Whiteless Pike
Knott Rigg
Starling Dodd
Robinson
High Stile
High Crag
Pillar
Red Pike
Kirk Fell
Great Gable
Scafell Pike
Glaramara
High Raise
Great Carrs
Pike o'Stickle
Dow Crag
Ullscarf

13
11
10
9 8 7
6
5 4 3 2 1

Maiden Moor
High Spy
King's How
Brund Fell
Great Crag
Sergeant's Crag

12

S

1 High Seat 2 High Raise 3 Grey Friar 4 Crinkle Crags 5 Bowfell
6 Esk Pike 7 Great End 8 Scafell 9 Lingmell 10 Dale Head 11 High Spy 12 Heather Knott 13 Great Borne

N

Lonscale Fell
Skiddaw Little Man
Jenkin Hill
Latrigg
Skiddaw
Carl Side
Long Side
Ullock Pike
Dodd
KESWICK
Walla Crag
Solway Firth
Lord's Seat
Barf
Whinlatter Fell
Griesedale Pike
Causey Pike
Swinside
Catbells

6 7
6
8

NW cairn and
path to Walla Crag

5
4
1 2 3

W

1 Wandope 2 Grasmoor 3 Eel Crag 4 Rowling End 5 Hopegill Head
6 Screel Hill 7 Bengairn in Dumfries & Galloway 8 Bassenthwaite 9 Sale Fell

BLEA RIGG

From the curious knob of Sergeant Man a long arm of fell draws essentially south-east off the high plateau of High Raise. Sustaining a plateau-like character this ridge terminates, after some five miles, on Loughrigg Fell above the confluence of the rivers Brathay and Rothay. There are numerous minor named and a few unnamed tops en route, Blea Rigg and Silver How the only two standing out as acknowledged summits. West from Swinescar Hause the ridge livens up as the dependant summits of Blea Rigg take charge, wet hollows and rocky crests, this section is great fun to explore.

From Great Castle How, Blea Rigg, in dark silhouette, looks every inch a bastion but from all other viewpoints its individuality is less obvious. To the north Blea Crag forms a solid buttress commanding attention from Easedale Tarn, Tarn Crag and surprisingly from high on Sergeant Man. While White Crag and Tarn Crag are eye-catching supporting acts to the stirring drama of the Langdale Pikes when viewed from the floor of Great Langdale.

The shortest climbs actually lead up from Great Langdale, most commonly via Stickle Ghyll, though one may opt for either the shy Swinescar Hause path from near Pye How, or the majestic intimacies with the rock-walls of Whitegill Crag. Easedale approaches from Grasmere have great charm and scenic mix. One may wander up by Blindtarn Moss and the extensive shrubberies of naturally toparied juniper to Swinescar Hause or, more directly follow the dale beck via Easedale. This latter route provides the greater contrast, from flower meadows to foaming falls, by lapping waters and barren fellsides,

556 metres   1,824 feet

SERGEANT MAN

Sour
Milk Gill

Codale
Tarn

Belles
Knott

Easedale
Tarn

Eagle
Crag

Blea
Crag

Blindtarn
Moss

PAVEY ARK

Great Castle How

Stickle
Tarn

Tarn Crag

Raw Pike

Stickle
Ghyll

Whitegill
Crag

Scout
Crag

Swinescar
Hause

Pye How

New Dungeon Ghyll Hotel
& Sticklebarn Tavern

29

Great Langdale

Harry Place

slopes of
LINGMOOR FELL

Great Langdale Beck

camp site

map continuation on page 46

Prehistoric
rock-art boulders

CHAPEL
STILE

culminating with the steady pull above Blea
Crag. Normally a ridge route is the reward for a
long and tiresome climb, but walkers may embark
from the top of Red Bank and follow the irregularities of
the ridge with minimal preliminary ascent. Though even this
approach can, and perhaps should, begin from either Grasmere,
via Allan Bank, or Chapel Stile, via Meg's Gill *see* SILVER HOW *page 236*.

ASCENT *from Great Langdale*

Choice of car parks : The National Trust Stickle Ghyll or National Park Langdale

There are three basic lines of approach from this dramatic valley
setting, in such surroundings scenic adventure must be anticipated for
all the subject summit sits well back from the percieved action.

1 Via Stickle Ghyll. Walk up the lane past the New Dungeon Ghyll
Hotel, from the gate head straight on through the small enclosures
and on beside the tree-shaded beck rising to a footbridge, beyond
this cross a stile to enter the main amphitheatre of this hugely
popular ravine. The path, for which much attention has necessarily been

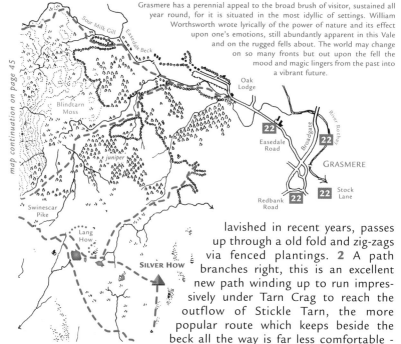

Grasmere has a perennial appeal to the broad brush of visitor, sustained all year round, for it is situated in the most idyllic of settings. William Worthsworth wrote lyrically of the power of nature and its effect upon one's emotions, still abundantly apparent in this Vale and on the rugged fells about. The world may change on so many fronts but out upon the fell the mood and magic lingers from the past into a vibrant future.

lavished in recent years, passes up through a old fold and zig-zags via fenced plantings. **2** A path branches right, this is an excellent new path winding up to run impressively under Tarn Crag to reach the outflow of Stickle Tarn, the more popular route which keeps beside the beck all the way is far less comfortable - troops of walkers heads bent, tend to go this way! **3** A far more pleasant less well-known alternative line is recommended. Directly after leaving the NDG, cross the footbridge located half-right after the initial gate, the path runs behind Millbeck Farm, enters an outgang lane rising thereafter onto the bracken rigg, keeping left to avoid outcropping. Either contour onto the main zig-zagging path, climbing off this as it shapes to towards Tarn Crag, wind up to the left of a walled enclosure. Or climb, with little initial evidence of a path in the bracken. On finding a green path skirt the

left-hand shoulder of a knoll above an incised gill, traverse the walled enclosure diagonally to join up with the upper section of the old shepherds' path, this then slips over a saddle depression to meet up with the path that runs along the southern shore of the tarn from the outflow. A clear, occasionally cairned, path leads north, then east, onto the plateau of Blea Rigg.

There are two approaches to Whitegill Crag *(see left)*, **4** the more direct route up behind the New Dungeon Ghyll Hotel, or **5**, the climbers' approach to Scout Crag, off the valley road.

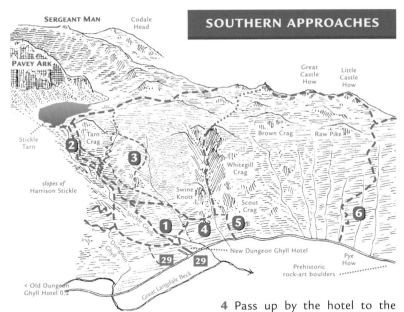

SERGEANT MAN   Codale Head

SOUTHERN APPROACHES

PAVEY ARK

Great Castle How   Little Castle How

Stickle Tarn   Tarn Crag

Brown Crag   Raw Pike

2

3

Whitegill Crag

slopes of Harrison Stickle

Swine Knott

Scout Crag

6

Stickle Ghyll

1   **4**   **5**

Dungeon Ghyll

New Dungeon Ghyll Hotel

Pye How

29   **29**

Prehistoric rock-art boulders ·····················

< Old Dungeon Ghyll Hotel 0.2

Great Langdale Beck

4 Pass up by the hotel to the bridle-gate, slant right in the triangular enclosure, cross the footbridge, the path rises above Millbeck Farm via a hand-gate with a walled gill gangway. Go through the kissing-gate after 100 yards on the right, keep the wall right passing through the foot of a larch plantation to cross a

Tarn Crag

Lingmoor and the Coniston Fells from within White Gill

low wall into the bouldery ravine. **5** Go right along the valley road passing the entrance to Millbeck Farm to reach a stile/gate with National Trust notice below a field-barn. Pass up above the field-barn to a wall-stile, climbing to the left of the lower buttress, a popular training ground for novice climbers. Cross the ladder-stile, ignore the climbers' path rising right to Scout Crag (which means '*projecting rock*'), instead follow the wall immediately left, little hint of a path to enter White Gill. The

combined effects of path and gill erosion ensures a loose clambering way, above the tree tend to the left for bigger boulder steps and more secure footing. Much of the gill-bed is dry, with subterranean flow. The view out of the ravine is superb leading the eye across Side Pike to Wetherlam. The natural exit draws into a short tight gully to the right, requiring a spot of mild scrambling, ignore the gill-head itself. The rock walls of Whitegill Crag are hugely impressive and can be best surveyed by wandering onto the open spur left once the hard work has been done (*see above - can you spot the climbers?*).

The summit of Blea Rigg beckons across undulating outcropped slopes. While there is no evident path a route is easily concocted, from this approach the perched summit cairn contrives to look like a bird of prey.

6 A footpath embarks from the valley road midway between Pye How and the Long House, the lack of immediate car parking and apparent plainness of the route, ensuring that it is more commonly used as a line of swift descent when inventing a circular walk from the New Dungeon Ghyll Hotel (NDG in conversation). It is nontheless a pleasing path, especially if time is taken for frequent pauses to look back upon the stunning surround of majestic fells. A kissing-gate gives entry into a pasture, initially keeping the wall to the left, ascend with half-a-dozen waymark posts as aids, cross broken intermediate walls with much mature scrub colonising the enclosures. A ladder-stile crosses the intake wall at the top. The path, at first stony, becomes a pleasant turf trail and beyond the solitary gill-shading holly, winds steadily to the ridge-top at Swinescar Hause. Joining the ridge path track left up from the marshy hollow by the old fold and curious cramped shelter. Traverse Little Castle How and Great Castle How passing cotton grass and bog bean adorned pools. From the vicinity of a cluster of quartz rocks admire a splendid view west to the striking dark profile of Blea Rigg, the obvious culmination of the northward plunging Blea Crag. The summit is confirmed by the presence of a walled rock shelter directly below. Though the ridge path waltzes by to the right, many a head-down fell-walker will have missed it, erroneously confusing the next prominent cairnless outcrop to the west as the ultimate point.

ASCENT *from Grasmere*

7 Follow Easedale Road via Goody Bridge, a few paces short of the Oak Lodge (teas), cross the Easedale Beck footbridge. A long view of Sour Milk Gill backed by Tarn Crag beckons across lovely flower meadows, the beginning of a fine wild trail. A part-paved path leads past New Bridge, reaching a gate (yellow footpath waymark affixed) the first route option begins. **8** Go through this gate entering a meadow pass, on by open woodland to join the access track at a gate leading to a pair of holiday cottages, glance by these to a gate. Beyond the gate the path trends up by the beck and left-ward to a footpath waymark post guiding right, into the hollow of Blindtarn Moss; the abundance of bushes ensures plenty of bird song during this approach. The term 'Blind' meaning obscure outflow. The scene is quite unique, a wild Chinese garden in the fells *(see right)*. The path climbs up through the juniper, higher up as the ground steepens the cairned path is worn to loose stones. Either follow the cairned path to the soggy saddle of Swinescar Hause or, just prior to the top, slant onto the right-hand side to follow the old green zig-zag path which offers sweeter footing to rise onto the westward climbing path above

Blindtarn Moss surrounded by juniper thicket, note path drainage channel in the foreground.

the quaint stone bivvy shelter *(see below)*. The ridge path weaves on, over Little Castle How and under Great Castle How, passing two sheets of water and a prominently perched rock to reach the summit bluff.

8 The popular path to Easedale Tarn leads to the next gate and over the Blindtarn Gill bridge heading straight across the open meadow (ignore the farm track right to Brimmer Head). Go through a gateway and sub-sequent kissing-gate, the paved path enters a lane which funnels, then opens, winding up above Sour Milk Gill. The best view of the falls is from the base of the sheepfold, though there is no ready path down. Only the upper fall can be easily reached from the path, its plunge pool can be the scene of much splashing and excited chatter on hot summer afternoons.

Shepherds' shelter on the rise to Little Castle How

The path has received considerable remedial paving, the final section to the tarn is presently in the course of construction. Easedale Tarn continues to attract walking visitors many of whom, as has long been the case, are quite content to make it the

The ridge path from Great Castle How

ultimate point of their walk, backtracking via the Stythwaite Steps foot-bridge at the foot of Far Easedale. Either side of the tarn conical drum-lins emphasise the glacial origins of this bleak amphitheatre. The domed top of Tarn Crag looms close right, while Blea Crag forms the southern sidewall, with the sub-edge peak of Belles Knott shielding Codale Tarn a little to its right. Follow the path above the tarn, watch for a small cairn where the Blea Rigg path very evidently branches left. This winds up above the drumlins seeking the natural dip in the ridge. Latterly one may either continue to the saddle close to the perched boulder or angle up right behind Blea Crag via a rake. **9** As a final option, continue

Blea Crag

Florally enchanting pool on Great Castle How

on the south side of Easedale Tarn. The path leads up beside the main feeder gill, with several essentially stepped sections beside the cascades, overlooked by the arresting peak of Belles Knott up to the right, a well respected scramblers' route and object of photographic composition. Above the falls a side path bears right, fording the gill, to visit the hanging waters of Codale Tarn with its tiny outflow and picturesque quaint isle set beneath the great slope of Codale Head. The main path zig-zags up to a ridge-top path interchange, turn left, south-east, wandering some half-a-mile to the summit.

North-east from Great Castle How

The Summit

There can be some doubt as to which is the highest point with several rocky tops vying for pre-eminence; conventional mapping offers only slack captioning to add to the confusion. The one sure clue is the presence of a cairn sitting on top of a blade of rock, directly above the shelter passed on the eastern approach. This is the culmination of outcropping above Blea Crag, and the high point seen from Great Castle How. The view is superb with Pavey Ark and Harrison Stickle the mighty neighbours. The Helvellyn chain rises invitingly eastward above the serried ridges overlooking Easedale and the Coniston Fells tantalise attention beyond Lingmoor Fell and Side Pike.

Walled rock shelter
tucked under the summit

Safe Descent

With crags close to the northern brink, great care is required in poor conditions. The ridge path is plain enough in most situations, but should the shelter of the valley be urgently required the best bet is to follow the ridge path running east. This leads under the summit by the walled shelter, down to the first depression bear left (north), descending north-eastwards through a shallow hollow east of Blea Crag and down to the popular path running close to Easedale Tarn. This path leads by Sour Milk Gill, the safety of the Easedale meadows and into Grasmere.

Ridge Routes

SILVER HOW   DESCENT 680ft   ASCENT 150 ft   2 miles

The twists and turns of the ridge trail ensure an entertaining march. En route pass two sizable pools and a cluster of quartz stones by the path, prior to crossing Great Castle How; deviate left to its top for a dramatic view of Codale Head, while the opposing and little visited Raw Pike also gives a fine view, over Great Langdale. Beyond Swinescar Hause the ridge is of a more rolling nature, though there are more pools, the largest being consumed to weed. The path runs under the higher top of Lang How (by 62ft) and traverses the headstream of Wray Gill to reach the scarp-top summit.

Seat Sandal and Fairfield from Little Castle How

SERGEANT MAN   DESCENT 50ft   ASCENT 680ft   1.3 miles

The occasional cairn indicates a surprisingly modest ridge trail. Immediately after the fourth mock summit knoll notice a small section of marsh, fenced-off to evaluate the effects of non-grazing. *A drastic reduction in sheep grazing would allow trees and shrubs to regain their ancient footing, after all they are only waiting in the wings for the day, though crucial minerals have been leached in the now acid grassland to further inhibit such a restoration.* Just short of the path interchange admire the rock-basin *(see right)* :

cairns now abound. Hereon the ridge narrows, with rocky outcrops, including one notable tilted slab, the path forks, then re-unites on the steady climb to the outflow of the marsh west of Codale Head, the summit is swiftly attained on the popular and worn final path.

Blea Crag from Easedale Tarn

PANORAMA

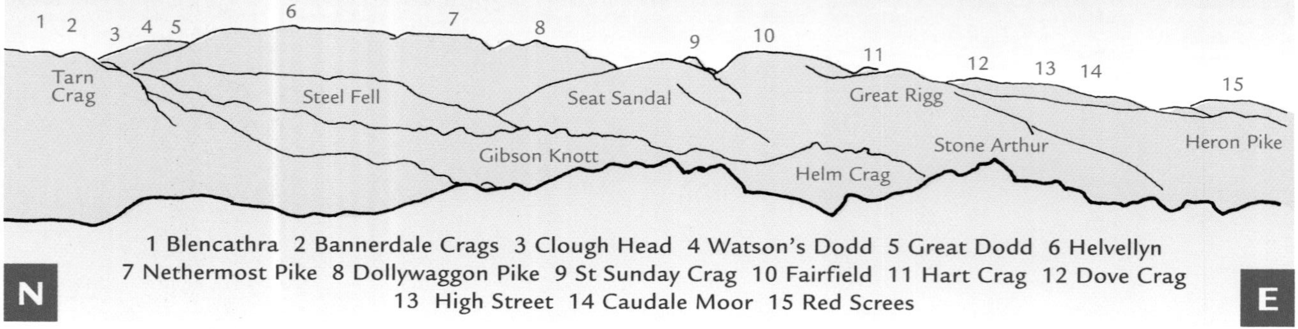

E

N

Heron Pike

15

14 13

12

11

10

9

8

7

6

5 4

3

2 1

Great Rigg

Stone Arthur

Helm Crag

Seat Sandal

Steel Fell

Gibson Knott

Tarn Crag

1 Blencathra 2 Bannerdale Crags 3 Clough Head 4 Watson's Dodd 5 Great Dodd 6 Helvellyn
7 Nethermost Pike 8 Dollywaggon Pike 9 St Sunday Crag 10 Fairfield 11 Hart Crag 12 Dove Crag
13 High Street 14 Caudale Moor 15 Red Screes

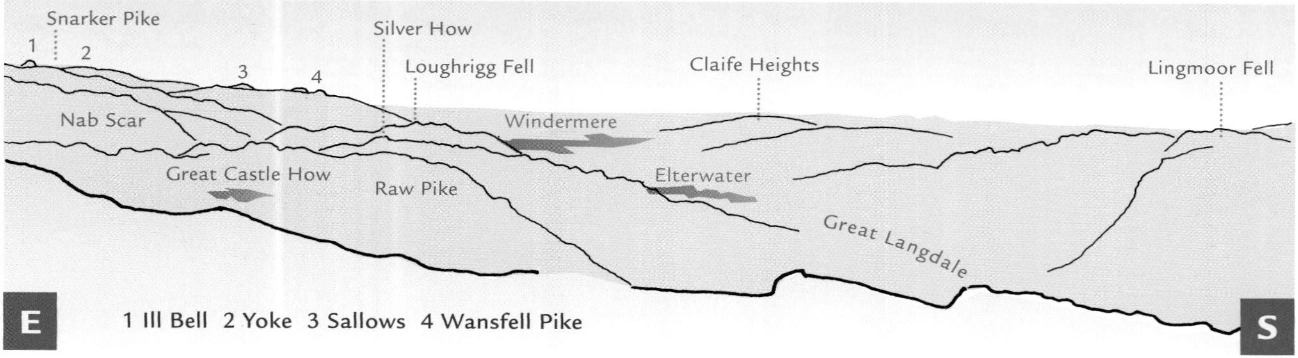

S

E

Lingmoor Fell

Great Langdale

Claife Heights

Elterwater

Windermere

Silver How

Loughrigg Fell

Snarker Pike

Nab Scar

Raw Pike

Great Castle How

1

2

3

4

1 Ill Bell 2 Yoke 3 Sallows 4 Wansfell Pike

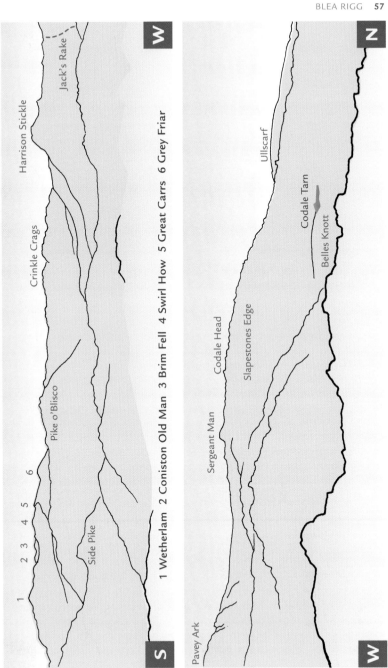

W

Jack's Rake

Harrison Stickle

Crinkle Crags

Pike o'Blisco

6

5

4

3

2

1

Side Pike

S

1 Wetherlam 2 Coniston Old Man 3 Brim Fell 4 Swirl How 5 Great Carrs 6 Grey Friar

N

Ullscarf

Codale Tarn

Belles Knott

Codale Head

Sergeant Man

Slapestones Edge

Pavey Ark

W

CALF CRAG

A curved ridge sweeps north-westward from the of Vale of Grasmere. It begins auspiciously with Helm Crag, probably Grasmere's best-known and best-loved hill, from where it takes a roller coaster ride over Gibson Knott climbing over Pike of Carrs to land eventually upon Calf Crag. This distance from valley affairs, lends the fell top a certain lonely mystique, in fact many fellwalkers may only vaguely remember climbing it once in all their adventures.

The summit forms the pivotal point on the Greenburn Dale horseshoe, which normally begins with a flourish, climbing onto Steel Fell and finishes with aplomb, upon Helm Crag. Though there is a warning for any walker approaching from Steel Fell in misty conditions, the lie of the land makes it all too easy to miss the top ending up at the pass at the head of Far Easedale. The Far Easedale horseshoe itself runs clockwise, climbing Tarn Crag first, from vicinity of Easedale Tarn. The notion of Greater Easedale Super-highway? Well now, that begins with Helm Crag, passes over Calf Crag climbing over Codale Head to Sergeant Man before heading for Blea Rigg and Silver How. This is a really excellent expedition, which might be made all the more sumptuous with the inclusion of High Raise. The fell-name, in common with Calfhow Pike and Calf Hole, refers to the frequent of red deer does and fawns, it would be a rare, though not an entirely impossible sighting today. The best view of the fell is from beneath Deer Bields Crag, its steep southern slopes spilling into the wild depths of Far Easedale. Apart from a moment of crag at the head of Greenburn Dale, the fell drifts soggily northward merging into the morass of upper Wythburn Dale.

537 metres   1,762 feet

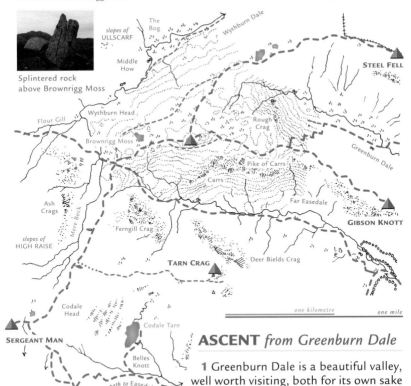

Splintered rock
above Brownrigg Moss

The
Bog

slopes of
ULLSCARF

Middle
How

Wythburn Dale

STEEL FELL

Flour Gill

Wythburn Head

Brownrigg Moss

Rough
Crag

Greenburn Dale

Pike of Carrs

Carrs

Ash
Crags

Mere Beck

Ferngill Crag

Far Easedale

GIBSON KNOTT

slopes of
HIGH RAISE

TARN CRAG

Deer Bields Crag

Codale
Head

Codale Tarn

one kilometre   _one mile_

SERGEANT MAN

Belles
Knott

path to Easedale Tarn >

ASCENT *from Greenburn Dale*

1 Greenburn Dale is a beautiful valley, well worth visiting, both for its own sake and as a route to Calf Crag. Start either from the bus stop above Town Head or from Mill Bridge following the minor road down to the bridge where Raise Beck becomes the River Rothay. Go right, passing Ghyll Foot. The two approaches merge as they turn up the drive leading over cattle-grids by Helmside, rising to Turn Howe and the subsequent gate onto the fell. Go forward with the green track, leading alongside a wall right, then through a gate into a short lane, emerging beyond the attractive waterfalls to continue as an unfettered track. Passing moraine the track bears left and crosses newly set stepping stones, going right contour past a neat sheepfold set between boulders. Watch for a cairn marking the point where the path climbs left, up a wet patch, zig-zagging to the saddle. Spot the cairn right, guiding onto the clear path climbing Pike of Carrs, sections of eroded peat intervene en route to the summit.

2 A most agreeable option from the same starting point is to gather in the Gibson Knott ridge. Branch left over the footbridge at GR 318104. The path climbs to cross an outgang lane, via facing hand-gates, ascending the steepening slope to Bracken Hause. Turn right, keeping to the obvious and delightful ridge path leading west over Gibson Knott.

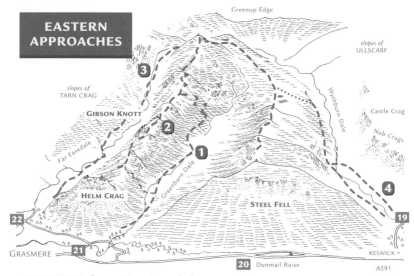

EASTERN APPROACHES

Greenup Edge

slopes of ULLSCARF

slopes of TARN CRAG

GIBSON KNOTT

Far Easedale

Wythburn Dale

Castle Crag

Nab Crags

HELM CRAG

Greenburn Dale

STEEL FELL

22

21

GRASMERE

20 Dunmail Raise

19

KESWICK >

A591

ASCENT *from Far Easedale*

3 Leave Broadgate, at the centre of Grasmere, along Easedale Road. This leads naturally onto the signposted bridle-path running into Far Easedale. Crossing Stythwaite Steps footbridge keep right, with the one clear path, which has a few rough sections en route to the saddle at the dale head. The metal stakes are all that remain of an old step stile. Bear acutely right, bound for the summit outcrop already in sight beyond the tarn in Brownrigg Moss.

Swirling surface to a pool in Far Easedale Gill

Tarn Crag and Deer Bields Crag from just below the summit

ASCENT *from Wythburn*

4 Consult the STEEL FELL map on page 245. Footpaths lead from either side of the road bridge spanning Wythburn Beck, opposite the Steel End car park. A further path follows a farm track via a lane stemming off the bridleway above West Head, formerly known as Steel End prior to the amalgamation of farm holdings. Negotiate the sequence of ladder-stiles by any path converging at the footbridge beneath Rake Crags, just where the valley begins to constrict. Follow the clear path climbing up the south side of the ravine below Black Crag. When the wind blows up the valley the fuming falls can be most impressive, the spray flying high. The dale opens becoming progressively more desolate, the beck slothfully winds through a gently curving tarn. Leave the obvious path, climb the easy slopes, no path, skirting to the west of the tarns in the wide shallow depression of the ridge, join the ridge path from Steel Fell heading damply south to the summit.

The Summit

A cairn rests aloft a pronounced upthrusting outcrop. The steep rock face on the Easedale side being of sufficient height to cause walkers to need to be wary in poor visibility. Being hemmed in by the bulky mass of High Raise and Ullscarf ensures the best elements of a disappointing view are eastward, to the long unflattering western wall of Helvellyn and Fairfield. The craggy façade to Tarn Crag, notably Deer Bields Crag, which can be seen across Far Easedale merits prime attention. As so often occurs, where summits are not prized by all, walkers create 'avoiding paths' from existing sheep trods, one such example runs below the summit on the southern flank.

Safe Descents

The ridge path east is reliable, if followed meticulously. Though in very poor conditions it may be prudent to head, initially west, by Brownrigg Moss to reach the saddle at the head of Far Easedale. At this point turn east to follow the valley path in comparative shelter and, importantly, greatest certainty of homing-in on Grasmere.

Looking to Rough Crag, the foreground boulder crowned with a dense crop of heather and bilberry flourishing beyond the reach of voracious sheep

Pike of Carrs from Far Easedale

Ridge Routes...

GIBSON KNOTT   DESCENT 400ft   ASCENT 100ft   1.3 miles

The path takes off east, traversing eroded peat before dipping more steeply off Pike of Carrs to a cairn in the depression. The ridge is sufficiently drawn in to give excellent views, though the path's southern bias tends to make Easedale the focus of attention. Passing a rock chair to the left, the ridge engages in several switchbacks to the summit.

SERGEANT MAN   DESCENT 50ft   ASCENT 700ft   2.1 miles

En route west, to the saddle between desolate Wythburn Dale and the deeply entrenched Far Easedale, the popular path negotiates some damp ground. The ridge path ignores both, marching due south largely in the company of what remains of the metal estate boundary stakes, leading via several pleasing pools, over Codale Head, rounding a marsh to climb the obvious, and certainly distinctive summit knoll.

STEEL FELL   DESCENT 100ft   ASCENT 350ft   1.5 miles

Leave the summit heading north, the route soon getting decidedly marshy, especially along the old fence line. The popular path keeps well to the right, in so doing enjoys the view into Greenburn Dale down to right. Curving north-east, the less well trod path, near the fence, merges from the left. Saunter on the south side of the two large, oddly nameless, tarns. Now going east, follow a fence ascending from the left to the acute corner by the summit cairn.

PANORAMA

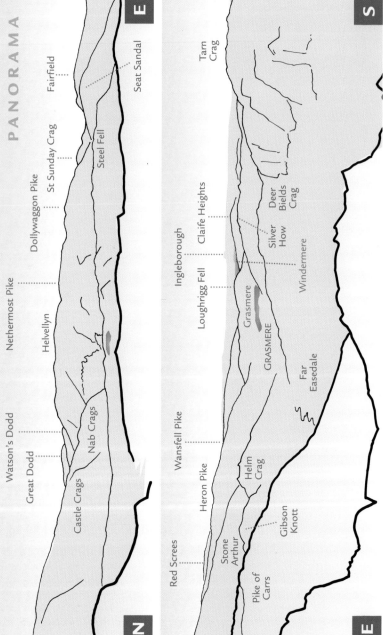

N

Great Dodd
Watson's Dodd
Nethermost Pike
Dollywaggon Pike
St Sunday Crag
Fairfield

Castle Crags
Nab Crags
Helvellyn
Steel Fell
Seat Sandal

E

E

Red Screes
Heron Pike
Wansfell Pike
Loughrigg Fell
Ingleborough
Claife Heights
Tarn Crag

Stone Arthur
Helm Crag
Grasmere
Silver How
Deer Bields Crag

Pike of Carrs
Gibson Knott
GRASMERE
Far Easedale
Windermere

S

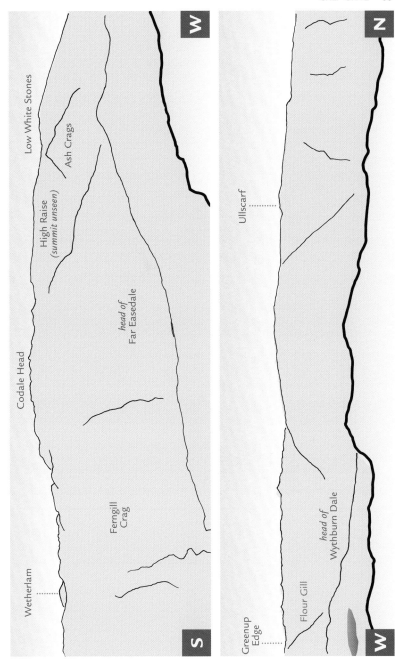

EAGLE CRAG

One can't help but wonder how many travellers venturing through Borrowdale for the first time swing through Rosthwaite, their minds perhaps intent on the impending challenge of Honister Pass, catch a sudden and unsuspected glimpse of Eagle Crag in the corner of their eye and yelp with delight. As the title view above confirms, it gives the Stonethwaite valley a stunning focal point, a real camera catcher. Walkers traversing the Central range via Greenup Edge see it much in the same light as Grasmere folk in reverse consider Helm Crag, it is a much-loved ingredient in an adorable fell landscape. The fell marks the termination of an extended limb descending directly from High Raise. A featureless ridge smartly coming to attention upon Sergeant's Crag, en route this grand finale.

There is but one prime ascent and one backdoor route best kept for descent, foul weather or not. Chances of spotting golden eagle, held in the fell-name are nigh on nil. It was documented in 1777 that "Here is every year an airy or nest of eagles .." they will have been persecuted to extinction, the valley folk mighty relieved with their. How times and perceptions change! The lower buttress, overlooking lower Langstrath, carries the name Heron Crag, the differentiation might be that it was the nesting-place of Sea Eagles.

520 metres **1,706** feet *(estimated height)*

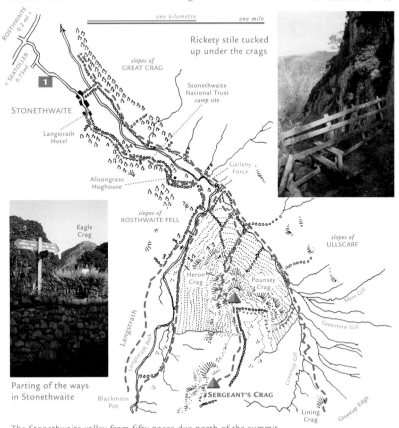

ROSTHWAITE 0.2 ml >
< SEATOLLER 0.75ml

one kilometre   one mile

1

STONETHWAITE

slopes of
GREAT CRAG

Stonethwaite
National Trust
camp site

Langstrath
Hotel

Galleny
Force

Alisongrass
Hoghouse

slopes of
ROSTHWAITE FELL

Rickety stile tucked
up under the crags

Eagle
Crag

slopes of
ULLSCARF

Heron
Crag

Pounsey
Crag

Mere Gill

Langstrath

Langstrath Beck

Greenhow Gill

Greenup Gill

Parting of the ways
in Stonethwaite

Blackmoss
Pot

SERGEANT'S CRAG

Lining
Crag

Greenup Edge

The Stonethwaite valley from fifty paces due north of the summit

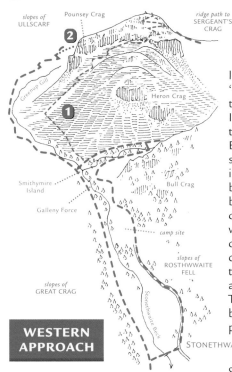

slopes of
ULLSCARF

Pounsey Crag

ridge path to
SERGEANT'S
CRAG

2

Greenup Gill

Heron Crag

1

Smithymire
Island

Galleny Force

camp site

Bull Crag

slopes of
ROSTHWWAITE
FELL

slopes of
GREAT CRAG

Stonethwaite Beck

**WESTERN
APPROACH**

STONETHWAITE

ASCENT
from Stonethwaite

1 From the centre of the hamlet, follow the lane signposted 'Greenup Edge' leading over the Stonethwaite Beck bridge. In winter, when the beckside trees have lost their foliage, Eagle Crag makes a fine subject. After the gate go right, in harmony with the gated bridle-track. Cross the footbridge immediately above the confluence of Greenup Gill with Langstrath Beck. Bear left, cross the fence stile, taking care to keep on the low side of the flush marsh which is abundant in delicate bog flora. The path brushes through bracken of potential monster proportions, keep parallel with the Greenup Gill fence.
Pass through a handgate in the down wall, while a

From Lingy End, Great Crag

Lining Crag

High Raise

Sergeant's Crag

Pounsey Crag

Heron Crag

Langstrath

path continues low beside the wall and gill, continue on the shepherd's path angling gently up the slope to a wall gap. At this point the climb proper begins. Keep the partly broken wall to the right, the path, confirmed by modest cairns of transitory existence, winds up to a fragile stile at the top of the rising wall hugging the undercliff. If one's temper has been tested by the sweaty ardour to this point, prepare for a fell ecstasy lift off. Smartly a narrow breach in the craggy defences permits a short stair climb. The way beyond suggests two options, but in reality there is only one. The path leading up left ends abruptly but gives a fine view of Pounsey Crag (see page 71), backtrack to continue - this is important as there is no safe fell-walking ground further left. The prime route goes

Key breach on the ascent

immediately right, along the ledge marked with ice-like fragments of quartz, terminating with a fine full height view of Sergeant's Crag. Now switch up, making several similar sharp turns to avoid rock bands with

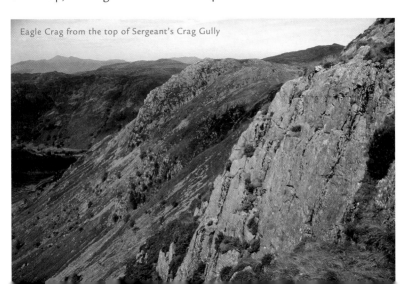

Eagle Crag from the top of Sergeant's Crag Gully

much heather underfoot, the immediate and outward scenery is consistently exciting. Duly, and with no little sorrow for an end to the fun, the tilted summit slab is rounded.

2 The fell has only one other tenable line of ascent for the ordinary mortal, one that is more likely to be used for descent by walkers wisely avoiding the risk of trying to unlock the intricacies of the principal ascent. Ignore the footbridge, continue up the Greenup Gill path via gates. The forbidding presence of Eagle and Pounsey Crags lend drama to the ascent along a bridle route made all the more popular since 'A Coast to Coast Walk' was established in 1972. Just short of the moraine branch right, ford the gill and make a steady ascent left, thereby avoiding serious outcropping and quickly beating the bracken. There is no path but follow the naturally line, which turns and contours to the base of the truncated wall above Pounsey Crag. Follow the wall to within ten yards of the wall corner and slip carefully through the fence at the small outcrop to complete the climb.

The Summit

A broad tilted rock outcrop surmounted by a small cairn forms the summit, heather abounds. A second natural block lies prostrate a few yards to the north, this has the appearance of fallen pillar, though of course it's nothing of the sort. The view concentrates north-westward, back from whence you came, through the Stonethwaite valley. The best place to see the valley is some fifty yards north, a thin path leads to the spot - this must not be misconstrued as a line of descent!

Safe Descents

Descend south from the summit, slipping under the fenced section of the wall just left of the wall corner, follow the wall down. Where the wall abruptly ends above a cliff, contour right until easier slopes permit you to complete the descent via a steep open fellside. There is no hint of path after leaving the wall-end. Ford Greenup Gill and join the bridle-path leading down into the Stonethwaite valley.

Ridge Route to...

SERGEANT'S CRAG   DESCENT 30ft   ASCENT 200ft   0.5 miles

Descend south, cross the stile to the right of the wall corner and follow the ridge wall. The path is clear enough, latterly it drifts half-right up to the summit, be mindful that cliffs line the near western slopes.

Pounsey Crag from the spur viewpoint

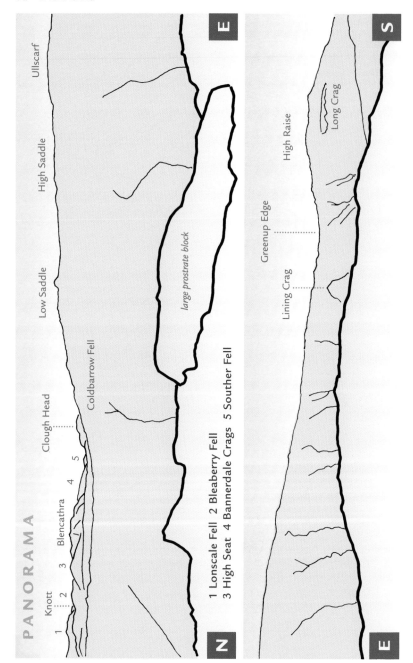

PANORAMA

Knott

1 2 3 4 5

Lonscale Fell Blencathra Clough Head Low Saddle High Saddle Ullscarf

Coldbarrow Fell

large prostrate block

N   E

1 Lonscale Fell 2 Bleaberry Fell
3 High Seat 4 Bannerdale Crags 5 Souther Fell

Lining Crag Greenup Edge High Raise

Long Crag

E   S

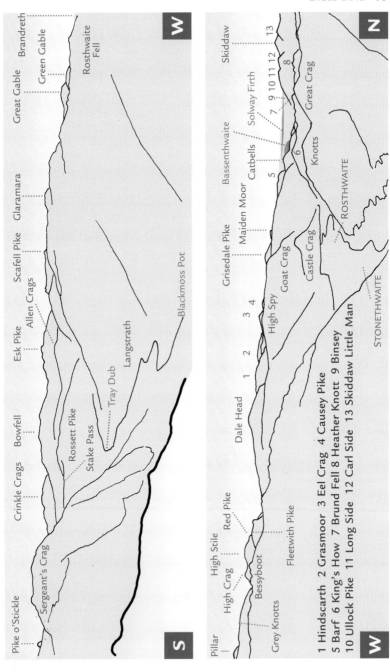

1 Hindscarth 2 Grasmoor 3 Eel Crag 4 Causey Pike 5 Barf 6 King's How 7 Brund Fell 8 Heather Knott 9 Binsey 10 Ullock Pike 11 Long Side 12 Carl Side 13 Skiddaw Little Man

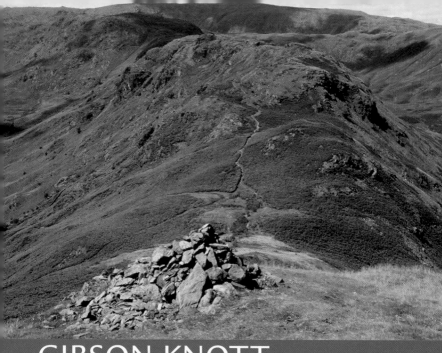

GIBSON KNOTT

Fells come in many guises, some are solitary summits while others, like Gibson Knott, are simply elements of a greater whole. The greater whole in question is the triple-topped ridge dividing Far Easedale from Greenburn Dale. As a ridge walk it is an undulating roller coaster ride that should put a smile on any fellwalker's face!

The southern slopes are rough and uninviting, with Horn Crag, the one major feature, tucked under the summit. There is but one line of approach from Far Easedale venturing to the Bracken Hause saddle. From Greenburn Dale, to the north, there are three comfortable lines; the corresponding route to Bracken Hause from the recently installed footbridge above Turn Howe, a pathless route from the stepping stones close to the moraines of the upper dale and a later shepherds' path reaching the depression below Pike of Carrs. Greenburn Dale deserves to be better known, a circuit concentrating on the valley is recommended using any two of these three routes, that can still include Helm Crag there and back from Bracken Hause.

From Town Head

421 metres   1,380 feet

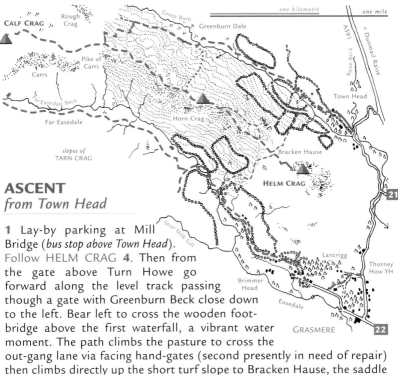

ASCENT
from Town Head

1 Lay-by parking at Mill Bridge (*bus stop above Town Head*). Follow HELM CRAG **4**. Then from the gate above Turn Howe go forward along the level track passing though a gate with Greenburn Beck close down to the left. Bear left to cross the wooden foot-bridge above the first waterfall, a vibrant water moment. The path climbs the pasture to cross the out-gang lane via facing hand-gates (second presently in need of repair) then climbs directly up the short turf slope to Bracken Hause, the saddle depression below Helm Crag. Turn right, the path avoids the early exchanges with the ridge, preferring to run along the southern flank with a bird's eye view over Stythwaite Steps into Far Easedale, before pitching onto the knobbly crest. Watch for the summit cairn, the path turns a 'blind-eye' at the critical moment.

2 Keep to the track via a second gate and short lane, pass above a more impressive waterfall, made all the more picturesque by the larch spinney and attendant ice-smoothed outcropping. The adjacent wall is lost, the track becomes a little less certain till, breaking through moraine, it encounters the large shallow basin of Greenburn Bottom. High to the right Blakerigg Crag presides over a lovely wild scene, the hollow once filled by a tarn. With some irony, comparable shallow pools adorn the flat ridge that forms the north-western headwall to this truncated dale. The fellwalker seeking peaceful sanctuaries will just love the upper reaches of Greenburn Dale. The path veers left to cross the newly set stepping stones. Bear left a matter of thirty yards downstream before bearing right to mount the obvious rounded grassy rigg, without a hint of a path. Climb, avoiding the skyline crags to the left, joining the ridge path at a marshy depression. Go left to reach the top after a tilted slab.

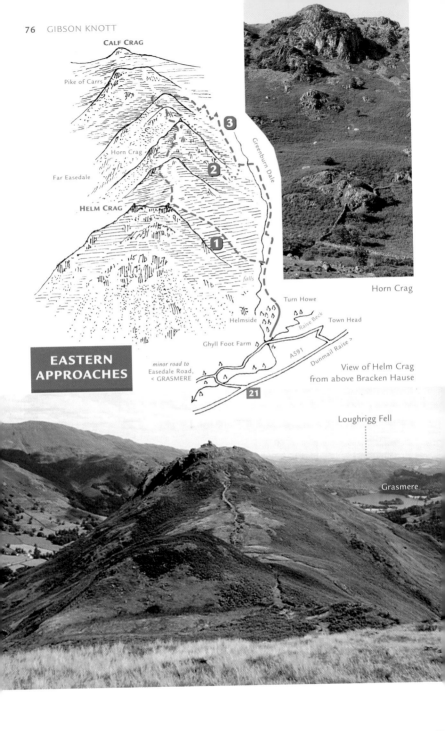

CALF CRAG

Pike of Carrs

Horn Crag

Far Easedale

HELM CRAG

Greenburn Dale

Horn Crag

falls

Turn Howe

Helmside

Ghyll Foot Farm

Raise Beck

Town Head

A591

Dunmail Raise >

EASTERN APPROACHES

minor road to Easedale Road, < GRASMERE

View of Helm Crag from above Bracken Hause

Loughrigg Fell

Grasmere

Helvellyn
Nethermost Pike
Dollywaggon Pike
Steel Fell
summit
Seat Sandal
Horn Crag
Easedale Tarn

From Blea Crag

3 Alternatively, from the stepping stones, bear right on a pleasing green way by an unusual triangular sheepfold built against three large boulders. The casual stroll is interrupted at a very modest six-stone cairn, from here the path heads uphill. Only after stepping over a marshy patch does the ascent ease onto a weaving trail that rises to the twin dip saddle on the ridge. Ahead, across Far Easedale, Deer Bields Crag is viewed as a striking cliff feature on the shadowy northern flank of Tarn Crag. While up to the right, the false summit of Pike of Carrs leads the eye westward up the ridge towards Calf Crag. Guided by the left-hand of two cairns, head east along the ridge. After some hundred yards spot an alcove 'throne' built into a ruckle of rocks to the left of the path *(see right)*. The ridge is entertainingly rocky, though there is one peaty interlude the path cannot avoid. As the path comes above a small crag watch for the summit cairn close to the left, easy to miss with attention fixed on maintaining a steady step!

See HELM CRAG page 121 for the ascent out of lower Far Easedale.

Boulder fold looking across Greenburn Bottom to Blakerigg Crag

The Summit

Perhaps it is fortunate that the consensus of visitor opinion has chosen a place for the summit cairn, one of several contending knobby knolls. The view is everything, especially over the wild bowl of Far Easedale, however, there is much else to enjoy; Helm Crag seems lowly backed by the might of the Helvellyn range; to the north the craggy face of Steel Fell and southwards the Coniston Fells beyond Blea Rigg. But it is to the rocky bulk of Codale Head that most attention will be given, with Harrison Stickle and Pavey Ark making guest appearances.

Safe Descents

From Pike of Carrs

Hold to the popular ridge path. If the need to leave the ridge is urgent then Bracken Hause to the east provides steep, but sure, lines to the foot of either Greenburn Dale for Town Head (north) and Far Easedale for Grasmere (south). There are two further reliable ways into Greenburn Dale, firstly from the first deep depression west of the summit, a path-less grass line down to the stepping stones, and secondly the old shep-herd's path further west, immediately before the climb to Pike of Carrs.

Ridge Routes to...

CALF CRAG   DESCENT 100 ft   ASCENT 480 ft   1.2 mile

The ridge path is clear cut, only becoming taxing with the climb to Pike of Carrs, from then on swathes of eroded peat lead to the summit outcrop. The views en route, particularly to Deer Bields, are excellent.

HELM CRAG   DESCENT 300 ft   ASCENT 330 ft   1 mile

The path dips from the summit with the main path trending onto the southern flank, though a slightly more taxing path continues along the ridge proper, if this has virtue then it is as means of side-stepping the inevitable drudgery of engaging with large walking parties. Helm Crag forms such a wonderful culmination to the ridge *(see book cover)*. The path slips straight across Bracken Hause and climbs directly to the foot of the massive jagged summit outcrop... and the decision to climb it or not!

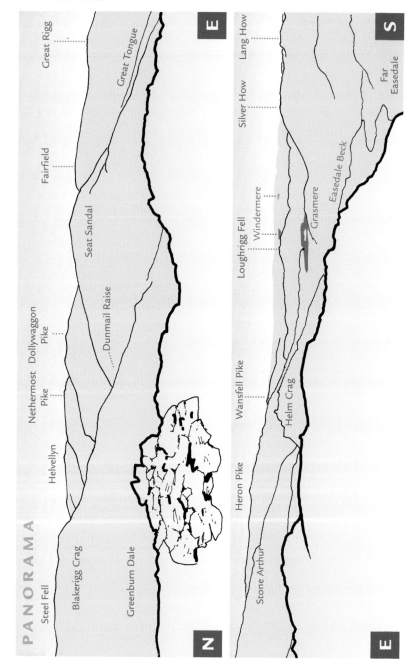

PANORAMA

Steel Fell · Blakerigg Crag · Helvellyn · Nethermost Pike · Dollywaggon Pike · Fairfield · Great Rigg

Greenburn Dale · Dunmail Raise · Seat Sandal · Great Tongue

N · E

Stone Arthur · Heron Pike · Wansfell Pike · Loughrigg Fell · Windermere · Silver How · Lang How

Helm Crag · Grasmere · Easedale Beck · Far Easedale

E · S

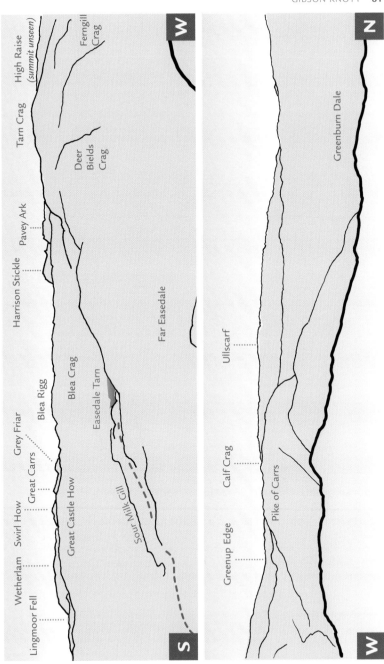

GRANGE FELL

The long perspective view above gives a strong clue to the rough nature of this tangled fell, which forms the steep verdant eastern cheek to the much adored Jaws of Borrowdale, where Derwentwater gives way to Borrowdale proper. To new eyes it must appear a confusing rocky height, birch, heather and bilberry clinging tenaciously to this knobbly irregular ridge where three summits vie for attention.

In terms of elevation and company this is a modest fell. What Grange Fell concedes in height is more than compensated by the infusion of the picturesque. Samuel Johnson said "he who tires of London, tires of life" - though he didn't have to park his car! Well the same may be said of Grange Fell. Climbers have long relished the accessibility and firm holds of Shepherd's, Black, Greatend, Bowder and Gowder Crags, while walkers have found comparable pleasure in unlocking its apparent labyrinth of paths combining the sylvan with a wild heatherscape.

Two summits are commonly sought, King's How and the actual top Brund Fell, while a third, Heather Knott set well to the north is invariably cold-shouldered, considered to be too much of a nuisance to bother with. Well, such weak-kneed thinking deserves to miss out, and duly does, for the traverse of this northern limb of the ridge from Lodore is delectably intricate. The climb onto the northern top of Brown Dodd deserves to be better known, though the going is tough over the ridge-top, here the heather has not been heavily grazed in recent decades and shows what a bit of healthy neglect can do for habitat diversity.

416 metres	BRUND FELL	1,365 feet
415 metres	HEATHER KNOTT	1,362 feet
392 metres	KING'S HOW	1,286 feet

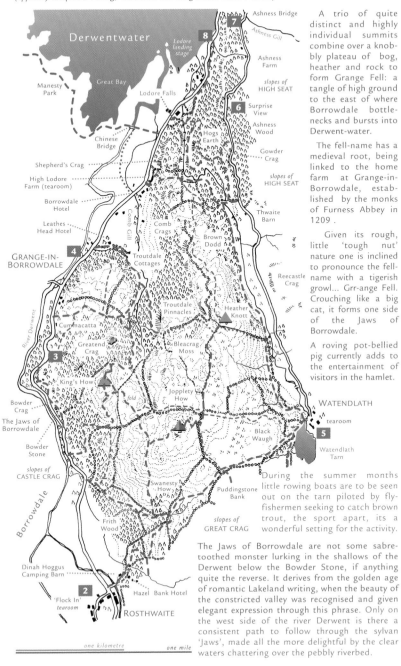

Derwentwater

Lodore landing stage

Ashness Bridge

Ashness Gill

8

7

Manesty Park

Great Bay

Lodore Falls

Ashness Farm

Chinese Bridge

slopes of HIGH SEAT

Shepherd's Crag

Hogs Earth

6

Surprise View

Ashness Wood

High Lodore Farm (tearoom)

Gowder Crag

Borrowdale Hotel

Comb Gill

slopes of HIGH SEAT

Leathes Head Hotel

Comb Crags

Thwaite Barn

GRANGE-IN-BORROWDALE

4

Troutdale Cottages

Brown Dodd

Reecastle Crag

Troutdale Pinnacles

Heather Knott

River Derwent

Cummacatta

Bleacrag Moss

3

Greatend Crag

King's How

Jopplety How

fold

Bowder Crag

WATENDLATH

The Jaws of Borrowdale

tearoom

5

Black Waugh

Bowder Stone

Watendlath Tarn

slopes of CASTLE CRAG

Borrowdale

Swanesty How

Puddingstone Bank

slopes of GREAT CRAG

Frith Wood

Dinah Hoggus Camping Barn

'Flock In' tearoom

2

Hazel Bank Hotel

ROSTHWAITE

one kilometre

one mile

A trio of quite distinct and highly individual summits combine over a knobbly plateau of bog, heather and rock to form Grange Fell: a tangle of high ground to the east of where Borrowdale bottlenecks and bursts into Derwent-water.

The fell-name has a medieval root, being linked to the home farm at Grange-in-Borrowdale, established by the monks of Furness Abbey in 1209 .

Given its rough, little 'tough nut' nature one is inclined to pronounce the fellname with a tigerish growl... Grr-ange Fell. Crouching like a big cat, it forms one side of the Jaws of Borrowdale.

A roving pot-bellied pig currently adds to the entertainment of visitors in the hamlet.

During the summer months little rowing boats are to be seen out on the tarn piloted by flyfishermen seeking to catch brown trout, the sport apart, its a wonderful setting for the activity.

The Jaws of Borrowdale are not some sabretoothed monster lurking in the shallows of the Derwent below the Bowder Stone, if anything quite the reverse. It derives from the golden age of romantic Lakeland writing, when the beauty of the constricted valley was recognised and given elegant expression through this phrase. Only on the west side of the river Derwent is there a consistent path to follow through the sylvan 'Jaws', made all the more delightful by the clear waters chattering over the pebbly riverbed.

BRUND FELL

This is the actual top of Grange Fell. Seen either from the Great Crag or Heather Knott it is identified by its bristly skyline. Two neighbouring outcrops vie for supremacy, with the jaunty sounding Jopplety How a passive onlooker, a shapely pike rarely, if ever, climbed.

HEATHER KNOTT

Merely a metre inferior to Brund Fell, but it attracts far fewer walkers, which is no bad thing for those who do make the effort. It is a real knott, particularly when seen from the south, a splendid objective, especially when combined in a triple-top traverse. The view north over Derwentwater to Skiddaw is marvellous, looking south-west from here there is a superb view of King's How. It culminates a tangled knot of heathery fell too, running over Brown Dodd, to the north liberally sprinkled with birch, quite a vision of what much of Lakeland could look like given reprieve from sheep grazing. In late summer its bracken slopes harbour massive, teeming ant hills, not evident where sheep maraud.

KING'S HOW

Named in 1910 as a memorial to King Edward VII, following its purchase by The National Trust. One might consider this the leading component of the Grange Fell massif, a craggy heavily wooded height, the compulsive objective for a climb out of the scenic wonderland that is the Jaws of Borrowdale. Many a walker who has climbed either via Troutdale or Red Brow has been more than content to leave the rest of the fell well alone. The view from the summit a rich reward, the eye is drawn south along the green strath of Borrowdale to the mighty Scafells, north beyond Derwentwater to Skiddaw and near west to the craggy

King's How from Heather Knott

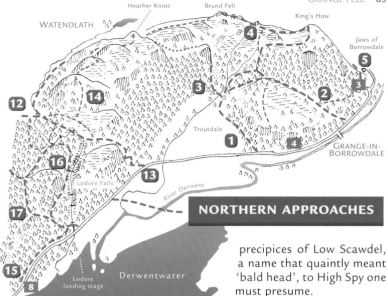

WATENDLATH

Heather Knott

Brund Fell

King's How

Jaws of Borrowdale

Troutdale

GRANGE-IN-BORROWDALE

Lodore Falls

River Derwent

NORTHERN APPROACHES

Lodore landing stage

Lodore

Derwentwater

precipices of Low Scawdel, a name that quaintly meant 'bald head', to High Spy one must presume.

The three component summits of Grange Fell have dedicated panoramas to instill those vivid scenes in the mind and gnaw at one's desire to return and claim them all.

ASCENT *from the Grange-in-Borrowdale*

1 Via Troutdale. Embark either from the Grange Bridge bus stop, or the small lay-by south of the Leathes Head Hotel. Walk beside the valley road to the bridle-lane branching right from behind the hotel. This leads to Troutdale Cottages and through a gate into Troutdale. A clear path runs on towards Comb Gill. Do not ford, keep right, rising into the woodland above the gill. The path rises to a hand-gate, bear left, fording a gill to rise into the birchwood shrouding the looming Greatend Crag. The path climbs purposefully on a stone-pitched staircase to heaven, for on a misty day there is a magical sense of being in the dwindling Costa Rican 'cloud forest'. The path winds up to a marshy hollow, keep right, climbing under a yew tree, ascend to the high point of the cross ridge wall: don't be tempted to follow this down it ends precipitously above Bowder Crag. Go left, joining the narrowing heather ridge

Grange-in-Borrowdale from Grange Crags

The Bowderstone

winding up to the summit.

From Quayfoot National Trust car park. There is a choice of two routes leading either north or south. **2** The more direct heads north. A hand-gate in the bounding fence marks an exit to the car park at its upper end. A minor path crosses the gill depression, passes a large erratic and slips through an old slate quarry to join the green bridle-path. This contours directly ahead above a damp slope, before climbing onto the ridge to a hand-gate in the saddle. Note: a spur path can be followed left, just prior to the hand-gate, it crosses a ladder-stile heading north to approach the birch fringed brink of Grange Crag: a little visited and quite enchanting viewpoint, especially notable for its bird's eye view of Grange Bridge. Backtrack to continue. Beyond the hand-gate in the saddle, a handsome view of Greatend Crag with an erratic in the foreground, advance till a path is spotted forking right, short of the next wall hand-gate, here join route **1**.

3 The stairway to heaven from Troutdale outlined in route **1**, can side-step King's How and progress directly to Brund Fell. Having completed the major stepped ascent, cross the fence stile left, the path running up a shallow side valley with a wall left, latterly curving right to join the direct path from King's How. Cross the ladder-stile to the left and rise to the next brow where the path bears acutely left climbing to the top of Brund Fell.

Brund Fell

King's How

Bleacrag Moss

Black Crag

Greatend Crag

South from Comb Crags

4 A beautiful approach to Heather Knott, based upon the path established by climbers to reach Black Crag and the famous Troutdale Pinnacles. Follow the path from Troutdale Cottages as in route **1**, only now stride across Comb Gill, climbing purposefully into the natural woodland on a well-made path to the base of Black Crag. A loose trail works up beneath the towering pinnacles to a notch beside a gill. Cross the fence tight by the rock. One may clamber left over the adjacent outcrop to discover a superb, if perilous, view down into Troutdale. The primary way follows the wall left beside Bleacrag Moss, curving up the rough valley head to the hand-gate, where the ridge path below Heather Knott is joined.

King's How

Puddingstone Bank

Bowder Stone

SOUTHERN APPROACHES

ROSTHWAITE

5 Via the Bowder Stone. Follow signs to the Bowder Stone, pass a fenced quarry via a gate on a surfaced pathway popular with all manner of appreciative visitors. Find the massive tilted boulder in a glade, the nearside angled sufficient to give climbers' scope for wet weather bouldering practice. It lies here not because it was plucked and tumbled from the crag above like so much of the rock in the vicinity, but rather as the random haul of a glacier, an Ice Age erratic. No Prehistoric rock-art has been recognised here, though that is not to say it does not exist. The flight of wooden steps gives access to the naturally notched top, countless visitors have made the rock slick, cautious visitors

Path above Red Brow

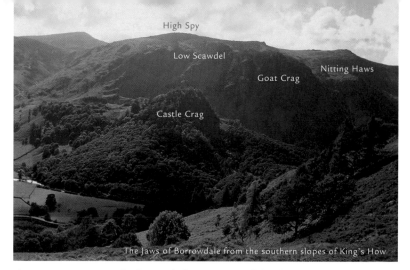

High Spy

Low Scawdel

Nitting Haws

Goat Crag

Castle Crag

The Jaws of Borrowdale from the southern slopes of King's How

do not venture too far beyond the security of the handrails! The path, a former quarry extraction track continues, declining to a hand-gate at the road. Follow the roadside verge path until a footpath sign and stile indicate the beginning of a path left. A clear path ascends through the bracken first onto the low rigg right, then curves left up through the bracken to slip under a yew tree, climbing to go through a broken wall winding up the steep lightly wooded fellside. The views improve as height is gained, particularly after coming above a wall, where they open to the south over the meadows of Borrowdale backed by the highest hills in England. This point can be reached by route **6**, an unusual and intriguing modern invention. Beginning a little further along the valley road at Red Brow, identified by the recessed lay-by, just where the road opens to the Borrowdale meadows. Go through the gate, ascend the bridle-path, a few yards short of a tiny gill ford, bear sharp left up the bank. An evident path leads uphill, ignore the early footpath right, which actually quickly becomes consumed by bracken, having fallen from favour. Continue climbing the wooded edge, the path persists to a wall gateway, link up with route **5** climbing the final open section of the south ridge to the top of King's How. **7** Continue up the bridle-path on a delightful woodland way ascending to a hand-gate. The path traverses a bracken fellside passing the cluster of rocks known as the Resting Stones, from here there is a lovely view down on the green Rosthwaite vale. Watch for the ladder-stile left before

Summit of King's How

Jopplety How

the conifer copse. One may continue to a kissing-gate to join the Puddingstone Bank path or cross this ladder-stile, climbing the slope beside the plantation, slanting left on a pronounced path. As King's How duly comes into view the path forks, go right climbing to the summit.

8 The popular bridle-path over Puddingstone Bank to Watendlath provides the ideal springboard for an ascent from Rosthwaite. Rosthwaite serves the visitor well, especially welcome the Flock-in tearoom. For the handful who find such things interesting, the village-name is thought to mean '*the enclosure surrounding a cairn*' – the stone piles engulfed by the jigsaw of walled enclosures in upper Wasdale being an elaborate expression of the same. Cross the Stonethwaite Beck bridge north of the Post Office, fork left facing the entrance to Hazel Bank Hotel. Passing above Dinah Hoggus camping barn, converted from a field hoghouse, originally winter housing for sheep, this is an aesthetically pleasing piece of farm diversification. The lane winds up to a gate. An open trail which has received some restorative treatment, leads up the slope. Take opportunities to look back from time to time as the view over upper Borrowdale improves with every

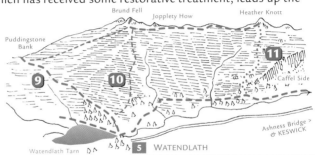

Brund Fell   Jopplety How   Heather Knott

Puddingstone Bank

9   **10**   **11**

Caffel Side

Watendlath Tarn   **5**   WATENDLATH

Ashness Bridge > & KESWICK

EASTERN APPROACHES

Brund Fell from the upper slopes of King's How, a rough fellscape in brown winter raiment which explains of the fell-name

stride and is quite superb. Two gates on, the track levels approaching the watershed. Bear left after the second gate, keeping the wall to the left to reach the low ladder-stile over the wall, duly cross and wind up to the summit outcrop.

ASCENT
from Watendlath

Heather Knott from the south

9 The easiest route of all strides out upon the bridle-path traversing Pudding-stone Bank. From The National Trust car park (with adjacent toilets and farmhouse tearoom) walk through the hamlet to cross the packhorse bridge at the outflow of Watendlath Tarn. Take the main path left via the hand-gate sign-posted to Rosthwaite, observing the antics of ducks and fly-fishermen afloat on the tarn. The track climbs steadily, with lovely views back upon the hamlet and tarn. Just short of the gate at the pass, go

Heather Knott and the Watendlath Beck valley from the knoll west of the hamlet

right accompanying route **8** to the top. Keeping the wall to the left, one may either cross the first ladder-stile on the left and ascend the pathless slope direct to the summit or, probably better, keep with the wall to the low ladder-stile at the top. **10** The direct ascent, avoiding the walking traffic on the Puddingstone Bank bridle-path. An early branch right, just above the tarn shore, leads up the bank, with a fine view down the Watendlath Beck valley towards Skiddaw *(see above)*. A narrow path leads through a hand-gate, ascend with a wall over to the right, sporadic evidence of a path. With some wet ground on the rise to the wall junction, go left along the ridge path, rounding the wall right to the low ladder-stile. **11** An unusual line of ascent to Brund Fell, which will inevitably turn into a circular walk as it first claims Heather Knott, a summit strikingly in view from Watendlath above the rugged Caffel Side. Go through the gate first right after the packhorse bridge and follow the path down the valley. Immediately before the second hand-gate and therefore before the short flight of steps, go left to clamber up the pathless rough fellside en route peering over the craggy ramparts of Caffel Side (*'deer calf's fellside'*). Climbing with a wall, then fence to the right, onto the upper slopes to reach the ridge-top stile at the fence junction to join the ridge path from Brund Fell. Cross the stile, work left, round and up the tough herbage to the summit of Heather Knott. Retrace your steps to the stile at the fence junction, head south keeping the fence to the right, ignore the hand-gate right in the dip, where route **4** joins from Bleacrag Moss. The undulating ridge is not only rough but very wet, a major contributory factor in the isolation of Heather Knott. Continue beside the fence negotiating marshy patches to a wall junction where there are two stiles. Cross the left-hand stile, keeping the wall to the right, round the right-hand corner to a low ladder-stile, cross and climb onto Brund Fell.

Daffodils at High Lodore Farm

ASCENT *from Lodore*

One may use the Ashness Bridge and Surprise View car parks as starting points for expeditions into the Watendlath valley. However, for the climb onto Brown Dodd, avoid road walking by passing through Hog's Earth wood to the footbridge at the foot of the upper valley meadows. Visitors to the Surprise View are both encouraged to revel in the view and given warning that it is the brink of a raw mountainside bereft of protection. It overlooks the great marsh running out into Derwentwater backed by Catbells and Skiddaw, a sumptuous scene, always rewarding and never the same with ever changing lighting and fell colour textures.

12 One may either follow the Watendlath road south through Ashness Wood, taking the first obvious track slip off right, through the woodland, dipping to a hand-gate adjacent to the Watendlath Beck footbridge. Or keep with the road past the finger rock to the cattle-grid,

Walkers conversing at Surprise View

turn immediately right, via the stile and steps descending to the footbridge. Spot the direction plate set in the ground at your feet on the western side. Keep the wall right, as to 'Lodore', but after 50 yards, before next hand-gate, go left, keeping the enclosure wall right. Go round the right-hand corner to reach a hand-gate where walls converge. Beyond, the footpath treads a small causeway, at the end turn acutely left.

13 This point can be reached on a more direct approach from High Lodore Farm. High Lodore Farm is quite a focus particu-

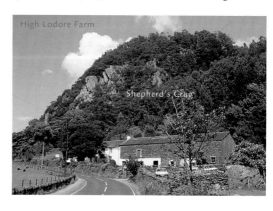

High Lodore Farm

Shepherd's Crag

larly for rock-climbers, the byre café used year-round by contingent's of agile rock-rats fresh from their routes on Shepherd's Crag. There is no casual parking in the vicinity, it is imperative to seek approval from the farm to use the farmyard for this purpose. Pass up the track behind the farm keep right, off the climbers' path, via a seat, then ascend to the saddle where paths radiate. Down to the left spot a dam at the head of the Lodore Falls gorge. The name Lodore actually describes this 'door', the main gorge of Watendlath Beck, while High Lodore, relates to the saddle you are standing on, the 'high low door'. One may continue, via the hand-gate, into the wood beside the tumultuous beck. Cross a fence stile to venture to the Watendlath Beck footbridge or go directly right, first with the wall right, then curve left, skip over a tiny gill to reach the neat wall running beside the causeway path.

14 The north ridge begins here, don't be under any illusion, while this is a fine route it is reminiscent of the Harlech Dome in Snowdonia, ankle twisting stuff. Re-ford that little gill and advance to a loose hand-gate in a wall. The path drives on through bracken aiming for the dip in the sky-line between outcropping, the view back over Derwentwater to Skiddaw from near the top makes a fine excuse for a brief breather! Once up bear half-left to thread through another outcrop gap. Again the path drifts left through the bracken and heather passing around a bluff, contouring by a tiny combe to reach a marshy tussocky hollow. Go forward to meet up with the wall and accompany this to where it curves right. Now bear left up a groove to follow the ridge-top path on Brown Knoll, again keep a left-hand bias over rank heather, avoid the second knoll, to a dip before the final pull to the top of Heather Knott via its western slope.

Derwentwater from Brown Dodd

Lodore Falls

Maps persist in naming this peak Ether Knott, reflecting local dialect. In Greek mythology ether was the upper atmosphere where heaven resided and, given the season and best of conditions, surely no more divine place exists!

ASCENT *from Kettlewell, Surprise View & High Lodore Farm*

15 Searches for a boiling spring will be in vain for all the name Kettlewell, delightfully situated on the south-eastern shores of Derwentwater. Cross the main road and follow the path right, weaving through the woods at the base of the Surprise View cliffs. This meets up with right-of-way at the back of the Hilton Lodore Hotel, signed off the road 'To Lodore Falls' leading through the backyard (akin an industrial works), passing the indoor swimming pool and over a footbridge. You might enjoy clambering into the chaos of boulders to view the 'fuming falls' by comparison with many a modest exhibition. The path climbs purposefully up the woodland bank, the first turn/s are the result of rock-climbers hasting down from Gowder Crag.

16 However, one may take a half-right branch to join the path leading

Watendlath, as seen during the descent from Brund Fell

up beneath the crag ascending above the gorge to a fence stile. **17** The same fence-line can be reached by continuing the initial ascent, the path switches right to cross a stile on the brink, all within woodland. This path continues forward to meet up with the Gowder route on a gentle curving path, by which means many strollers make a simple loop back. If the beck is low, and only then, one may venture to balance on the irregular stones to ford Watendlath Beck down to the right. Otherwise go left, south-east through Hog's Earth (which means '*the shelter of over-wintering hoggets*'), exiting the woodland at a hand-gate, joining route **12**, go right to cross the footbridge over Watendlath Beck.

Brund Fell summit

A question mark hangs over the summit. To be precise, which of two contending outcrops can claim superiority? The summit adopted by walkers *(see right)* is abrupt and only large enough to form a base to a small cairn. The irregular outcrop features several intriguing igneous medallions which take on artistic shapes looking as if they could have been chiselled. Old survey maps lead to the view that the outcrop a little to the west is one foot higher (hence the Brund Fell panorama is taken from that spot).

Safe Descents

The roughness and confusing terrain of the upper fell may be a concern in misty conditions. The easiest line of escape is east, cross the low ladder-stile thereon aim south, beside the descending wall to the top of Puddingstone Bank. On meeting the track, either go right (west) to Rosthwaite 1 mile, or left (east) to Watendlath 0.5 mile.

Ridge Routes to...

GREAT CRAG   DESCENT 300 ft   ASCENT 130 ft   1.3 miles

Begin upon the route to the top of Puddingstone Bank just described. A continuing path leads south, via the hand-gate, winding across intermittently marshy ground with patches of bog myrtle to a further hand-gate in a cross-ridge wall. The path bears slightly left to link up with the path rising from the lane on the west side of Watendlath Tarn. Now bear right, skirting the marsh to a hand-gate. Thereon the path climbs towards Dock Tarn, take the first clear turn right before the tarn to up to the top.

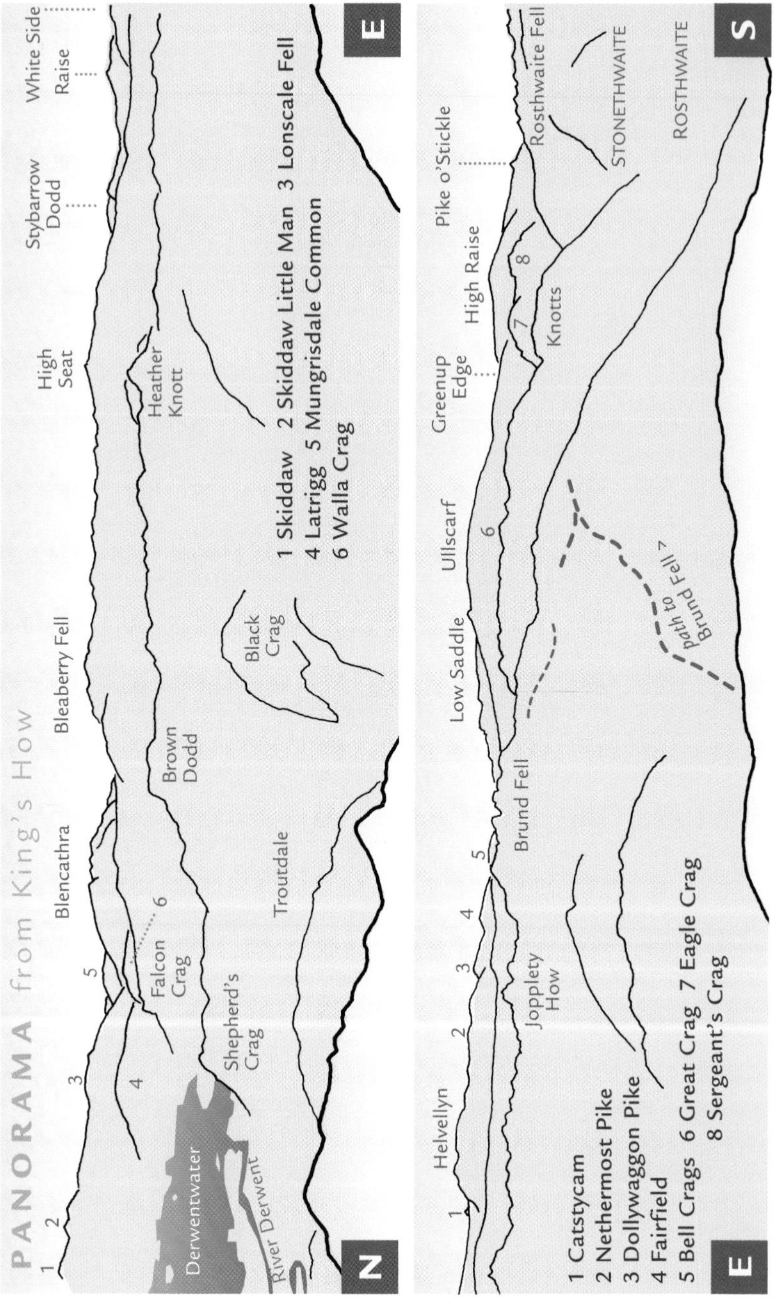

PANORAMA from King's How

Top panel (E / N):

White Side
Raise
Stybarrow Dodd
High Seat
Heather Knott
Bleaberry Fell
Blencathra
Brown Dodd
Black Crag
Troutdale
Falcon Crag
Shepherd's Crag
Derwentwater
River Derwent

1 Skiddaw 2 Skiddaw Little Man 3 Lonscale Fell
4 Latrigg 5 Mungrisdale Common
6 Walla Crag

Bottom panel (S / E):

Rosthwaite Fell
Pike o'Stickle
STONETHWAITE
ROSTHWAITE
High Raise
Greenup Edge
Knotts
Ullscarf
Low Saddle
Brund Fell
path to Fell
Joppolety How
Helvellyn

1 Catstycam
2 Nethermost Pike
3 Dollywaggon Pike
4 Fairfield
5 Bell Crags 6 Great Crag 7 Eagle Crag
8 Sergeant's Crag

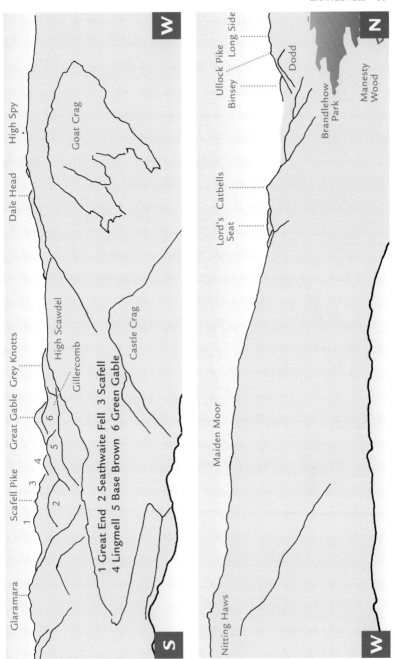

W

High Spy

Dale Head

Goat Crag

Glaramara   Scafell Pike   Great Gable   Grey Knotts

High Scawdel

Gillercomb

1   3   4   5   6
  2

1 Great End 2 Seathwaite Fell 3 Scafell
4 Lingmell 5 Base Brown 6 Green Gable

Castle Crag

S

N

Ullock Pike   Long Side

Binsey

Dodd

Lord's   Catbells
Seat

Brandlehow
Park

Manesty
Wood

Maiden Moor

Nitting Haws

W

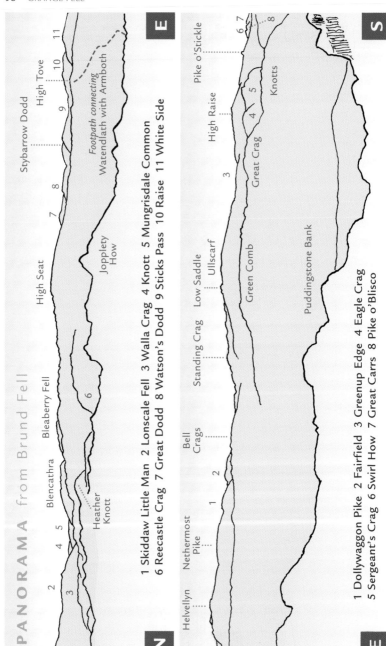

PANORAMA from Brund Fell

Helvellyn · Nethermost Pike · Bell Crags · Standing Crag · Low Saddle · Ullscarf · High Raise · Pike o'Stickle

Puddingstone Bank · Green Comb · Great Crag · Knotts

1 Skiddaw Little Man 2 Lonscale Fell 3 Walla Crag 4 Knott 5 Mungrisdale Common
6 Reecastle Crag 7 Great Dodd 8 Watson's Dodd 9 Sticks Pass 10 Raise 11 White Side

1 Dollywaggon Pike 2 Fairfield 3 Greenup Edge 4 Eagle Crag
5 Sergeant's Crag 6 Swirl How 7 Great Carrs 8 Pike o'Blisco

Helvellyn · Stybarrow Dodd · High Tove · High Seat · Bleaberry Fell · Blencathra · Heather Knott · Jopplety How

Footpath connecting
Watendlath with Armboth

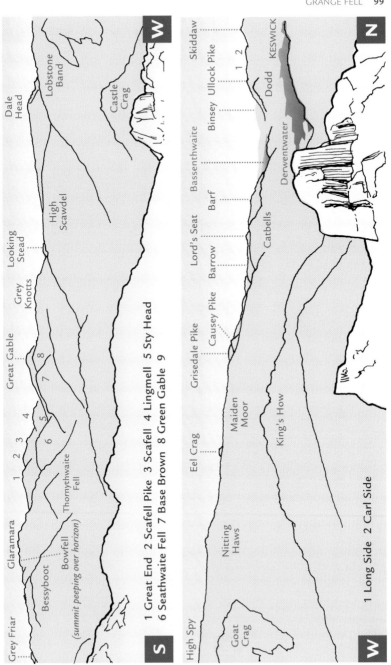

W

Dale Head

Lobstone Band

Castle Crag

Grey Friar

Glaramara

Bessyboot

Bowfell
(summit peeping over horizon)

Thornythwaite Fell

Great Gable

Looking Stead

Grey Knots

High Scawdel

S

1 Great End 2 Scafell Pike 3 Scafell 4 Lingmell 5 Sty Head
6 Seathwaite Fell 7 Base Brown 8 Green Gable 9

N

Skiddaw

Binsey Ullock Pike

Dodd KESWICK

Bassenthwaite

Barf

Derwentwater

Lord's Seat

Barrow

Catbells

Grisedale Pike

Causey Pike

Eel Crag

Maiden Moor

King's How

High Spy

Nitting Haws

Goat Crag

W

1 Long Side 2 Carl Side

PANORAMA from Heather Knott

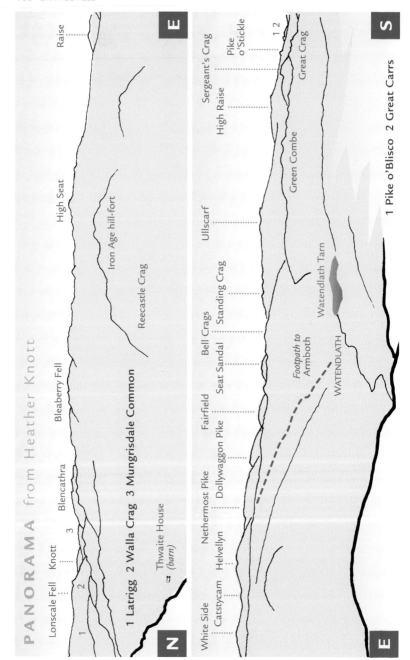

N

Lonscale Fell   Knott   Blencathra   Bleaberry Fell   High Seat   Raise

1 Latrigg **2** Walla Crag **3** Mungrisdale Common

Thwaite House *(barn)*

Reecastle Crag

Iron Age hill-fort

E

E

White Side   Nethermost Pike   Fairfield   Bell Crags   Ullscarf   High Raise   Sergeant's Crag

Catstycam   Helvellyn   Dollywaggon Pike   Seat Sandal   Standing Crag   Green Combe   Pike o'Stickle

Great Crag

Footpath to Armboth

Watendlath Tarn

WATENDLATH

1 Pike o'Blisco **2** Great Carrs

S

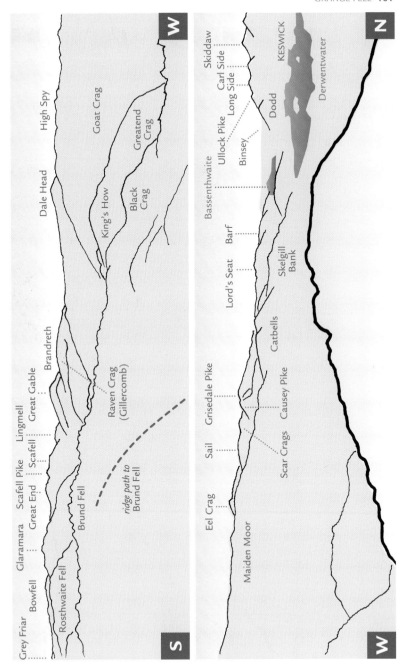

W

Grey Friar
Bowfell
Glaramara
Scafell Pike
Great End
Scafell
Lingmell
Great Gable
Brandreth
Dale Head
High Spy

Goat Crag

King's How

Greatend Crag

Black Crag

Raven Crag (Gillercomb)

Rosthwaite Fell

Brund Fell

ridge path to Brund Fell

S

N

Skiddaw
Carl Side
Ullock Pike
Long Side
Dodd
KESWICK
Binsey
Derwentwater

Bassenthwaite

Barf

Lord's Seat

Skelgill Bank

Catbells

Griesdale Pike

Causey Pike

Sail

Scar Crags

Eel Crag

Maiden Moor

W

GREAT CRAG

Observed from Stonethwaite the fell appears to be a mass of trees, a gloriously pleated deciduous skirt, such sylvan tapestries deserve to be revived elsewhere for the benefit of whole-fell diversity. Hidden are its roughly textured upper slopes luxuriant with heather, marsh and volcanic rock. Paths are few. Indeed, apart from the north/south traverse by Dock Tarn and sundry minor diversions to the summit the fell is bereft of confidence-giving trails, the fell-walker relying most on the instinctive twists and turns of sheep for any comfort.

The fell forms an intriguingly rough bridge between Grange Fell and the high central plateau of Ullscarf and is a backdrop to the much-loved lake-end scene at Watendlath. If your idea of a good time on the fells includes a spot of intense tanglefoot exploration, then this is your kind of top. It attracts few visitors, most actually ignore the summit, content with the shy charm of Dock Tarn on the lovely path between Stonethwaite and Watendlath. The tarn has irregular shores and is resplendent with reeds and one massive fairy circle of water lilies set over on the eastern side: the origin of the tarn name - from the Old English 'docce'. An unusual, yet fascinating excursion, when the heather is at its best, is to wander around the ring of little tops surrounding Dock Tarn, by High Crag, Green Comb, Black Knott and Great Crag (no path).

452 metres   1,483 feet

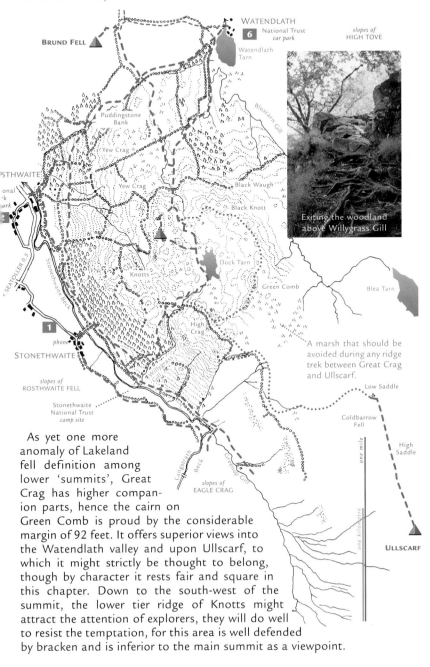

WATENDLATH
6 National Trust
car park

slopes of
HIGH TOVE

BRUND FELL

Watendlath
Tarn

Puddingstone
Bank

Yew Crag

Bleatarn Gill

STHWAITE

onal
k
rk

Yew Crag

Black Waugh

Black Knott

Exiting the woodland
above Willygrass Gill

Dock Tarn

< SEATOLLER O.S.

Stonethwaite Beck

Knotts

Green Comb

Blea Tarn

1

phone

STONETHWAITE

High
Crag

A marsh that should be
avoided during any ridge
trek between Great Crag
and Ullscarf

slopes of
ROSTHWAITE FELL

Stonethwaite
National Trust
camp site

Low Saddle

Coldbarrow
Fell

As yet one more
anomaly of Lakeland
fell definition among
lower 'summits', Great
Crag has higher compan-
ion parts, hence the cairn on
Green Comb is proud by the considerable
margin of 92 feet. It offers superior views into
the Watendlath valley and upon Ullscarf, to
which it might strictly be thought to belong,
though by character it rests fair and square in
this chapter. Down to the south-west of the
summit, the lower tier ridge of Knotts might
attract the attention of explorers, they will do well
to resist the temptation, for this area is well defended
by bracken and is inferior to the main summit as a viewpoint.

High
Saddle

Langstrath Beck

Greenup Gill

slopes of
EAGLE CRAG

one mile

one kilometre

ULLSCARF

Green Comb   High Crag   Dock Tarn   Knotts

4

Bleatarn Beck

2

3

Puddingstone Bank

5

Watendlath Tarn

WATENDLATH

Lillie ring Dock Tarn

ASCENT *from*
Rosthwaite & Watendlath

Cairn on Green Comb

Low Saddle

1 The perennially popular path over Puddingstone Bank to Watendlath provides the ideal springboard for an ascent. Cross the Stonethwaite Beck bridge north of the Post Office, fork left facing the entrance to Hazel Bank Hotel. Passing above Dinah Hoggus camping barn, the lane winds up to a gate. An open trail

leads up the slope, take opportunities to look back from time to time as the view over upper Borrowdale is quite superb. Two gates on, the track levels approaching the watershed. Bear right, off the bridle-path to the kissing-gate. **2** From the National Trust car park, behind the farmhouse tearoom, cross the packhorse bridge at the outflow of the tarn. Follow

Dale Head

High Scawdel

Dock Tarn from Green Comb

either the main path up to the watershed branching south via the aforementioned kissing-gate, along a clear path over boggy ground with a considerable growth of bog myrtle, noted for its midge-deterrent properties. At another kissing-gate the trail drifts left to meet up with the path climbing direct from Watendlath Tarn. **3** Or from the fork in the track beyond the initial gate after the packhorse bridge, follow the gated lane rising above the tarn, latterly winding up a pasture via gates onto the marshy ground meeting up with the former ridge-top path. One path leads on via yet

more marsh, curving right to a wall stile, climbing through a weakness in the Great Crag façade. The main thrust of the path wanders on towards the western shore of Dock Tarn, watch for the cairned branch path right, climbing onto the first top, the second is the true summit.

ASCENT *from Stonethwaite*

4 Car parking along the approach road, not in the hamlet please! Entering the community bear left at the kiosk, signed 'Greenup and Grasmere'. Cross Stonethwaite Bridge to a gate and join the main valley bridle-path, co-incident with Wainwright's *A Coast to Coast Walk*. Go right, via the gate. After the sheepfold, which forms a delightful foreground to views of Eagle Crag, the lane dips. At the low wall opening, after some fifty yards, bear half-left rising up the pasture on a turf trod between swathes of bracken to a wall-stile. The path goes left, rising to a wall-stile. Hereon the path climbs purposefully through the deciduous woodland, on a stony staircase, switching away from Willygrass Gill. The coppice trees are of comparable age, suggesting they were largely clear-felled within the last hundred years - oddly the wood is nameless. Emerging from the canopy take an approving view south to Eagle Crag and Sergeant's Crag, dramatically seen at their very best. Rising onto the appropriately named Lingy End, climb by the heather banks and ruined shepherd's shelter. Skirt round the re-entrant of Willygrass Gill, the view is of the inaccessible High Crag above the eastern fork of the cascading gill. Cross over the wall stile continuing to the shores of Dock Tarn, seek the path leading left at the northern end of the tarn. On a path wind north-westward to the summit.

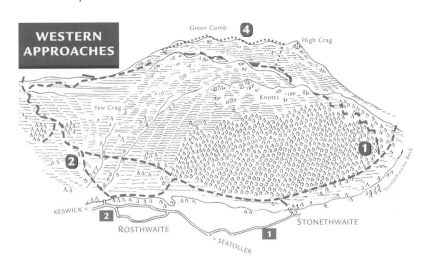

WESTERN APPROACHES

Green Comb

High Crag

Knotts

Yew Crag

Stonethwaite Beck

KESWICK <

ROSTHWAITE

> SEATOLLER

STONETHWAITE

Eagle and Sergeant's Crags from the ruined bothy on Lingy End

The Summit

Heather, sadly deficient on so many fells makes repose in this vicinity quite delightful, notably when in full late-summer bloom. To the north, beyond a short depression, a large cairn rests on a rock step. Further cairns mark a subsidiary top, blessed with a superior northward prospect towards Grange Fell and Skiddaw.

Safe Descents

The consistent path running alongside Dock Tarn gives security for descents to Watendlath 1.3 miles, Rosthwaite (north) 2 miles or Stonethwaite (south) 1.4 miles, so head east from the summit to join it.

Ridge Routes to...

GRANGE FELL   DESCENT 130 ft   ASCENT 300 ft   1.3 miles

A path leads north over an adjacent cairned top then bears right, dropping north-east to join the path from Dock Tarn. This now continues down to a wall-stile, bearing half-right avoids marshy ground resplendent with bog myrtle. At the path fork go half-left to a kissing-gate, more marshy ground crossed en route to a second kissing-gate. Cross the Puddingstone Bank track, ascending with the wall left to a low ladder-stile, cross and wind up to the summit, which is the second top after the apparent summit, marked by a cairn on a sharp pike.

Watendlath from the summit

(right) Igneous rings on Black Knott

ULLSCARF
ASCENT 1,300 ft

DESCENT 50 ft
2.8 miles

To minimise rough and seriously boggy ground head south-east to follow the main path beyond the outflow of Dock Tarn. Where a wall is seen rising left, bear off, ford the outflow gill, ascending with the wall to the right, cross the saddle, to the left of High Crag. Descend, enjoy the marvellous views of Eagle and Sergeant's Crag as well as the long view up Langstrath to Bowfell. The wall dips right, contour to pick up the wall again along the edge above Greenup Gill. Rising and falling as some latterday Hadrian's march, follow the wall until rounding a knoll, one may spin off east climbing the fellside to Low Saddle and, picking up the ridge path, continue south-south-east to High Saddle and the ridge fence. Cross the flimsy stile near the acute corner to reach the summit.

Borrowdale

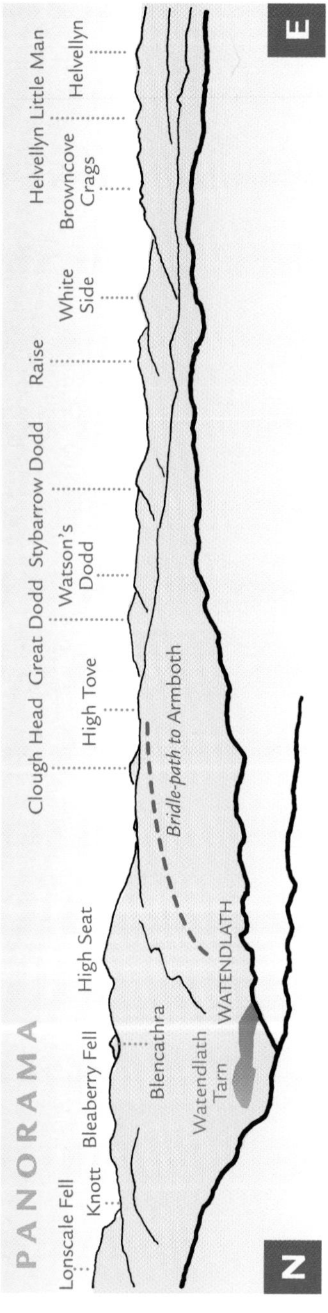

PANORAMA

N

Lonscale Fell · Knott · Bleaberry Fell · High Seat · Blencathra · Watendlath Tarn · WATENDLATH · Bridle-path to Armboth · High Tove · Clough Head · Great Dodd · Stybarrow Dodd · Watson's Dodd · Raise · White Side · Browncove Crags · Helvellyn Little Man · Helvellyn

E

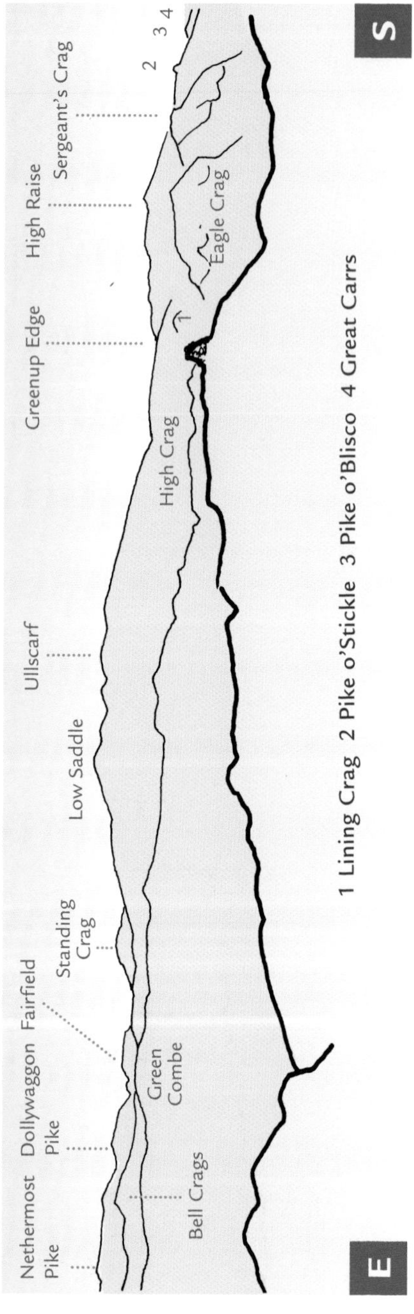

E

Nethermost Pike · Dollywaggon Pike · Fairfield · Standing Crag · Green Combe · Bell Crags · Low Saddle · Ullscarf · High Crag · Greenup Edge · High Raise · Sergeant's Crag · Eagle Crag · 2 · 3 · 4

S

1 Lining Crag 2 Pike o'Stickle 3 Pike o'Blisco 4 Great Carrs

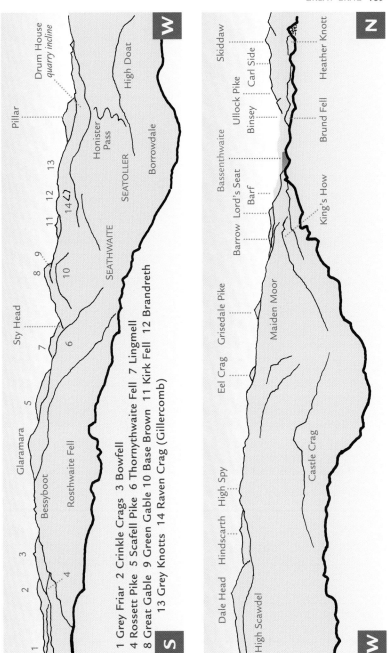

W

S

1 Grey Friar 2 Crinkle Crags 3 Bowfell
4 Rossett Pike 5 Scafell Pike 6 Thornythwaite Fell 7 Lingmell
8 Great Gable 9 Green Gable 10 Base Brown 11 Kirk Fell 12 Brandreth
13 Grey Knotts 14 Raven Crag (Gillercomb)

Drum House *quarry incline*
Pillar
High Doat
Honister Pass
SEATOLLER
Borrowdale
SEATHWAITE
Sty Head
Glaramara
Bessyboot
Rosthwaite Fell

N

W

Skiddaw
Ullock Pike
Carl Side
Bassenthwaite
Binsey
Barrow Lord's Seat
Barf
King's How
Heather Knott
Brund Fell
Grisedale Pike
Eel Crag
Maiden Moor
Dale Head Hindscarth High Spy
Castle Crag
High Scawdel

HARRISON STICKLE

The Langdale Pikes are up there with Skiddaw and Great Gable as Lakeland landscape icons. On travelling along the winding road up Great Langdale one turns that corner out of Chapel Stile to suddenly comprehend the majesty of the Langdale Pikes, it's one of the most marvellous mountain moments any visitor can have (*see above*).

Harrison Stickle is central, lord and master of a noble group of highly individual fells. The company, composed of the four 'pikes' Loft Crag, Pike o'Stickle and Pavey Ark, with Thunacar Knott at back stop. An expedition to any one will turn into a four-top-trip, they have that effect. Why resist such a heady cocktail of thrilling situations?

The craggy head of Harrison Stickle throws down steep slopes to Stickle Tarn, a tendril ridge reaching down to the valley held tight in the vice by Dungeon and Stickle Ghylls. This rigg has its own moment of exuberance in the little peak of Pike How. Although it always seems such an obstacle from the valley floor, it melts away into insignificance once height is gained, then the real contenders faced.

In the title view above notice the figure in the foreground is bouldering on the Copt How erratics. This practice should be considered in the light of the recent discovery of six thousand year old rock-art at this precise spot, probably allied to the stone axe factory on Pike o'Stickle.

736 metres   2,415 feet

ASCENT *from New Dungeon Ghyll*

Millbeck Farm

The ultra-popularity of the Langdale Pikes has ensured a plethora of paths, the line of every desire expressed as a trail of some sort or other.

1 Go either directly up the bridle-path from the hotel or ascend from Stickle Ghyll car park information shelter. The paths meet up by the fenced gap, follow the paved path beside Stickle Ghyll. Cross the footbridge rising to a stile. Keep to the right-hand side of the valley winding through a fenced area shielding the slope from erosion, the fencing has been compromised by sheep thus minimising any bene-fits of grazing relief. Higher up, after mounting a rock step the path fords the gill and completes to the dam before Stickle Tarn. Ahead the massive crag of Pavey Ark frowning down on the cool dark waters of Stickle Tarn and high to the left Harrison Stickle. Go left on the obvious path, which has received some restorative paving, more is needed. Work up the slope to the right of the buttresses. On meeting the contouring path from Pavey Ark, head left with two optional paths to the very top, the left-hand is marginally easier.

Loose scree renders the exit to the top ravine of Dungeon Ghyll unstable. In the interests of reducing wear and tear give it a miss. **THUNACAR KNOTT**

Look at the title picture to get a real impression of the scale of the fell, the map scaling does not do it justice.

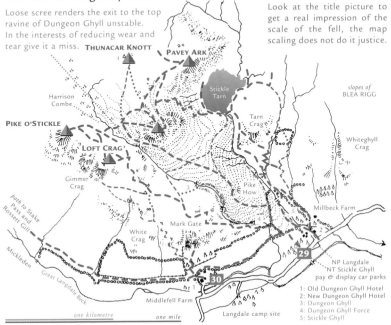

PAVEY ARK

Stickle Tarn

slopes of BLEA RIGG

Harrison Combe

PIKE O'STICKLE

Tarn Crag

Whiteghyll Crag

LOFT CRAG

Gimmer Crag

Pike How

Millbeck Farm

path to Stake Pass and Rossett Gill

Mark Gate

White Crag

29

Mickleden

30

NP Langdale
NT Stickle Ghyll
pay & display car parks

Great Langdale Beck

Middlefell Farm

Langdale camp site

1: Old Dungeon Ghyll Hotel
2: New Dungeon Ghyll Hotel
3: Dungeon Ghyll
4: Dungeon Ghyll Force
5: Stickle Ghyll

one kilometre   *one mile*

Bog-bean in a pool overlooked by Harrison Crag

2 The Pike How route leads off left from the fence gap, rising to a hand-gate, turn right passing a seat to a stile. Keep the wall right, do not ford Dungeon Ghyll. The well-marked path bears left mounting the steep slope in steady stages, much of it re-engineered to cope with the inevitable heavy foot traffic. Many walkers use this as their return leg after the ascent via Stickle Ghyll, though they would be better resorting to the Mark Gate path off Loft Crag, it has the best base. Climbing up to the saddle behind Pike How, make the move right to stand on top, it is a super viewpoint. Note: a minor path advancing north from Pike How along the rim of the slope on a right-hand curve to reach the Stickle Tarn dam, this path might appeal to walkers as an honourable retreat, having ascended Stickle Ghyll only to find the higher fells consumed in threatening cloud.

PAVEY ARK

Thorn Crag

2

1

> path to SERGEANT MAN

> path to BLEA RIGG

Stickle Tarn

Tarn Crag

path to LOFT CRAG and Gimmer Crag <

Pike How

Stickle Ghyll

Mark Gate

3

Dungeon Ghyll Force

SOUTHERN APPROACHES

path to the ODG Hotel < and Mickleden

Millbeck Farm

29

Old Dungeon Ghyll Hotel & Little Langdale <

New Dungeon Ghyll Hotel & Sticklebarn Tavern

The main path proceeds across the open pasture aiming west-north-west for the high shoulder above the deep upper gorge of Dungeon Ghyll. The aggressive slope beneath Harrison Crag affords the path little room, so take your time, watch your footing, as there is loose ground to negotiate. Entering Harrison Combe come to the path junction above the peat-hopping stepping stones. Either turn sharp right, this route has a rock step half-way up, or curve round to the right to approach the summit from the north-west, without such an obstacle.

3 For those attuned to wild ravines Dungeon Ghyll (*see right*) has an aura that is at the same time forbidding and fabulously attractive. The lower section, shrouded in bracken and trees, is a tight gorge, wherein lurks the actual dungeon. There is no way through, not even the most agile, aquatic gill-scrambler can force through. The route begins by fording Dungeon Ghyll on the recently re-engineered path on course for Loft Crag.

However, at the next easing of the ravine above Dungeon Ghyll Force one may cautiously enter, watching not to trip on tree roots as you do. Scramble over the mid-gill rocks to follow the right bank up to the first mare's tail waterfall. Scramble dexterously up the right-hand outcropping. The scenery is superb. Keep to the right bank until forced onto the left side, climb up through the large boulders to reach the baulking upper fall. A thunderous scene, the water crashing into a pool before finally spilling to the gill floor. The exit is the unlikely looking gully left, a sinister but safe scramble leads onto the tame fell pasture. Hold to the trod bearing right from the popular path to Loft Crag, angle gently down to ford Dungeon Ghyll in this tame intermediary phase. The path quickly joins route **2**, alternatively, continue across the slope to Stickle Tarn and link with route **1**.

The Summit

Given the visibility it would be hard not to enjoy a visit to this place. Being part and parcel of one of England's finest landscapes does ensure it quite some dignity. There are cairns on the north and south tops, the former being the actual summit. Rock abounds, the most threatening on the southern rim, so be wary. The view should make you linger and look long and hard. Pavey Ark is subservient but no less impressive, its relationship to Stickle Tarn seen at its best (*see right*). The blue ribbon of Windermere draws the eye east, can you spot Low Wood Hotel gleaming white on its far shore? Its is a wonderful spot to witness how the fells rise from the Silurian south and east to an heroic volcanic girdle of high fells crowding above Great Langdale.

Safe Descents

Just make sure you leave the summit on a northern bias, there is nothing but peril to the south. Paths are well enough marked by constant use.

The steep, rough descent to Stickle Tarn is sheltered from a western breeze. The easier route takes the path trending north, as if to Thunacar Knott, taking a left curving line from west to south into Harrison Combe. The narrow trod above the upper gorge of Dungeon Ghyll demands care. Beyond, the way is simple, heading SE to round Pike How to the right.

Ridge Routes to...

LOFT CRAG DESCENT 345 ft ASCENT 200 ft   0.3 miles

Two popular paths lead either west, with a rock-step to carefully negotiate, or north, curving left over easier slopes down to the stepping-stones. Cross the large boulders, to help avoid further erosion in the peaty hollow of Harrison Combe. Take the first path left, then angle right on the path mounting the prominent ridge to the cairn.

PAVEY ARK DESCENT 190 ft ASCENT 95 ft   0.6 miles

Either slip down the north-east path which contours just below the edge over rough ground or keep to the ridge via the north path, passing a rock tor before drifting right to join a more definite path. The coarse rocks, obviously abrasive, are a fascinating feature of this locale and may tempt many a photographer to reach for their camera seeking to use the textured rocks as foreground subjects. Cross the wall to reach the cairnless summit.

PIKE O'STICKLE DESCENT 345 ft ASCENT 250 ft   0.5 miles

From the stepping-stones in Harrison Combe, continue west on the worn path to the base of the summit stack. It's a 'hands on' rock all the way to the top, a compulsive climb to a stunning, scenic station.

THUNACAR KNOTT DESCENT 190 ft ASCENT 150 ft   0.5 miles

Take the north path, dipping to skirt to the left of the rock tor, not being on a main ascent route the path is less than convincing. The first cairn is the summit, the cairn beyond the pool, elsewhere cited as the summit, is several feet lower.

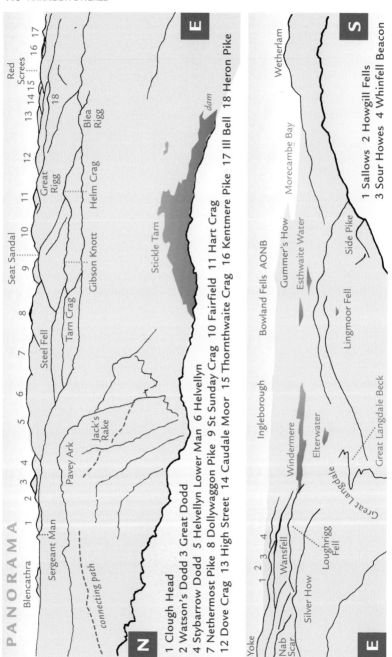

PANORAMA

N

Blencathra
Sergeant Man
connecting path

Red Screes
13 14 15 16 17
18
Seat Sandal
Great Rigg
Steel Fell
Tarn Crag
Pavey Ark
Jack's Rake
Gibson Knott
Helm Crag
Blea Rigg
Stickle Tarn
dam

E

1 Clough Head
2 Watson's Dodd 3 Great Dodd
4 Stybarrow Dodd 5 Helvellyn Lower Man 6 Helvellyn
7 Nethermost Pike 8 Dollywaggon Pike 9 St Sunday Crag 10 Fairfield 11 Hart Crag
12 Dove Crag 13 High Street 14 Caudale Moor 15 Thornthwaite Crag 16 Kentmere Pike 17 Ill Bell 18 Heron Pike

E

Yoke
Nab Scar
Wansfell
Silver How
Loughrigg Fell
Windermere
Elterwater
Great Langdale
Great Langdale Beck
Ingleborough
Bowland Fells AONB
Esthwaite Water
Gummer's How
Morecambe Bay
Lingmoor Fell
Side Pike
Wetherlam

S

1 Sallows 2 Howgill Fells
3 Sour Howes 4 Whinfell Beacon

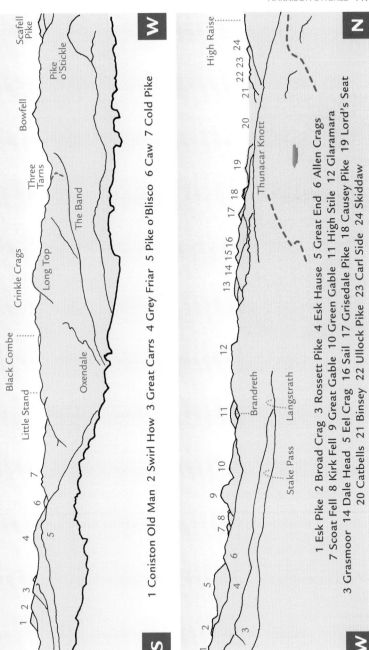

W

S

1 Coniston Old Man 2 Swirl How 3 Great Carrs 4 Grey Friar 5 Pike o'Blisco 6 Caw 7 Cold Pike

Scafell Pike · Pike o'Stickle · Bowfell · Three Tarns · The Band · Long Top · Crinkle Crags · Black Combe · Little Stand · Oxendale

N

W

High Raise

Thunacar Knott

Brandreth · Langstrath · Stake Pass

1 Esk Pike 2 Broad Crag 3 Rossett Pike 4 Esk Hause 5 Great End 6 Allen Crags
7 Scoat Fell 8 Kirk Fell 9 Great Gable 10 Green Gable 11 High Stile 12 Glaramara
3 Grasmoor 14 Dale Head 5 Eel Crag 16 Sail 17 Griesdale Pike 18 Causey Pike 19 Lord's Seat
20 Catbells 21 Binsey 22 Ullock Pike 23 Carl Side 24 Skiddaw

HELM CRAG

Intrinsic to the Vale of Grasmere. Yet for all the greater bulk of surrounding fells more regularly lose their heads in cloud, it is no wonder that this modest height is known as the cloud-capped hill. People have travelled over Dunmail Raise for countless centuries, the main north/south road through the wild fells of Cumbria for lords and the lorded, all eyes turning in recognition to this one knobbly fell. It was always a landmark, the one fell everyone knew by sight, so if lost in mist, with its head in the clouds it was considered 'helmeted'.

Of more recent centuries those travellers have been tourists, who found irresistible the biblical analogy in the likeness of the summit rocks to a lion lying down with the lamb. The rocks on the southern skyline joining in with the fun and games by giving observers from the village a second, perhaps even more convincing, Leo profile. How many visitors have thought they were looking at the same group of rocks they saw on their journey south into the valley upon the A591? Casually it appears a singularity, but fell-walkers know the fell's connectedness with the delightful roller coaster ridge running over Gibson Knott to Calf Crag ending at the saddle at the very top of Far Easedale.

405 metres   1,329 feet

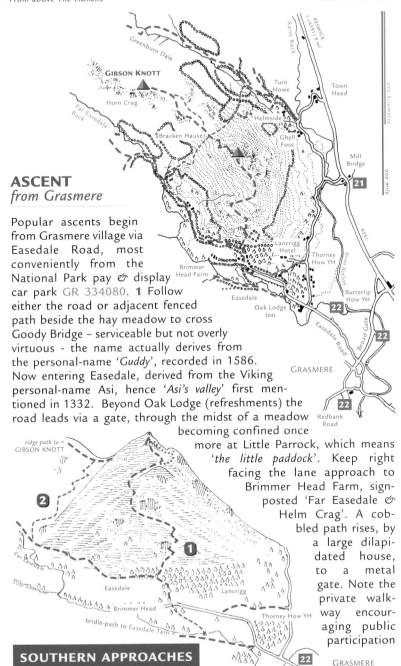

ASCENT
from Grasmere

Popular ascents begin
from Grasmere village via
Easedale Road, most
conveniently from the
National Park pay & display
car park GR 334080. **1** Follow
either the road or adjacent fenced
path beside the hay meadow to cross
Goody Bridge – serviceable but not overly
virtuous - the name actually derives from
the personal-name 'Guddy', recorded in 1586.
Now entering Easedale, derived from the Viking
personal-name Asi, hence 'Asi's valley' first mentioned in 1332. Beyond Oak Lodge (refreshments) the
road leads via a gate, through the midst of a meadow
becoming confined once
more at Little Parrock, which means
'the little paddock'. Keep right
facing the lane approach to
Brimmer Head Farm, sign-
posted 'Far Easedale &
Helm Crag'. A cob-
bled path rises, by
a large dilapi-
dated house,
to a metal
gate. Note the
private walk-
way encour-
aging public
participation

SOUTHERN APPROACHES

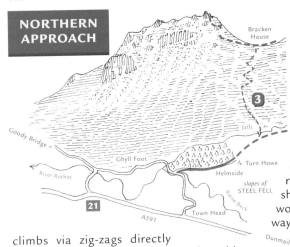

NORTHERN APPROACH

signed right to Lancrigg. Known as the 'Poet's Walk' this leads through pleasant woodland to the guest house - where scrumptious teas are served! From the metal gate two routes diverge. Trend right, through the short lane flanked by woodland, taking the waymarked path which climbs via zig-zags directly ahead above an old quarry. Note that older guides and maps indicate a path taking a right slant, this has been rested. Time, toil and no little funds, some the from readership of *The Great Outdoors* magazine, went into engineering a new 'popular' path up the fell. This path is an excellent piece of re-thinking, actually a better route than the old way, enjoying superb views into Far Easedale. Ascending over bare rock at one point before switching right on turf to a saddle

Far Easedale from the summit >

From above Winterseeds

(where the old route joined the ridge proper). Head north up the ridge, scramble over the southernmost skyline lion outcrop en route to the summit – and, for most walkers, this will be the base of the summit how-itzer. Immediately to the east an ancient landslipped sub-tier gives scope for a spot of exploration. Even if you feel making it to the very top knot is not your cup of tea, this rough slope will give you a sense of elation and adventure, as not too many visitors venture away from the ridge proper.

2 Go left with the bridle-path, again initially flanked by woodland. This track-cum-lane being the age-old pony trail up Far Easedale, destined for Borrowdale via the high watershed of Greenup Edge. The profile of the route elevated in recent years when Alfred Wainwright created his 'A Coast to Coast Walk'. The rough tracked lane passes a vernacular barn en route, to come alongside Far Easedale Beck. As the right-hand wall bears up right follow suit, with little early evidence of a path but one does materialise winding up onto a knoll to mount the steep bracken slope. Pass a lone thorn at a spring to reach the saddle of Bracken Hause, how appropriate after that climb! Go naturally right with the ridge path to the top.

From higher up Far Easedale

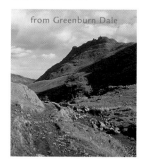

from Greenburn Dale

ASCENT *from Town Head*

This is the nippy route, catching the fell unawares! **3** There is a bus stop on the A591 above the Town Head Farm, or use the Mill Bridge verge parking space and follow the minor road down over the Rothay bearing right by Ghyll Foot to reach the drive access to Helmside. Ascend the metalled lane, via its cattle-grids, to the gate beyond Turn Howe. Go forward along the level track passing though a

gate with Greenburn Beck close down to the left. Bear left to cross the wooden footbridge above the first waterfall (*see right*). The path climbs the pasture to cross the out-gang lane, via facing hand-gates, climbing directly up the steep short turf slope to Bracken Hause.

The Summit

The ordinary mortal might feel cheated, having struggled up the confounded hill only to find that some clown has built a unassailable fortress on top, complete with a moat! Steady headed scramblers will think nothing of the twenty-four

summit outcrop from the west

lines of ascent

The Grasmere 'Lion & Lamb'

foot climb, with either a rib to the south, or north-west groove as their choice; the author has made it to the top on three occasions, each time via the latter line. Console yourselves, there is little extra merit in the ultimate view, though the panorama is concocted from a composite of images taken from the actual top - during the author's tentative retreat, his camera received a severe blow, though mercifully it survived to take the title view of Gibson Knott!

Safe Descents

Both conventional lines of ascent give secure footing, the route north from Bracken Hause to the footbridge spanning Green Burn is steep but most free of rock hazard.

Ridge Route to...

GIBSON KNOTT   DESCENT 330 ft   ASCENT 300 ft   1 mile

Descend NW to the saddle depression of Bracken Hause, the ridge path proceeds less than faithful to the ridge keeping a southern bias, though one may tackle the ridge proper with no hazard.

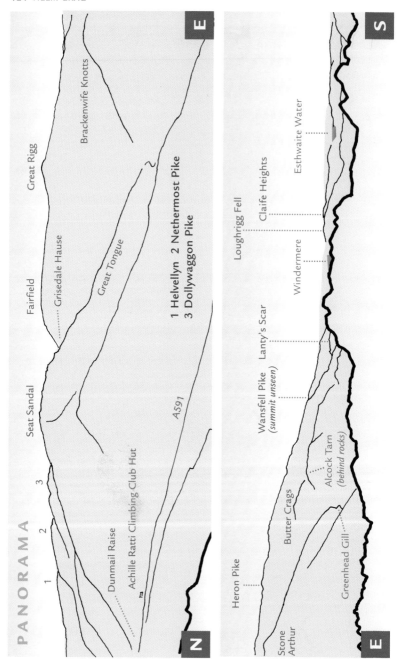

P A N O R A M A

N

E

1 Helvellyn 2 Nethermost Pike
3 Dollywaggon Pike

Great Rigg

Brackenwife Knotts

Fairfield

Grisedale Hause

Great Tongue

A591

Seat Sandal

3

2

1

Dunmail Raise

Achille Ratti Climbing Club Hut

S

E

Loughrigg Fell

Claife Heights

Esthwaite Water

Windermere

Lanty's Scar

Wansfell Pike
(summit unseen)

Heron Pike

Butter Crags

Alcock Tarn
(behind rocks)

Stone
Arthur

Greenhead Gill

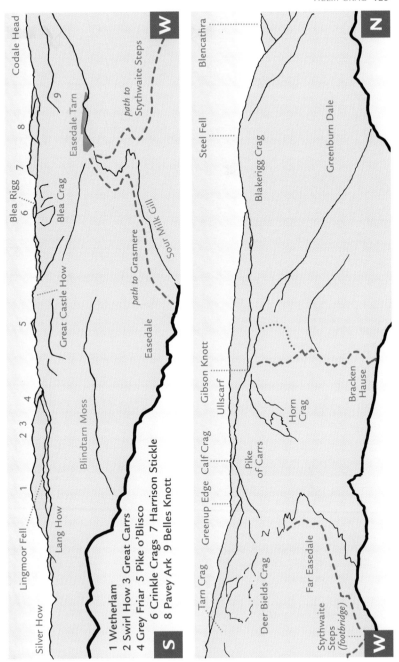

S

1 Wetherlam
2 Swirl How 3 Great Carrs
4 Grey Friar 5 Pike o'Blisco
6 Crinkle Crags 7 Harrison Stickle
8 Pavey Ark 9 Belles Knott

W

N

W

HIGH RAISE

Rosthwaite, in the depths of Borrowdale, meant 'the raise or cairn within an enclosure'. From the village the distant cairn on the south-eastern skyline would be the high cairn, hence High Raise. The main body of the fell has a simple symmetry, content with its role as a range-top, scarp-top viewpoint, reserving all flamboyance for its ancillary parts. It lies unabashed at the solar plexus of mountain Lakeland, surrounded by far finer specimen heights, a rather plain broad plateau pasture bursting into momentary life on the brink above Langstrath.

Given half decent visibility High Raise performs a noble duty as a major panoramic station. The view in the western arc beyond Langstrath and Glaramara features Bowfell, Scafell Pike and Great Gable, with the consistently high switchback skyline of the Helvellyn and Fairfield range forming the eastern horizon.

Invariably visitors make this the turning point of their day's walk, a chance to lengthen the stride after a tough pull onto any one of the Langdale Pikes, backtracking to Sergeant Man or Thunacar Knott.

By its nature and superior situation it gives a solid reason for any number of radial approaches and circuits, a natural crescendo, drawing out a walk that may otherwise have timidly turned forfeiting a precious hour on the roof of the range. High Raise is a reward, not an irksome addition, for seasoned fellwalkers this is an oft repeated royal balcony.

762 metres   2,500 feet

As High Raise and Sergeant Man are Siamese twins, the physical fusion is such that no contour break has been shown on the map in the interests of clarity and safe navigation.

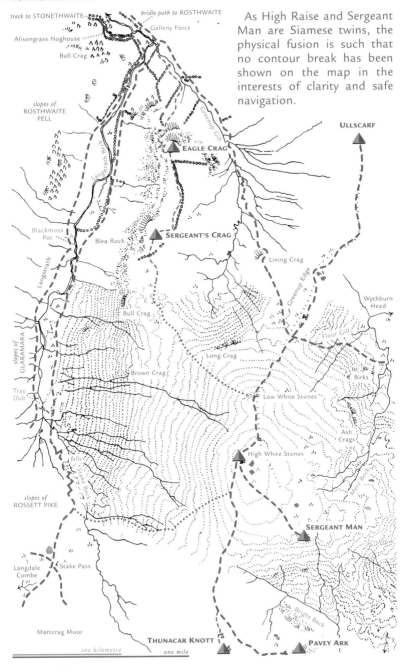

track to STONETHWAITE

bridle-path to ROSTHWAITE

Galleny Force

Alisongrass Hoghouse

Bull Crag

slopes of ROSTHWAITE FELL

Langstrath Beck

Greenup Gill

ULLSCARF

EAGLE CRAG

Blackmoss Pot

Blea Rock

SERGEANT'S CRAG

Lining Crag

Langstrath

Greenup Edge

Wythburn Head

Bull Crag

Flour Gill

slopes of GLARAMARA

Long Crag

Brown Crag

Birks

Tray Dub

Low White Stones

Ash Crags

Wern Beck

falls

Stake Beck

High White Stones

slopes of ROSSETT PIKE

SERGEANT MAN

Langdale Combe

Stake Pass

Bright Beck

Martcrag Moor

one kilometre   one mile

THUNACAR KNOTT

PAVEY ARK

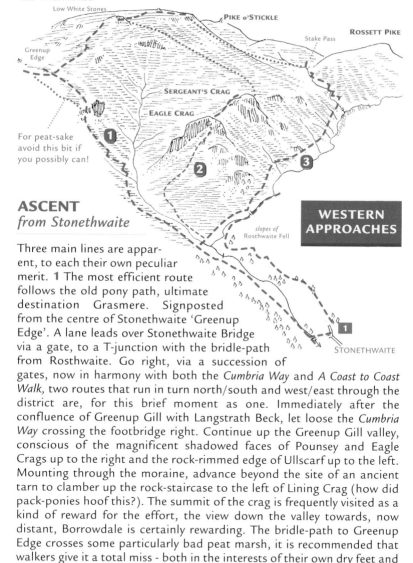

Low White Stones

PIKE o'STICKLE

ROSSETT PIKE

Stake Pass

Greenup Edge

SERGEANT'S CRAG

EAGLE CRAG

1

For peat-sake avoid this bit if you possibly can!

2

3

slopes of Rosthwaite Fell

ASCENT
from Stonethwaite

Three main lines are apparent, to each their own peculiar merit. **1** The most efficient route follows the old pony path, ultimate destination Grasmere. Signposted from the centre of Stonethwaite 'Greenup Edge'. A lane leads over Stonethwaite Bridge via a gate, to a T-junction with the bridle-path from Rosthwaite. Go right, via a succession of

1

STONETHWAITE

gates, now in harmony with both the *Cumbria Way* and *A Coast to Coast Walk,* two routes that run in turn north/south and west/east through the district are, for this brief moment as one. Immediately after the confluence of Greenup Gill with Langstrath Beck, let loose the *Cumbria Way* crossing the footbridge right. Continue up the Greenup Gill valley, conscious of the magnificent shadowed faces of Pounsey and Eagle Crags up to the right and the rock-rimmed edge of Ullscarf up to the left. Mounting through the moraine, advance beyond the site of an ancient tarn to clamber up the rock-staircase to the left of Lining Crag (how did pack-ponies hoof this?). The summit of the crag is frequently visited as a kind of reward for the effort, the view down the valley towards, now distant, Borrowdale is certainly rewarding. The bridle-path to Greenup Edge crosses some particularly bad peat marsh, it is recommended that walkers give it a total miss - both in the interests of their own dry feet and for the welfare of the terrain - by climbing directly up to the ridge-top from Lining Crag (no path), then going right, with the line of metal fence posts as guides on the ridge path off Ullscarf, crossing the Greenup Edge depression bound for Low White Stones. The climb includes some further peaty ground and an interim rocky ledge, before arrival at the Stones gives renewed elation for it is but a short traverse of the easily angled plateau to gain the summit.

2 Via Eagle Crag and Sergeant's Crag - the adventurer's route, full of drama in the preliminary climb, tailing off on the final pull to the ultimate top. Follow the descriptions EAGLE CRAG 1 (page 68) and the ridge routes to Sergeant Crag (page 228), then those subsequently to High Raise.

3 This accompanies the *Cumbria Way*. From the footbridge at the confluence with Greenup Gill wend up the long Langstrath valley via Blea Rock, a startling upstanding rock beneath the slabs of Sergeant's Crag and Blackmoss Pot (stile). The beck interspersing meandering shingle beds with water shoots and rocky channels on an eventful journey upstream to the footbridge at the foot of Stake Beck. Cross the bridge and zig

zag up the old pony route, witnessing some quite amazing water cascades close to the path (*see right*). As the path eases, branch off left at will, to follow a gill ESE, as it is eventually lost make for the skyline and join the path from Thunacar Knott, going left to the summit.

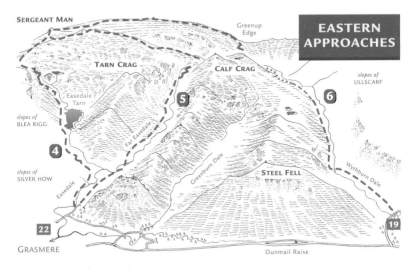

ASCENT *from Grasmere*

The high plateau is hidden from the east by the headwall of Codale Head, which appears to be the conclusive termination of the high ground above Easedale Tarn. **4** Sergeant Man perched over the shoulder from Codale Head, is the crucial link point, enabling walkers to attain the plateau with minimal difficulty - follow the SERGEANT MAN route 4 (page 220) and the ridge route. There are several ridge connections to Sergeant Man, via Blea Rigg, Tarn Crag and Calf Crag, but the natural valley alternative **5** wanders up Far Easedale, takes a left turn at the saddle, then climbs in the company of the few forlorn metal stakes that once formed a fence marking the Cumberland/Westmorland county boundary. An off-the-beaten track variation to this for adventurous types is to drop over the saddle into the head of Wythburn Dale and follow the rough courses of either Mere Beck and Deep Slack or Birks Gill directly onto the plateau.

6 In many eyes the most drear route, which wends up the lonely wastes of Wythburn Dale linking to the old pony path at Flour Gill then climbs onto Greenup Edge. The route contrives to avoid all hint of rocky out-cropping so may appeal as a simple means of reaching the roof of the range. Consult CALF CRAG route 4 (page 57), though the essence of the High Raise route would keep with the faltering path, up the southern side of the valley avoiding the worst of the peaty ridge-top, unless, of course, Calf Crag might be thought worthy inclusion - and it is.

Codale Head, Ash Crags and Birks at the head of Wythburn Dale

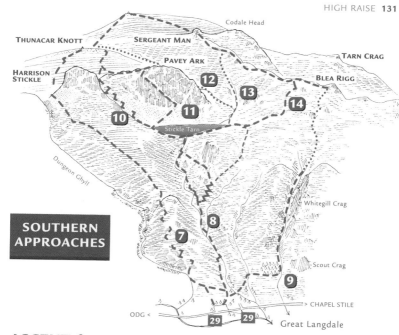

THUNACAR KNOTT

SERGEANT MAN

Codale Head

TARN CRAG

HARRISON STICKLE

PAVEY ARK

BLEA RIGG

12

13

14

10

11

Stickle Tarn

Dungeon Ghyll

Whitegill Crag

SOUTHERN APPROACHES

8

7

Scout Crag

9

ODG <

29   29

CHAPEL STILE

Great Langdale

ASCENT *from Great Langdale*

The Langdale Pikes are but a front to a massif that has it's crown on High Raise. In the traditional spirit of fell-walking this should be considered the ultimate point when setting out on any expedition to climb Harrison Stickle, Pavey Ark, or even Blea Rigg and Sergeant Man. As the diagram reveals there are a number of braided routes, though only route **12** can claim to be exclusive to High Raise. **7** Follow the one path exclusive to HARRISON STICKLE route 2 (page107/108) rising above Dungeon Ghyll and through Harrison Combe onto THUNACAR KNOTT route 1 (page 262), thereon following the ridge route. **8** Climbs Stickle Ghyll, though even here there are three lines, the new zig-zag path which draws under Tarn Crag is better than that unflinching gill path, with the green trod climbing on from the zig-zag an altogether quieter option still. **9** The Whitegill Crag route see BLEA RIGG route 4/5 (pages 47/48) makes an exciting variant, side-stepping Stickle Tarn.

From the shores of Stickle Tarn five routes spring. **10** The eastern approach to Harrison Stickle climbs the scree slope, with evidence of recent path repair, see HARRISON STICKLE route 4 (page 111). As the contouring path from Pavey Ark joins go straight up onto the saddle. Keep right, rounding a tor to cross the shoulder of Thunacar Knott, now

Pool approaching the summit rocks

upon the ridge path. **11** Jack's Rake, all true mountaineers take this as their royal route to High Raise, see PAVEY ARK (page 195). **12** Either follow Bright Beck from the the head of the tarn, through its upper ravine to the broad depression north of Thunacar Knott. **13** Ford Bright Beck making for the rounded summit of SERGEANT MAN. **14** Take the line of least resistance, suitable for those long summer days when one has time to dawdle, see BLEA RIGG route 2 (page 46), ignore the summit of Blea Rigg, climb left onto the ridge bound for Sergeant Man and the plateau beyond.

The Summit

Aptly called High White Stones. Among the pale surface rocks resides a capacious wind-shelter within which half-a-dozen may huddle when all about is torrid and foul, and a stone-built Ordnance Survey pillar to lean against when fortune brings a barmy sun. This is a place of congregation and expansive scenic pleasure. While some walkers, having gained their bearings, speed on to craggier attractions elsewhere those who adore just being on top of the world dally long, soaking up this the purest of Lakeland fellscapes, with Glaramara centre-stage (*see above*) setting the inspirational tone across the obscured depths of Langstrath. On the broad front the fell-top has more in common with the Far Eastern Fells, being an almost pancake flat pasture where sheep wander at will.

Safe Descents

The remote situation carries a price. Innocuous though the broad peaty-pastured top appears to be do not be tempted to bee-line N as Long Crag is a nasty trap. The surest recourse is to Greenup Edge, joining the well-marked range-crossing pony path. Head slightly E of N for 600 yards to High White Stones, then NNE down to the damp depression. For Grasmere turn right, E, descending initially beside Flour Gill, in crossing the rough slope at the head of Wythburn Dale fording Mere Beck then rising to the low saddle at the very top of Far Easedale. The path runs securely down this wild dale via the Stythwaite Steps footbridge. For Borrowdale, go left NNW watchful to keep to the right at Lining Crag, descending a gully, the path runs down the Greenup Gill valley bound for Stonethwaite 3.2 miles and Rosthwaite 3.7 miles.

The Stake Pass is certainly a safe line for either Borrowdale or Great Langdale, but it almost doubles any journey and on such grounds should be a last recourse. Best reached (no path) from the depression at the head of Bright Beck. Southbound routes engage in more tricky terrain, though remember that Sergeant Man is the key for Easedale and Thunacar Knott for Langdale, via Harrison Combe and the Pike How route leading down from the head of Dungeon Ghyll to Pike How.

Ridge Routes to...

SERGEANT MAN DESCENT 100 ft ASCENT 25 ft   0.5 miles

Walk SSE passing the shallow pools and peaty ground to join the vestige of the metal fence. The summit coming into view as the plateau unfolds.

SERGEANT'S CRAG DESCENT 640 ft ASCENT 30 ft   1.5 miles

Advance to Low White Stones, from here leave the plateau WNW on a rough, pathless descent, mindful that Long Crag lurks to the NW. There is little evidence of a ridge until the reedy depression at the foot of the slope is reached then one materialises, as too now a path, leading to the stile in the summit embracing wall.

THUNACAR KNOTT DESCENT 400 ft ASCENT 150 ft   1 mile

The main path leads S, gently declining to a broad depression, as the first rocks are encountered along the easy rise, bear off right from the main trail, otherwise the path makes for Pavey Ark.

ULLSCARF DESCENT 500 ft ASCENT 390 ft   2.3 miles

Head NNE for 600 yards to High White Stones, then descend NNE to Greenup Edge. Go straight on accompanying the the line of metal stakes. Sweep to the right of at least one notable pool before rising onto the drier ridge. Aim N with only the merest of stumps (watch you don't stumble on them) for guides to the solitary summit cairn.

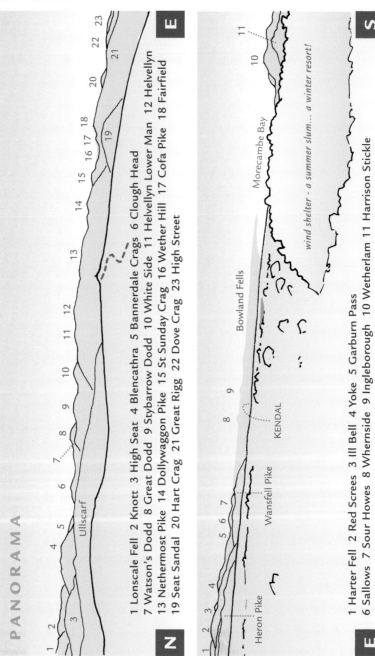

PANORAMA

N

E

Ullscarf

1 Lonscale Fell 2 Knott 3 High Seat 4 Blencathra 5 Bannerdale Crags 6 Clough Head
7 Watson's Dodd 8 Great Dodd 9 Stybarrow Dodd 10 White Side 11 Helvellyn Lower Man 12 Helvellyn
13 Nethermost Pike 14 Dollywaggon Pike 15 St Sunday Crag 16 Wether Hill 17 Cofa Pike 18 Fairfield
19 Seat Sandal 20 Hart Crag 21 Great Rigg 22 Dove Crag 23 High Street

E

S

Morecambe Bay

Bowland Fells

KENDAL

Wansfell Pike

Heron Pike

wind shelter - a summer slum.... a winter resort!

1 Harter Fell 2 Red Screes 3 Ill Bell 4 Yoke 5 Garburn Pass
6 Sallows 7 Sour Howes 8 Whernside 9 Ingleborough 10 Wetherlam 11 Harrison Stickle

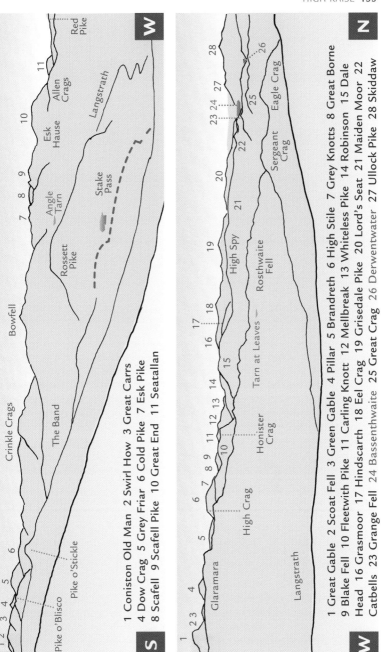

W

Red Pike
Allen Crags
11
Esk Hause
10
Langstrath
9
8 7
Angle Tarn
Rossett Pike
Stake Pass
Bowfell
Crinkle Crags
The Band
Pike o'Stickle
Pike o'Blisco
6
5 4 3 2 1

S

1 Coniston Old Man 2 Swirl How 3 Great Carrs
4 Dow Crag 5 Grey Friar 6 Cold Pike 7 Esk Pike
8 Scafell 9 Scafell Pike 10 Great End 11 Seatallan

N

28
27 24 23
26
25
22
20
21
High Spy
Rosthwaite Fell
Sergeant Crag
Eagle Crag
19
18 17 16 15
Tarn at Leaves
14 13 12 11 10
Honister Crag
High Crag
Glaramara
9 8 7
6
5
4 3 2 1
Langstrath

W

1 Great Gable 2 Scoat Fell 3 Green Gable 4 Pillar 5 Brandreth 6 High Stile 7 Grey Knotts 8 Great Borne
9 Blake Fell 10 Fleetwith Pike 11 Carling Knott 12 Mellbreak 13 Whiteless Pike 14 Robinson 15 Dale
Head 16 Grasmoor 17 Hindscarth 18 Eel Crag 19 Grisedale Pike 20 Lord's Seat 21 Maiden Moor 22
Catbells 23 Grange Fell 24 Bassenthwaite 25 Great Crag 26 Derwentwater 27 Ullock Pike 28 Skiddaw

HIGH RIGG

I magine a single distillation of the Lakeland fells, difficult I know, but traverse High Rigg and you'll get pretty close to it. So it lacks height, is not connected to anything, has no famous climbs on its crags, in fact barely causes one to break into a sweat in climbing at all! Nevertheless, this is the meat and matter of the district sublime, here one is exposed to all the ingredients that make up the fell montage. Take the three-mile ridge-top stroll from Legburthwaite to Tewet Tarn and you'll love every stride and wish it never to end! Naturally you'll be tempted there and then just to turnabout and repeat whole thing, and why not for it more surely consolidates the whole wonderful setting in one's mind.

Travellers whether speeding along the A591 heading for Keswick or adhering to the 40 mph limit on the St Johns-in-the-Vale road, will notice the fell sure enough, its steeply tilted rock ribs and switch-back skyline sitting like a masterpiece model beneath the massive buttresses of Clough Head. As an introduction to fell-walking it must have long served. The Carlisle Diocese Youth Centre beside St John's Church, charmingly set in the hause below the summit, ensures that each year a fresh influx of youngsters are infused with the magic of these surroundings. Very much in context they look in awe at Blencathra, and can be told that the second element of the name 'cathra' comes from the same root as Cathedral, meaning high seat (in the latter case Bishop's throne). High Rigg is a stepping stone to greater things.

355 metres   1,165 feet

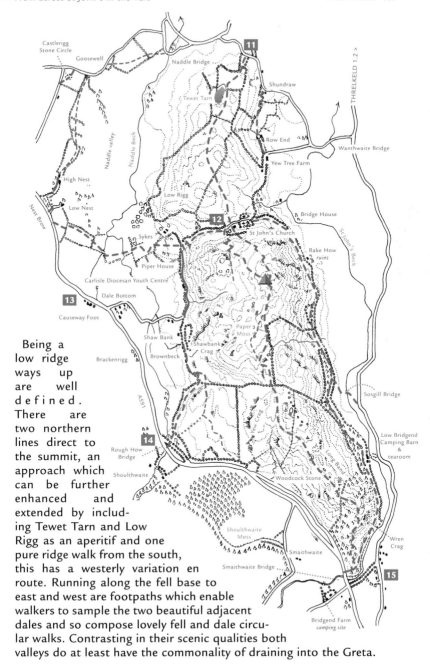

Being a low ridge ways up are well defined. There are two northern lines direct to the summit, an approach which can be further enhanced and extended by including Tewet Tarn and Low Rigg as an aperitif and one pure ridge walk from the south, this has a westerly variation en route. Running along the fell base to east and west are footpaths which enable walkers to sample the two beautiful adjacent dales and so compose lovely fell and dale circular walks. Contrasting in their scenic qualities both valleys do at least have the commonality of draining into the Greta.

A winter view of the fell's tilted profile, as seen to travellers in St John Vale

The grandest circuit would introduce Castlerigg Stone Circle into the equation across Naddle Beck, taken in this manner the sight and siting lend the stones greatest power. Bus stops on the A591 at Thirlmere Dam Road End (*shelter*) and Shoulthwaite lay-by underpin these as the best starting points for circular footpath tours. The Shoulthwaite route given added charm by beginning upon the newly surfaced forest track skirting Shoulthwaite Moss, passing old Smaithwaite to reach Bridge End (*working farm and camp site*).

ASCENT *from St John's Church*

3 Car parking - defer to Centre visitors. Embark upon either the path rounding the west end of the main Centre building which leads up to a kissing-gate and continues as a steady uphill trod. The bracken suppressed by the regular pounding, latterly the path swings round the left-hand side of final summit knoll, thereby approaching the cairn from the south. **4** Alternatively, go a further along the hause road to the kissing-gate where the road deteriorates to a track 'unsuitable for motor vehicles'. Now bear left by the seat, rising above the enclosure copse and water tank on a zig-zagging path which straightens onto a semblance of a ridge making the top with alacrity and no little elation.

NORTHERN APPROACHES

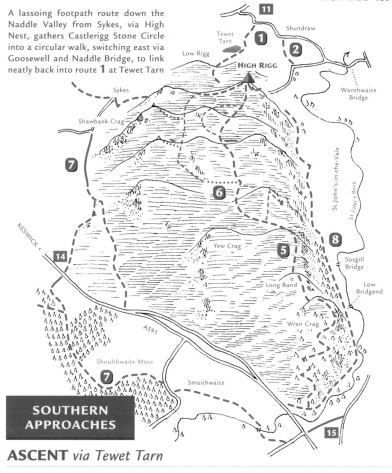

A lassoing footpath route down the Naddle Valley from Sykes, via High Nest, gathers Castlerigg Stone Circle into a circular walk, switching east via Goosewell and Naddle Bridge, to link neatly back into route **1** at Tewet Tarn

SOUTHERN APPROACHES

ASCENT *via Tewet Tarn*

Verge parking GR306239 (avoid blocking field-gate access). **1** A footpath is signed from a gate up a small field to a gateway, continue guided by a wooden waymark post by a curious rift feature, presumably laboriously cut for piping linked to the tarn. Aim left of the sheet of water and cross the wall-stile left of the fenced gateway. Quite naturally many visitors encircle the tiny tarn, admire the backdrop of Blencathra and watch the coots weaving among the weed. It is a place of quiet repose and fun. Here children may laugh and play and courting couples sit and dream. The tarn-name refers to the frequent of green plover or lapwing, colloquially called 'tewet' from their distinctive call. The path strides on via a fence-stile, over a dip in the Low Rigg ridge to a wall-stile and on down to a stile opposite St John's Church, resting among a shroud of trees. **2** The footpath linking Yew Tree farm with Shundraw is useful as an alternative back-tracking route from the summit (hence is described south/north). From the church follow the approach road down, via the gate by the tiny Yew Tree Cottage, and at the road bend bear off left through the double gates signed to Row End. The track leads between the house and barn to the gate with a 'footpath' plate. Head straight across the ensuing rushy field skipping over the open ditch mid-course, to a stepped wall-gate. Keep the wall close right to a short gated lane beside the huge bank-barn at Shundraw, replicating the barn back at Yew Tree Farm.

Wren Crag from Legburthwaite

ASCENT *from Legburthwaite*

See the very best of High Rigg, a journey given impetus by the magnificent surroundings with eyes inevitably drawn with admiration to the most handsome fell of all, Blencathra. The epitome of Lakeland grander the fell backing views down the green strath of St John's-in-the-Vale, exalting attention all the way to Tewet Tarn. The walk leaves the A591 at a ladder-stile/hand-gate at GR315196 one hundred yards north of the bus shelter; to reach this spot from the Legburthwaite NWW car park follow the old road Cycle Way lane. **5** A popular path sets off, ultimately bound for St John's Church neatly slipping by Low Bridge Farm (tea garden), but within fifty yards the ridge path branches left, for the time being putting appetising thoughts onto the back-burner. The early relish a delightful rising ridge garnished with Scots pines giving superb views of Castle Rock of Triermain. Coming above the pines the first knoll provides a stunning panorama. In view are Helvellyn and its mighty supplicants overbearing to the south-east, the conifer-draped Thirlmere fells to the south-west beyond Great How, with Raven Crag an imposing feature above the dam, while to the north the Skiddaw massif, Great Calva and Blencathra, beyond St Johns-in-the-Vale, are beautiful compositions, stirring stuff. The path, showing signs of erosion, slips through a dip in the ridge, via a wall gap, and clambers onto an attractive rocky step in the ridge. Passing a cairn perched on a splintered rock the path strides along a lovely narrowing of the ridge above Long Band. At a wooden post

St John's church - a romantic setting perfect for that romantic wedding

the path is ushered left to a fence stile. The regular path sweeps to the left of the next knoll, while one may stroll up with the fence to the right onto a cairned top above a pool, following its outflow to re-join the main path leading down to a ladder-stile at a wall junction. Note the fine construction of the enclosure walling in this vicinity. Once over the stile there are two options. The ridge path heads up with the wall to the right. At the marshy hollow skirt left to cross the narrow outflow stones under Moss Crag then either curve right resuming beside the wall, or climb straight up the fell to the ridge-top bearing right to re-join the main path beyond the wall-end, the summit beckons ahead. **6** From the ladder-stile branch left across the bracken slope, on a sheep trod. Once level with the ash tree, curve right under the outcrop onto a shallow rigg rising to the saddle. Briefly bear left to a viewpoint cairn with adjacent pool. Continuing from the saddle with the slightly more apparent sheep path at the next saddle spur left again to the cairn at the top of Shawbank Crag. Both cairns enjoy lovely views across the Naddle valley to the shapely prow of Dodd Crag, foremost limb of Bleaberry Fell. The path even more sure advances across the broad hollow to link up with the popular path at the last lower saddle, this the path rising from the St John's Church hause, via the water tank.

There are two valley variation returns. **7** The western route turns down the road left from St John's hause, from the gate the road is unsuitable for wheeled traffic at the foot of the zig-zags follow the tarmac road left. Pass Piper House, a quintessential Lakeland cottage with a superb backdrop of Bleaberry Fell (cameras out!). Where the road turns right ignore this, keep the wall right in following the by-way past Shaw Bank, overlooked by Shawbank Crag, and Brownbeck. Soon after the road ends forking as two bridle-paths. The left-hand path rising invitingly to a ladder-stile, but there is little merit in the succeeding trail across a

High Rigg across the Naddle valley from Dodd Crag

bracken hollow, though a footpath veers right along the back of the rigg may come to your rescue if by error you chose the wrong option at the fork. Better take the right fork via a stile, a rocky path dips to a smooth green track and a gate where the footpath reunites from over the brow left. The track leads through open woodland, spot the old arched Rough How Bridge spanning Shoulthwaite Gill at the point where it becomes Naddle Beck, this is the original crossing point, truncated, even its successor road is sidelined by the wide A591, where traffic speeds with no sense of the former orientation of travel, as the path just followed was the old 'main road' to Keswick. Cross the road and follow the lane to Shoulthwaite Farm, passing through by the camp site to enter Thirlmere Forest at a hand-gate. A path leads on, merging with a track from the right, this is now a well-graded track leading past Shoulthwaite Moss onto a minor road, go right and first left with the signposted footpath which leads via gates through the part-restored Smaithwaite farmyard leading down by a fence to a footbridge over St John's Beck, rising to meet the road at Bridgend Farm (*camping site opposite*).

8 The eastern trail is part bridle-path, part footpath, while sheltered and shady it does have two notably appealing pluses, its fine view of Wanthwaite and Bram Crags, invariably bathed in afternoon sunlight....

and the Low Bridgend tea-garden! The green track starts down immediately east of the church via a gate/stile. Thereon, navigation is an unnecessary fussiness, the paths just flow, which isn't bad bearing in mind you are effectively walking upstream!

Castlerigg backed by High Rigg and the Helvellyn range in evening light

(*left*) Low Bridge End tea-garden/room and camping barn
(*middle*) Castle Rock of Triermain from Wren Crag
(*right*) The summit peeping through a notch by the ridge wall

The Summit

A solitary cairn rests among the outcropping on a modest top, sufficient in area to give a party plenty of room to sit and consider the feast before them, more's the point all round them! A large shapely rock no doubt taking centre stage for photographic compositions.

Safe Descents

The main caution is that serious crags bound the fell to east and west. The palpable paths leading smartly down NNE to St John's Church and Youth Centre are without question the best options if in doubt or deteriorating weather. While the ridge path south has little to cause trepidation, it is nicer in foul conditions to trace the fell foot trails, with particular encouragement on the eastern trail with Low Bridgend tea garden offering beverages and fayre to suit prevailing conditions, as the notice on the gate informs 'if its hot' or 'if it cold'!

PANORAMA

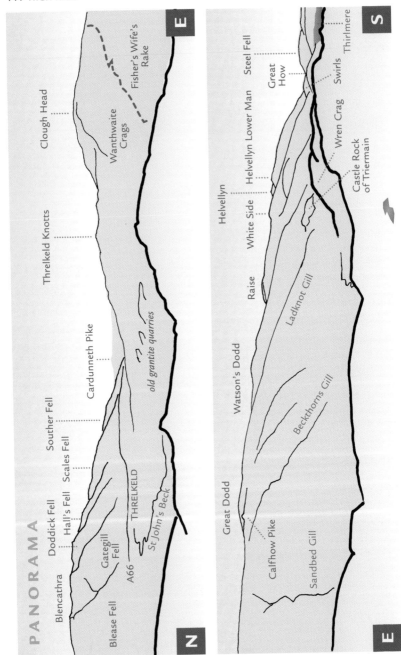

N / **E**

Blencathra
Doddick Fell
Hall's Fell
Scales Fell
Souther Fell
Cardunneth Pike
Threlkeld Knotts
Clough Head

Blease Fell
Gategill Fell
A66
THRELKELD
St John's Beck
old grantite quarries
Wanthwaite Crags
Fisher's Wife's Rake

E / **S**

Great Dodd
Watson's Dodd
Raise
Helvellyn
White Side
Helvellyn Lower Man
Steel Fell
Great How
Swirls
Thirlmere

Calfhow Pike
Sandbed Gill
Beckthorns Gill
Ladknot Gill
Castle Rock of Triermain
Wren Crag

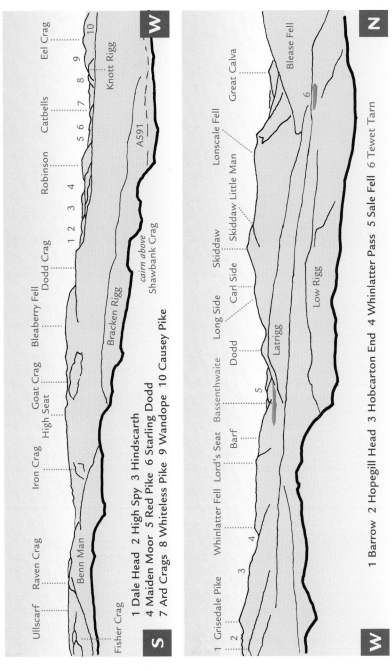

W **S**

Ullscarf · Raven Crag · Iron Crag · Goat Crag · High Seat · Bleaberry Fell · Dodd Crag · Robinson · Catbells · Eel Crag

Benn Man · Fisher Crag

Knott Rigg

Bracken Rigg

A591

cairn above Shawbank Crag

1 Dale Head 2 High Spy 3 Hindscarth
4 Maiden Moor 5 Red Pike 6 Starling Dodd
7 Ard Crags 8 Whiteless Pike 9 Wandope 10 Causey Pike

N **W**

Grisedale Pike · Whinlatter Fell · Lord's Seat · Bassenthwaite · Long Side · Skiddaw · Lonscale Fell · Great Calva · Blease Fell

Barf · Dodd · Carl Side · Skiddaw Little Man

Latrigg · Low Rigg

1 Barrow 2 Hopegill Head 3 Hobcarton End 4 Whinlatter Pass 5 Sale Fell 6 Tewet Tarn

HIGH SEAT

The spine of the Central Fells dips from Ullscarf, switching north-east on Bell Crags and runs, or should that be squadges, its way due north, raising its head, like a butterfly swimmer, upon three summits, the middle, the subject of this chapter, being the highest.

From a distance the fell top does indeed look like a bench therefore the 'seat' analogy is appropriate, a definite knoll perched above a general undulating marshiness. To the east of the ridge fence a cairned knoll bears the name Man, harking back to pre-Viking days, before the term raise was applied to significant cairns. That numerous summits are called 'high' is of parochial relativity, they meant quite simply the top pasture. With impudence and disdain, the eastern slopes drain into the Naddle valley via Shoulthwaite Gill, giving Thirlmere short shrift. The contrast between east and west could hardly be greater. The western slopes spread along the road all the way from Ashness Bridge to the hamlet of Watendlath with Gowder and Reecastle Crags the main sporting outcrops. The lovely native woodland about Surprise View and Hogs Earth softening Watendlath Beck's break for freedom through the Lodore gorge.

Of all the ascents that from Reecastle Crag is the most direct and least prone to wet ground. The more commonly followed climbs from Ashness Bridge, the best of this journey experienced to the edge at Dodd, the moor beyond being peaty indeed. The back route from Shoulthwaite is peaceful and an ideal out of the way experience. Middlesteads Gill provides a novel quiet line too, with all the excitement confined to the gill and its minor arete, the slopes thereafter are plain.

608 metres 1,995 feet

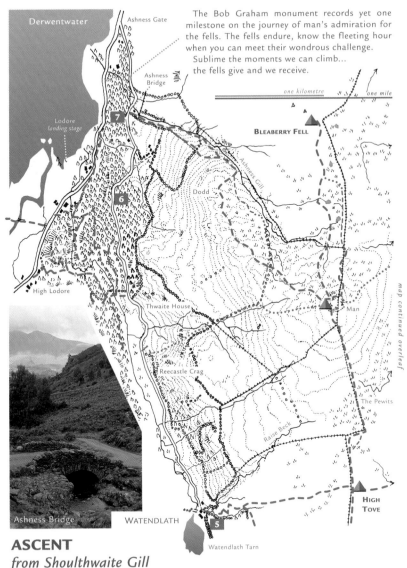

Derwentwater

Ashness Gate

The Bob Graham monument records yet one milestone on the journey of man's admiration for the fells. The fells endure, know the fleeting hour when you can meet their wondrous challenge. Sublime the moments we can climb... the fells give and we receive.

Ashness Bridge

one kilometre   one mile

BLEABERRY FELL

Lodore landing stage

7

6

Dodd

Ashness Gill

High Lodore

Thwaite House

Man

Reecastle Crag

The Pewits

Raise Beck

map continued overleaf

Ashness Bridge   WATENDLATH   5

HIGH TOVE

Watendlath Tarn

ASCENT
from Shoulthwaite Gill

Eastern ascents inevitably stem from Shoulthwaite Gill, a valley whose praises are seldom sung, and yet there is no doubting its beauty, hemmed-in between sheer cliffs and dense forest. The gill shakes off an unprepossessing start in life upon austere moorland at a peaty waste enchanting called The Pewits, and generates a special visual energy during this impressive passage towards the Naddle vale.

Shoulthwaite Gill looking to Iron Crag

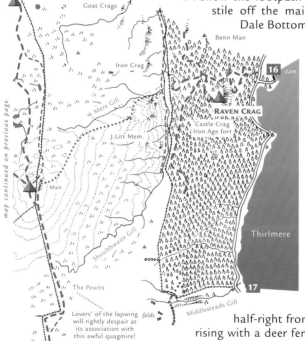

BLEABERRY FELL
Goat Crags
Benn Man
Iron Crag
16 dam
Mere Gill
RAVEN CRAG
Castle Crag
J.Litt Mem. Iron Age fort
Man
Shoulthwaite Gill
Thirlmere
The Pewits
17
Lovers' of the lapwing folds
will rightly despair at Middlesteads Gill
its association with
this awful quagmire!

map continued on previous page

I Follow the footpath from the ladder-stile off the main road south of Dale Bottom. This runs above Brackenrigg to a gate beside the footbridge and old weir. **2** This point can more efficiently be reached starting from the Rough How Bridge lay-by, passing up the lane by Shoulthwaite Farm and on through the farmyard to a kissing-gate entering Thirlmere Forest. Branch immediately half-right from the lower path, rising with a deer fence right to a forest track, go right to where the track forks, bear right exiting the forestry via the tall kissing-gate to cross the bridge. It is not unreasonable to consider following the forest track up to the Raven Crag and Castle Crag viewpoints and either beating a way down from the duckboarding to a ladder-stile directly beneath Castle Crag, or continue to exit the forestry off the track near the head of the gorge. The preferred route keeps with the footpath running up the west side of the gill itself. The cliffs above are striking, notably spot the fall spilling from a high crag then the bold profile of Iron Crag. Pass an old sheepfold close to where the route of Castle Crag is met, soon after encounter Mere Gill. **3** Ford and follow this impressive little ravine climbing quite steeply west, with the minimum of inconvenience, as the gill opens bear left to a cairned knoll below which are located two slate slabs, like fairy gateposts. This is the Litt Memorial, a person of no known significance, one stone carries a fanciful poem telling of the gathering of the stone in Mere Gill, while the other has a brass disc inscribed 'In memory of J.Litt who died March 9, 1880'.

There is nought but a sheep trod pursuing the shallow ridge, as best as may avoiding damp ground on the rise south-westward to the outcrop isle of Man! **4** Alternatively, continue with the gillside path, which falters as it moves away from the proximity of the forest. This is just as well, as the upper reaches of Shoulthwaite Gill promise no more than peat and mire. So make a random right-hand move heading due east for the skyline fence and the summit.

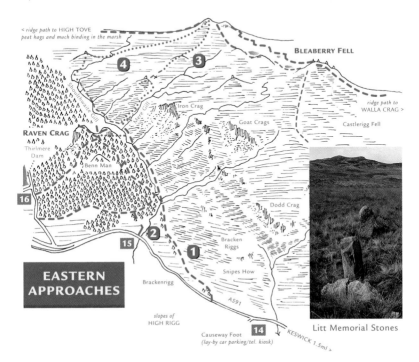

Litt Memorial Stones

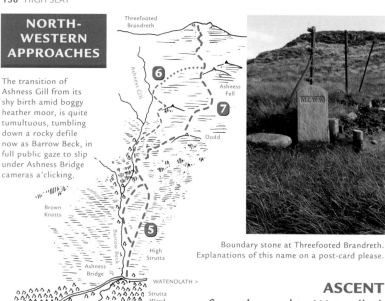

The transition of Ashness Gill from its shy birth amid boggy heather moor, is quite tumultuous, tumbling down a rocky defile now as Barrow Beck, in full public gaze to slip under Ashness Bridge cameras a'clicking.

Boundary stone at Threefooted Brandreth.
Explanations of this name on a post-card please.

ASCENT
from the road to Watendlath

Two routes depart from the Watendlath road, one the common way, the other far less so, both benefit from good early stages, the second gains commendation for having the driest line. **5** From Ashness Bridge (car park) a footpath climbs direct beside the wall via an early stile. As the wall gives way to a fence either continue ahead climbing to a ladder-stile spanning the intake wall climbing on by a solitary rowan to come level with the brink of an impressive waterfall. Or, bear half-left to accompany Barrow Beck up to a hand-gate rising through the bracken along the edge

overlooking the formidable dale-head to unite with the main path. The more intrepid may fancy keeping even closer to the beck's bouldered course though nearing the top the going gets tricky. The waterfall makes a worthy spot to pause and admire the broader scene, both gloriously back over Derwentwater and near at hand, peering down the upper cleft and across the cascading slab (*see left*) above. Hereon the headwaters are called Ashness Gill and are tightly fenced to the north conclusively denying access to Bleaberry Fell from this side. **6** The old path, less obvious and therefore less commonly trod, keeps strict

Derwentwater from the head of Barrow Beck

company with the beck a little further, before drawing out onto the heather moor to pass to the left of a knoll crowned by a cairn. Continue again quite near the gill until an old wall is met. Keep close to the wall's foundations, useful where it crosses bog, to reach the point where the popular path crosses near the ridge-top. **7** Alternatively, this place may be gained by climbing the initially eroded path leaving the environs of the waterfall, the path easing as it approaches the prominent cairn on the brink of the fell. Evidenced by a path some walkers, not aware of the

From the path to Great Crag

craggy edge below, appear to have tried to descend directly, they must have rued their lack of wisdom! The path is caused to meander by encounters with marsh in following on up the ridge to the wall crossing. Note the two cairned tops are by-passed to reach this point. The fell summit is clearly in view but more marsh has to be rounded before the final rise to the old stone-built trig point. **8** Quite the most direct route to the summit is to be found taking a surreptitious line out of the Watendlath valley from the foot of the imposing Reecastle Crag ridge. Park either at Watendlath or Surprise View car parks. The popular road climbing into the hanging valley from Derwentwater, via Ashness Bridge, twists and turns through gorgeous woodland to emerge at a cattle grid. Ahead a succession of meadows grazed by cattle, sheep and ponies is flanked by rough fellsides, those to the west a tangle of trees and crags falling from Grange Fell, while to the east lies bracken-clad Thwaite Bank. The road is unenclosed on this side. Passing the Thwaite House (barn - useful shelter in a downpour) the road crosses Thwaitehouse Beck and rounding the next bend, short of the cattle grid, find a short

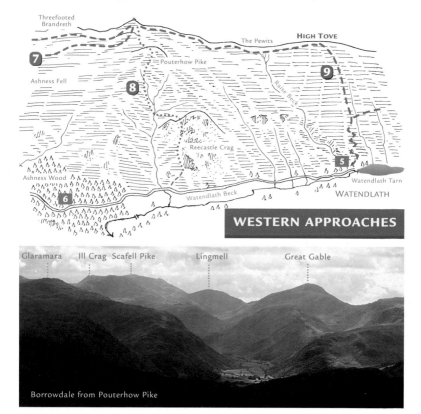

Borrowdale from Pouterhow Pike

pull-off where lazy rock climbers' slot their cars. You'll not need me to point out that cars are like litter in this setting and walkers with an ounce of sense will prefer to park a mile distant at either of the two parks hitherto mentioned. The climbers' approach is the key to this ascent, a path rising with a gill to the marsh beneath Reecastle Crag. The crag forms a broad buttress wall alternat-

Reecastle Crag backed by Heather Knott

ing damp and dry lines for the exclusive delight of the accomplished rock gymnast. However, this is of no matter, for the route keeps left. Eye and aim for the skyline dip between two outcrops, there is no path, keep to the rough line of thorns en route passing a large fractured boulder. At the top ignore the hand-gate in the enclosure wall. Bear left along the edge, enjoying handsome views back over Reecastle Crag to Grange Fell. Pass an old sheepfold and ford Thwaitehouse Gill to reach a ladder-stile in the intake wall. Go half-right and ascend beside the gill and broken wall. Nearing the skyline, as the wall curves left, slant right to crest the prominent outcrop, this is Pouterhow Pike, a excellent viewpoint (*see below left*). The summit is in view ENE, the intervening ridge has but one small marsh and the occasional sheep path. **9** From Watendlath High Seat is within range, if not exactly within means. Follow the Armboth path onto High Tove, then follow the ridge fence north, easier said than done - bring back the pewits please as a distraction from the mire!

High Seat from Dodd

The Summit

Formerly open grazing, unfortunately now crossed by a fence, albeit periodically graced by stiles. One may consider the fence a blessing in mist to act as a guide, in the main it would be deemed an eyesore, for all its practical stock-proofing intent. It partitions off the summit from the eastern knoll, called Man, the older British name, which simply meant '*the stones*' (*see below the present heap of stones looking to the summit*). High Seatt's (sic) earliest written record being 1569. The boss of rock that forms the summit is marked with a stone-built Ordnance Survey pillar (*see right*). The science of surveying may have rendered it redundant, with triangulation a thing of the past, yet this well-made pillar lends a touch of order to the scene. And what a scene it is too, an unusually good all-round panorama sufficient to cause one to idle many minutes mentally ticking off the tops... *while your mates plough on up through the bogs!*

Safe Descents

All lines of ascent work in reverse, the quickest route to a useful road is due W via Pouterhow Pike and route **8** slipping below Reecastle Crag.

Ridge Routes to...

BLEABERRY FELL   DECENT 100 ft   ASCENT 170 ft   1.3 miles

In years gone by the normal practice was to follow the general line of the fence, but it has to be admitted this is now less satisfactory, except in mist, encountering the worst of the marsh. Better, avoid crossing the

fence, instead dip off the NW edge of the summit on a path that admittedly slodges through some pretty appalling peat to a stile at the head of Ashness Gill and below Threefooted Brandreth. Thereafter it winds N with varying degrees of peatiness keeping left of a large pool to duly rise onto the dry summit ridge.

HIGH TOVE   DECENT 330 ft   ASCENT 25 ft   1 mile

Head S and cross the fence stile at the fence junction. Keeping to the E side of the fence all the way, though the path through The Pewits is a trial not a trail. Deep sqidgy peat, invariably with the consistency of muck, turns the outing into an outrageous quest for a moment's firm footing. Where the fence turns some over-eager folk short-cut through yet more peat, the advantage is paltry, if not fowl! The heave-hove to High Tove ends on dry ground... *what blessed relief.*

Cairn on the knoll between Dodd and the summit

PANORAMA

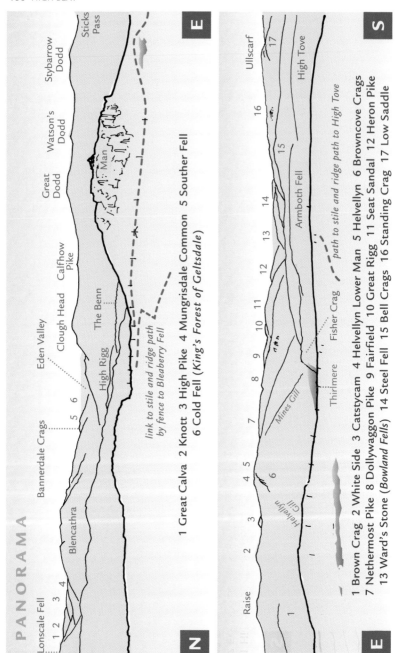

N

Lonscale Fell 1 2 3 4 Bannerdale Crags Blencathra High Rigg Eden Valley Clough Head Calfhow Pike The Benn Great Dodd Watson's Dodd Man Stybarrow Dodd Sticks Pass

E

link to stile and ridge path by fence to Bleaberry Fell

1 Great Calva 2 Knott 3 High Pike 4 Mungrisdale Common 5 Souther Fell
6 Cold Fell (*King's Forest of Geltsdale*)

E

Raise 1 2 3 4 5 6 Helvellyn Gill Mines Gill 7 8 9 10 11 12 13 14 15 16 Ullscarf 17 Thirlmere Fisher Crag Armboth Fell High Tove

S

path to stile and ridge path to High Tove

1 Brown Crag 2 White Side 3 Catstycam 4 Helvellyn Lower Man 5 Helvellyn 6 Browncove Crags
7 Nethermost Pike 8 Dollywaggon Pike 9 Fairfield 10 Great Rigg 11 Seat Sandal 12 Heron Pike
13 Ward's Stone (*Bowland Fells*) 14 Steel Fell 15 Bell Crags 16 Standing Crag 17 Low Saddle

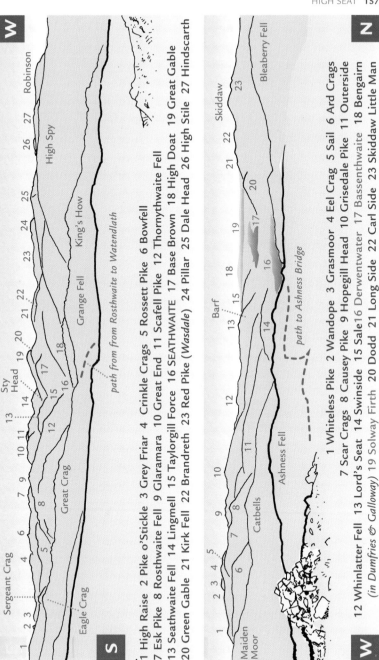

W

Sergeant Crag

Eagle Crag

Great Crag

Sty Head

High Spy

Grange Fell

King's How

Robinson

S

path from from Rosthwaite to Watendlath

1 High Raise 2 Pike o'Stickle 3 Grey Friar 4 Crinkle Crags 5 Rossett Pike 6 Bowfell
7 Esk Pike 8 Rosthwaite Fell 9 Glaramara 10 Great End 11 Scafell Pike 12 Thornythwaite Fell
13 Seathwaite Fell 14 Lingmell 15 Taylorgill Force 16 SEATHWAITE 17 Base Brown 18 High Doat 19 Great Gable
20 Green Gable 21 Kirk Fell 22 Brandreth 23 Red Pike (*Wasdale*) 24 Pillar 25 Dale Head 26 High Stile 27 Hindscarth

N

Maiden Moor

Catbells

Ashness Fell

Barf

Skiddaw

Bleaberry Fell

path to Ashness Bridge

W

1 Whiteless Pike 2 Wandope 3 Grasmoor 4 Eel Crag 5 Sail 6 Ard Crags
7 Scar Crags 8 Causey Pike 9 Hopegill Head 10 Grisedale Pike 11 Outerside
12 Whinlatter Fell 13 Lord's Seat 14 Swinside 15 Sale 16 Derwentwater 17 Bassenthwaite 18 Bengairn
(*in Dumfries & Galloway*) 19 Solway Firth 20 Dodd 21 Long Side 22 Carl Side 23 Skiddaw Little Man

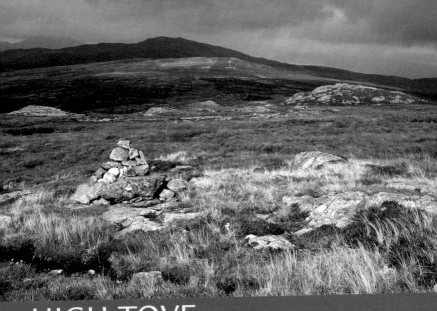

HIGH TOVE

The age-old cross-ridge footpath which linked Armboth Hall beside Leathes Water - now lost under the lapping waters of Thirlmere - and the hamlet of Watendlath contradicted convention. Instead of seeking a low point in the ridge, it slipped precisely over the summit of High Tove, the reasoning, eminently sane, for just one moment, on this otherwise soggy trail, it is high and dry! There are moments when webbed feet would be a distinct advantage, the Watendlath ducks would be in their element! The tough tussocks of heather and rush must always have been taxing to the stride; hence the fell-name Tove, a variant of 'tuft', descriptive of those very clumps of rushes.

To north and south the ridge's easy gradients should give cause for a little questioning. Journeys to either Bell Crags or High Seat look nothing on the map, but there is dismay awaiting the ill-prepared. Good gaiters a basic, bare necessity, particularly at the worse of 'the sponge', encountered at the ornothologically disarmingly-named hollow The Pewits, at the source of Shoulthwaite and Raise Gills, which is more than a match for any Pennine peat bog! A period of drought or intense frost is a distinct advantage for any degree of comfort. 'Pewit' being a variant for the green plover or lapwing, one of the most enchanting of native British birds, the name mimics the bird's distinctive 'pee-wit' call. Water from the fell initially flows without due haste, then smartly spills into both Thirlmere and into the exquisitely shy, but far from secret, Watendlath Tarn... everyone's quintessential idea of a Lakeland tarn.

515 metres   1,690 feet

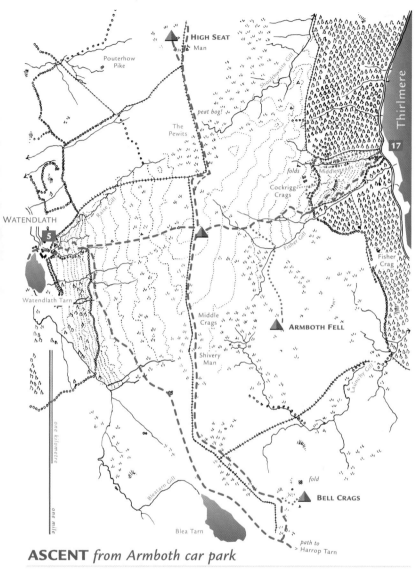

ASCENT *from Armboth car park*

The creation of the reservoir and, in particular, the planting of forestry inevitably effected the early course of this old path. Evidence of its route survives rising as a forest track beginning a short distance south of the entrance to the Armboth car park effectively climbing on the south side of Fisher Gill, though the higher section now runs through a young plantation and for all that high ladder-stiles have been inserted, this is most

EASTERN APPROACHES

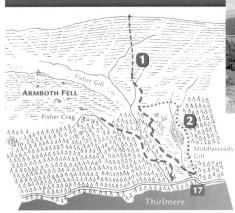

Boulder frozen in rolling motion

definitely not a recom-mended line of approach. **1** Leave the car park turning right to the hand-gate, footpath sign 'Watendlath', at the first bend in the road. There are two lines of ascent from this point. The made-way pass-es over the little bridge spanning Middlesteads Gill, to a hand-gate rising through the hurdle sheepfold on a green trail. As the forestry wall comes near pass a distinctive group of large boulders after which the wall is replaced by a fence partitioning the path from Fisher Gill. As the slope steepens below Cockrigg Crags, the name a reference to *'the lekking place of black cock'*, it makes exaggerated zig-zags and passes under a sycamore tree with some juniper evident, rising to a wall-gap at the top of the forestry.

2 This point can be reached with more interest - and effort – from the hand-gate off the road by ascending by the right-hand forest fence, steep and no path. As the slope scoops angle half-left onto the arete over-looking the impressively deep Middlesteads Gill ravine, natural tree growth enhancing the view to Fisher Crag (*see this view in the* ARMBOTH FELL *chapter, page 20*) and across Thirlmere to Helvellyn. Keep to the rim of the gill, latterly angle right to slip round the right-hand end of the fell-bounding wall where it all-but abuts the forest fence. Go left, keeping this wall to the left to reach the gap mentioned earlier. Now follow the well-defined path leading west, avoid fording the tributary gill as bracken is entered, keep uphill fording a little higher. The path becomes far less certain and contrives to deliver damp ground underfoot nearing the top, even in dry weather, though nothing to match the de-boggy debacle of The Pewits. The summit cairn your skyline target.

ASCENT *from Watendlath*

Start from the National Trust car park crossing the ladder-stile or go right from the point of entry, by either means reach a gate. The way marked footpath fords Raise Beck, soon commencing the zig-zag ascent of the steep bank, grooved by centuries-old sled trails conveying peat from High Tove for domestic heating. The path is in a well-repaired state rising onto the pasture beyond the wall corner, where the old bridle-path tops, Harrop Tarn departs right. Continue up the easier ground due east. The occasional cairn reflect the idle boredom of pedestrians, not navigational need, though in mist the lack of landmarks lend them a certain credibility. There are worn sections higher up, watch for sly holes, the author managed to 'lose' a leg down one providing a moment of surprise and jocularity on an otherwise dead-beat journey to the hand-gate in the ridge fence.

WESTERN APPROACH

The Pewits

Raise Beck

3

> path to Blea & Harrop Tarns

WATENDLATH

road to < KESWICK

Watendlath Tarn

5

> path to Great Crag

slopes of GRANGE FELL

> path to Rosthwaite

High Tove from Green Comb

The Summit

A solitary cairn (*see below*) rests on the eastern edge of the summit as a skyline marker and sure guide for wayfarers traversing the ridge east to west. Splitting hairs the hand-gate in the fence some 50 yards further west rests on slightly higher ground. The view is remarkably good for all the modesty of the setting, westward the array of tops will keep you amused for several minutes, though the stronger horizon is east from Blencathra through Helvellyn to Heron Pike. Catstycam makes a cheeky appearance over the saddle south of White Side, in much the same way as Raven Crag and Castle Rock of Triermain raise their respective heads further north above the thoroughly hidden Thirlmere. In fact, the only named water in view is the Solway Firth sneaking into shot over the left shoulder of High Seat.

Safe Descents

Compass bearings due east for the Armboth road and, better, due west ensuring restoration with habitation at Watendlath (*see right*), are the only sane options, all else is ankle-twisting, bewildering misery in mist.

Middle Crags on the ridge path to Bell Crags

Ridge Routes to...

ARMBOTH FELL DESCENT 250 ft   ASCENT 130 ft   1 mile

Dismiss all thoughts of the bee-line. The heather is cruelly rank and the hollow at the source of Fisher and Launchy Gills is on a par with The Pewits, which IS saying something! Follow the eastward course of the traversing footpath, bearing SE after the first hint of a gill to meet, ford and follow upstream Fisher Gill bearing half-left to the prominent summit outcropping.

BELL CRAGS   DESCENT 30 ft   ASCENT 160 ft   2 miles

The ridge fence S provides the guide, there are too many marshy moments to call this a joyous escapade.

HIGH SEAT   DESCENT 10 ft   ASCENT 300 ft   1 mile

Again the fence does the navigation for you, but a religious faith in an ultimate salvation would be useful personal strength through The Pewits!

High Seat from The Pewits - a monsterous mire

PANORAMA

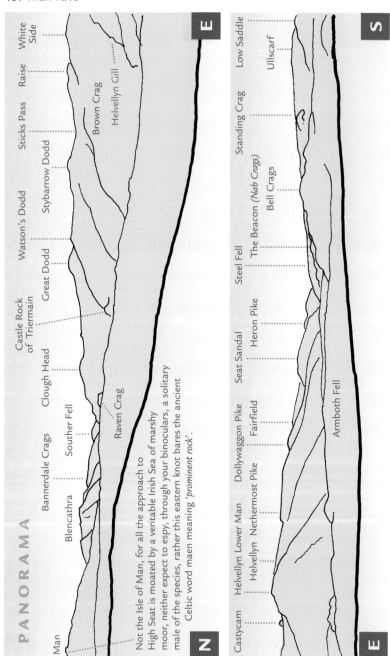

Not the Isle of Man, for all the approach to High Seat is moated by a veritable Irish Sea of marshy moor, neither expect to espy, through your binoculars, a solitary male of the species, rather this eastern knot bares the ancient Celtic word maen meaning '*prominent rock*'.

E

Man · Bannerdale Crags · Blencathra · Souther Fell · Clough Head · Castle Rock of Triermain · Raven Crag · Great Dodd · Watson's Dodd · Stybarrow Dodd · Sticks Pass · Brown Crag · Helvellyn Gill · Raise · White Side

N

S

Low Saddle · Ullscarf · Standing Crag · The Beacon (*Nab Crags*) · Bell Crags · Steel Fell · Heron Pike · Seat Sandal · Fairfield · Dollywaggon Pike · Helvellyn Nethermost Pike · Helvellyn Lower Man · Castycam · Armboth Fell

E

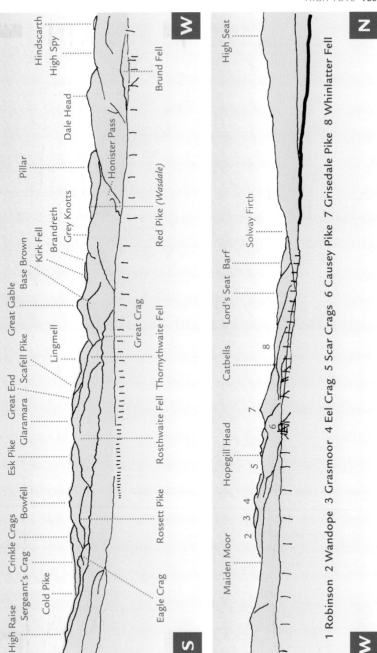

S — **W**

High Raise · Sergeant's Crag · Crinkle Crags · Bowfell · Cold Pike · Esk Pike · Great End · Glaramara · Scafell Pike · Lingmell · Great Gable · Base Brown · Kirk Fell · Brandreth · Grey Knotts · Pillar · Dale Head · Hindscarth · High Spy

Eagle Crag · Rossett Pike · Rosthwaite Fell · Thornythwaite Fell · Great Crag · Red Pike (Wasdale) · Honister Pass · Brund Fell

W — **N**

Maiden Moor · Hopegill Head · Catbells · Lord's Seat · Barf · High Seat · Solway Firth

1 Robinson 2 Wandope 3 Grasmoor 4 Eel Crag 5 Scar Crags 6 Causey Pike 7 Grisedale Pike 8 Whinlatter Fell

LOFT CRAG

To rock-climbers this is the ultimate point of Gimmer Crag, a loft in the attic of a famous and much revered cliff. To fell-walkers it is the central component of the trinity of peaks, along with Harrison Stickle and Pike o'Stickle, collectively known as the Langdale Pikes. Its underling top, Thorn Crag, cramping the top ravine of Dungeon Ghyll, cannot properly be called a pike, though many find it difficult to exclude Pavey Ark from any expression of the ensemble.

A long facade of crags and scree forms an impressive wall above Mickleden between Dungeon Ghyll and Troughton Beck, supremely judged during an ascent of The Band. However, in isolation the best view of the fell is from Pike o'Stickle (*see above*). From this location tiers of rock spill impressively down its southern flank towards Mickleden, backed by Lingmoor Fell and the distant Windermere.

One cannot know the fell by allegiance to the ridge-top alone, a spot of exploration is called for. Follow the climbers' traverse off the Mark Gate path to admire Gimmer Crag from below. Then, with a modicum of effort, clamber up beside the easternmost gully and venture onto the tiny col where Junipal (*the most striking feature in the view above*) and South-eastern Gullies converge. It will come as no surprise to learn that this is the most thrilling spot to admire Pike o'Stickle. The fell has a short northern slope, craggy at first, descending to the marshy hollow of Harrison Combe.

692 metres **2,270** feet (*estimated height*)

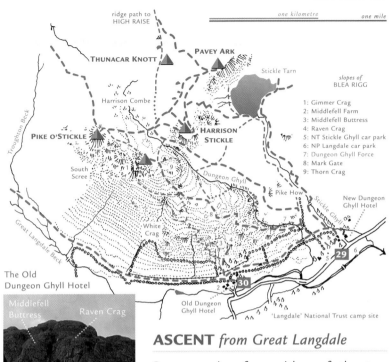

ridge path to
HIGH RAISE

one kilometre

one mile

THUNACAR KNOTT

PAVEY ARK

Stickle Tarn

slopes of
BLEA RIGG

Harrison Combe

1: Gimmer Crag
2: Middlefell Farm
3: Middlefell Buttress
4: Raven Crag
5: NT Stickle Ghyll car park
6: NP Langdale car park
7: Dungeon Ghyll Force
8: Mark Gate
9: Thorn Crag

PIKE O'STICKLE

HARRISON
STICKLE

Troughton Beck

South
Scree

Dungeon Ghyll

Pike How

New Dungeon
Ghyll Hotel

Great Langdale Beck

White
Crag

Stickle Ghyll

The Old
Dungeon Ghyll Hotel

Middlefell
Buttress

Raven Crag

Old Dungeon
Ghyll Hotel

'Langdale' National Trust camp site

ASCENT *from Great Langdale*

Routes spring from either of the two Dungeon Ghyll Hotels. The most secure path, known as Mark Gate, is in receipt of a tremendous amount of sturdy structuring, sufficient pitching and paving that might lead one to believe one is climbing a castle rampart rather than a wild fell. **1** Start from either of the pay *&* display car parks and walk up behind the New Dungeon Ghyll Hotel. Keep left in rising to a hand-gate, go right past the seat, clamber over the stile. Turn left, dipping to ford Dungeon Ghyll now properly upon Mark Gate, respect those sections shut-off to nurture turf recovery. As the path veers from the wall one may slip into the ravine to squint into the dark recesses of Dungeon Ghyll Force - no way through at this point. Backtrack, follow the path winding uphill. At the next relaxation in the ravine, directly upstream of the 'dungeon' section, one may either keep with Mark Gate or take the opportunity to enter the ravine proper. Mark Gate is the unambiguous high way to the top, winding steeply above the lower tier of buttresses and pell-mell of outcrops that bear down on the ODG. **2** The middle section of Dungeon Ghyll runs so deep into the breast of the Pikes that

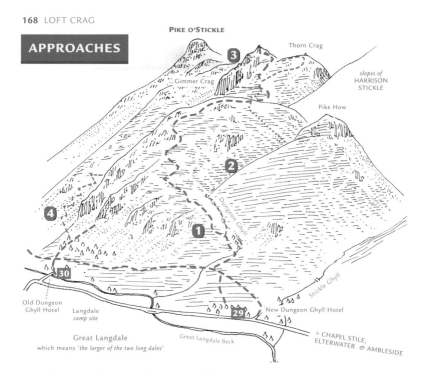

PIKE O'STICKLE

APPROACHES

Thorn Crag

slopes of
HARRISON
STICKLE

Gimmer Crag

Pike How

Dungeon Ghyll

Stickle Ghyll

Old Dungeon
Ghyll Hotel

Langdale
camp site

New Dungeon Ghyll Hotel

> CHAPEL STILE,
ELTERWATER & AMBLESIDE

Great Langdale
which means *'the larger of the two long dales'*

Great Langdale Beck

one feels one is venturing beyond the limits of reason to end in some
hidden kingdom of doom - so do not enter unless you are confident in
such surroundings. Cautiously enter, beware of the tree roots as you do.
Scramble over the mid gill rocks to follow the right bank up to the first

Looking up at Gimmer Crag from Mickleden

Loft Crag from Thunacar Knott

mare's tail waterfall. Scramble dexterously up the right-hand outcropping. The scenery is superb. Keep to the right bank until forced onto the left side, climb up through the large boulders to reach the baulking upper fall. A thunderous scene: water crashing into a pool before finally spilling to the gill floor. The exit is the unlikely looking gully left, a sinister but safe scramble leads onto the open fell pasture to join Mark Gate – so is vanquished the kingdom of doom!

Mark Gate duly arrives onto this moor and advances WNW to a sheepfold and cairn where outcropping resumes. This is a significant point. Hereon the slope steepens once more bringing further paving either leading directly onto the saddle overlooking Harrison Combe or, rounding

the first outcrop, bear up right onto Thorn Crag on a faint path, passing the cairn with its fine view of Harrison Crag across the gulf of the upper gorge of Dungeon Ghyll. The paths reunite, contour then bear up left on a loose stony bedded path to access the summit. **3** From the cairn the climbers' traverse to the famous buttresses of Gimmer Crag may be pursued. While confident climbers may tackle the Southeastern Gully, those less adept should divert earlier off the path aiming up to the much shorter easternmost gully. Even this has a ten-foot chockstone 'bad step' (*see left*), side-stepped up easily handled rocks on the right-hand side. Once above one may simply follow the grassy ledge above

the North-western Gully to join the ridge west of the summit or take the opportunity to visit the thrilling col at the actual top of Gimmer Crag. Incidentally, in case you were wondering, the crag-name derives from the term for a '*ewe-lamb between its first and second shearing*'. Look for, then follow, the short tilted rock and grass rake to the left, switching precisely at its top. Zig-zag through the early outcropping, contour along a ledge right to arrive at the tiny col immediately above the plummeting Junipal Gully, from here Pike o'Stickle seems to soar! Look back up the fellside, a solid mass of banded rock suggests you are crag-bound, well you would be... but for the knowledge of your approach! Before you retreat, gaze behind you down South-eastern Gully (*see left*).

4 From the Old Dungeon Ghyll car park follow the path up behind the hotel, via a gate. Cross directly over the bridle-way to the ladder-stile. Winding up the light plantation, bear left just as the flight of steps begin – for the express use of rock-climbers accessing Middlefell Buttress and Raven Crag. Ford the tiny gill to reach a stile in the fence at the top of the wall. The path, never in doubt, tackles the scree slope progressively firmer footing is found though the mild outcropping and light bracken climbing to a obvious fork. The climbers' path rather oddly chooses to follow the initially inviting ledge path left, falling foul of steep ground as a gill re-entrant is neared, causing it to climb steeply before slanting left beneath the upper fall angling up towards Gimmer. The immeasurably better route is straight up, being an easy grassy slope directly to the cairn, where the climbers' traverse leaves Mark Gate.

The top of Dungeon Ghyll

The Summit

The ideal summit in many respects, quite small, yet with ample room for a party to sit and drool over the view. Great Langdale is especially prominent, with Mickleden far below, Bowfell forming the dark majestic backdrop. Ahh, the stuff of fell-walking dreams, don't you just love it?

Pike o'Stickle from the top of Junipal Gully

Wetherlam

Blake Rigg

The west face of Gimmer Crag

(*above*) Summit backed by Harrison Stickle

(*left*) Summit ridge from the west

Safe Descents

For all the ferocity of tiered crags directly beneath one's feet the walker has a sure recourse in Mark Gate. Leave the summit on the path SE. Bear left down the stony trail, at the foot of this short ramp the stones at their loosest. Join the contouring path below the northern slope of the summit, go right, the evident cairned path soon begins its newly-paved descent, destination NDG.

Ridge Routes to...

HARRISON STICKLE   DESCENT   200 ft   ASCENT 345 ft   0.5 miles

Splitting hairs this is not strictly a ridge route, rather these are two summits with a natural harmony. You climb one... you want to climb the other! Go NW off the summit ridge to join the worn trail from Pike o'Stickle, go right to cross the large boulders in the peaty hollow of Harrison Combe, two paths lead to the summit. The direct route encountering an easy rock step, whilst the left-hand route sweeps up and round to approach from the NW over easy ground every step of the way.

PIKE O'STICKLE   DESCENT 80 ft   ASCENT 200 ft   0.3 miles

Leave the summit NW, following the undulating ridge to the top of South Scree. From where there are at least four lines of scrambly ascent up the massive summit cone – *how many can you discover?*

PANORAMA

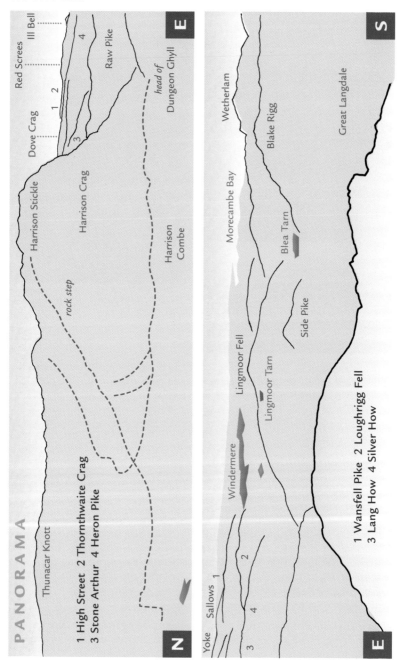

E

Ill Bell
Red Screes
Raw Pike
4
1 2
Dove Crag
3
head of
Dungeon Ghyll
Harrison Crag
Harrison Stickle
Harrison Combe
rock step
Thunacar Knott

N

1 High Street 2 Thornthwaite Crag
3 Stone Arthur 4 Heron Pike

S

Wetherlam
Blake Rigg
Great Langdale
Morecambe Bay
Blea Tarn
Side Pike
Lingmoor Fell
Lingmoor Tarn
Windermere
Sallows
Yoke
1
2
4
3

E

1 Wansfell Pike 2 Loughrigg Fell
3 Lang How 4 Silver How

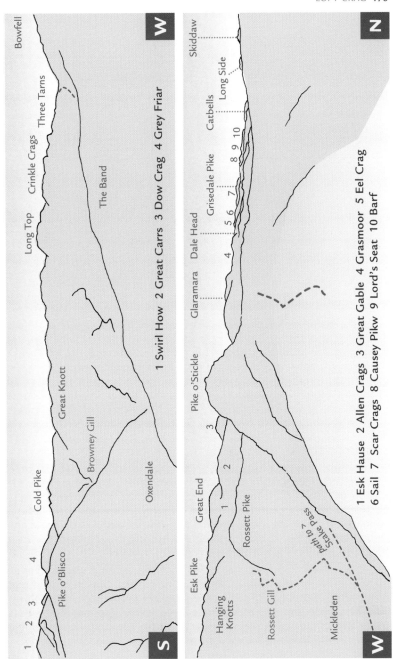

W

Bowfell
Three Tarns
Crinkle Crags
Long Top
Great Knott
The Band
Cold Pike
Browney Gill
Pike o'Blisco
Oxendale
1 2 3 4

1 Swirl How 2 Great Carrs 3 Dow Crag 4 Grey Friar

S

N

Skiddaw
Long Side
Catbells
Grisedale Pike
Dale Head
Glaramara
Pike o'Stickle
Great End
Esk Pike
Hanging Knotts
Rossett Pike
Rossett Gill
path to Stake Pass
Mickleden
4 5 6 7 8 9 10
1 2 3

1 Esk Hause 2 Allen Crags 3 Great Gable 4 Grasmoor 5 Eel Crag
6 Sail 7 Scar Crags 8 Causey Pikw 9 Lord's Seat 10 Barf

W

LOUGHRIGG FELL

At the point where the rivers Rothay and Brathay meet to infuse Windermere, the Central Fells are born in the irregular form of Loughrigg Fell. Climbing above Clappersgate and the site of Galava Roman Fort onto Todd Crag, a lowly, but strategic viewpoint for the great lake. Trending north-westward, a gently undulating mass of bracken-clad fell and pasture, including the former site of Ambleside golf course, a further ridge rises from the vicinity of Rydal village running south-westward over Lanty Scar. The two ridges converge at a damp amphitheatre beset with bracken before climbing more confidently over Ivy Crag to the triple-top summit.

The fell-name means 'ridge above the lake'. Sweetly cradled in a bowl of trees and green pastures on the southern flank is Loughrigg Tarn, the lake in question. Curiosity is aroused by the use of the term 'lough', absent elsewhere in Lakeland, might it betray an ancient Irish cultural connection? From the vicinity of the tarn the fell appears compact and characterful, other aspects are less convincing, apart from the neat backdrop profile in views across Grasmere (*see above*).

Well endowed with paths at every level the fell is a parade for all manner of walks and walkers. By Rydal Water and Grasmere, and that near perfect expression of the picturesque, the promenade of Loughrigg Terrace. While the higher portions have wilder ground, harbouring pools and undulations, where, were it not for the bracken, one might wander at will enjoying the exceptionally lovely outlooks.

335 metres   1,099 feet

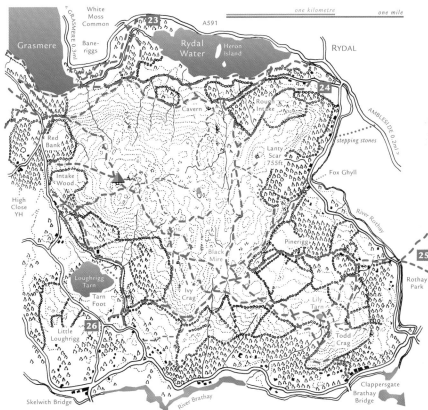

one kilometre   one mile

Grasmere

White Moss Common

Bane-riggs

Rydal Water

Heron Island

RYDAL

23

A591

24

Cavern

Rough Intake

AMBLESIDE 0.2ml

stepping stones

Red Bank

Lanty Scar 755ft

Fox Ghyll

Intake Wood

River Rothay

High Close YH

Pinerigg

Black Mire

25

Loughrigg Tarn

Ivy Crag

Lily Tarn

Rothay Park

Tarn Foot

26

Little Loughrigg

Todd Crag

Clappersgate

Skelwith Bridge

River Brathay

Brathay Bridge

The fell also has one great work of audacious quarrying, Loughrigg Cavern above Rydal Water. For anyone nervous of caves and dark places, here is a dank, eerie hollow you can stroll into with the minimum of claustrophobia and sense of chill.

Rydal Water

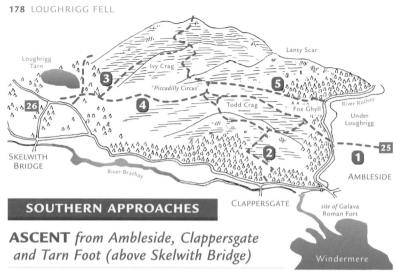

Loughrigg
Tarn

Ivy Crag

Lanty Scar

'Piccadilly Circus'

3

26

4

Todd Crag

Fox Ghyll

River Rothay

Under
Loughrigg

5

River Brathay

2

1

25

SKELWITH
BRIDGE

AMBLESIDE

CLAPPERSGATE

site of Galava
Roman Fort

Windermere

SOUTHERN APPROACHES

ASCENT *from Ambleside, Clappersgate and Tarn Foot (above Skelwith Bridge)*

Ambleside, for all the congregation of casual visitors has got rich pickings beyond the shops, cafes and sundry innocent diversions of the pocket and flesh. Fells rise in such a way to ensure the fell-walker may quickly escape to loftier thoughts and scenes. One is reminded of William Blake's poem "*Great things are done when men and mountains meet, This is not done by jostling in the street*". Loughrigg is pronounced '*luff-rigg*', it is also usual to drop the 'Fell' in conversation. By comparison with many a neighbour, such as Red Screes or Wansfell Pike even, this may be a lowly fell, but has so many paths that encounters with fellow walkers are relatively infrequent and normally pleasant events. From the town, Todd Crag is the first fell-top port of call, certainly a high point in terms of its superb position at the head of Windermere.

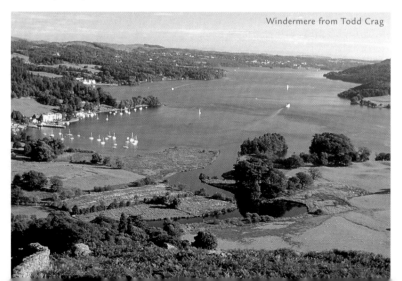

Windermere from Todd Crag

Loughrigg Tarn from Ivy Crag

1 Either leave the Rydal Road car park left, following the footway turn left into Stoney Lane (cul-de-sac), leading onto a path direct to Miller Bridge; or one may also get to this point from Zeffirellis pizzeria & cinema, by following Vicarage Road, signed 'Rothay Park, Loughrigg' leading between the spired parish church of St Mary's and the primary school to a gate into the park, continue via the open metalled path. Cross Miller Bridge and turn right, taking the metalled lane rising left signed to 'Browhead and Pinerigg'. One may follow the road and subsequent track via gates above Pinerigg through the old golf course, as the direct route for the fell proper. However, Todd Crag should not be flippantly dismissed. A footpath is signed 'Clappersgate' at the first bend above Browhead up the wall steps. Pass through a wood to a squeeze

Great Langdale from below Ivy Crag

stile, ascend keeping left to pass a large cairn, viewpoint for Ambleside. Advance to a ladder-stile then onto the prominent top, the second being the main Todd Crag viewpoint (*see page 186*). **2** This top can be reached from Clappersgate. A footpath signed from the main road leads up a narrow walled path to a gate then winds up by the 'Sid Cross Memorial Seat', dedicated to the former landlord of the ODG and much-loved doyen of Langdale climbing society who died in 1998 at the age of 85. The plaque reads 'A true Westmerian who loved his Langdale' how ironic the seat predominantly overlooks the soft wooded hills of old Lancashire's Furness!

The ridge walk by Lily Tarn is a very pleasant stroll leading via a hand-gate in the cross ridge fence where the enclosure walls bottleneck. Either cross the next knoll or skirt to the left to reach a 'Piccadilly Circus' of path-

Miller Bridge

Black Mire

ways. Cross the bridle-path from Pinerigg to Tarn Foot en route to the main body of the fell. Climb from the bracken beset hollow, appropriately known as Black Mire, onto the ridge, a left-hand spur leading to the Ivy Crag viewpoint.

A popular route onto the fell begins from the vicinity of the Tarn Foot camp site, close to Loughrigg Tarn. A small car park GR 346039 provides a useful start point up the lane under Little Loughrigg from Skelwith Bridge. 3 Follow the bridle-lane from Tarn Foot Cottage via two gates leading east, after the second gate with slate sign 'Ambleside' go just 100 yards and with a walled-up gate visible right branch up left through the bracken, soon climbing steeply with a wall to the left and the Ivy Crag ridge above right up the ridge path, turn left to reach the summit, via a lateral trough hollow.

4 Or, more simply, keep along the track to the 'Piccadilly Circus' of paths and streams. Bear left onto the ridge, as with the route off Todd Crag. 5 From the Under Loughrigg road a footpath is signposted south-west, behind Fox Ghyll (house) and up beside the gill itself to reach the aforementioned path-interchange.

Hart Crag Dove Crag High Pike
Low Pike
Cairn on Lanty Scar

Loughrigg Tarn

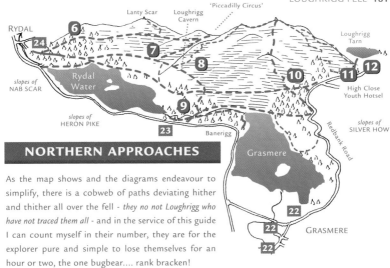

'Piccadilly Circus'

Lanty Scar   Loughrigg
                Cavern

RYDAL

24   **6**

7

8

Rydal
Water

slopes of
NAB SCAR

Loughrigg
Tarn

12

11

10

High Close
Youth Hostel

slopes of
HERON PIKE

9

23   Banerigg

slopes of
SILVER HOW

Redbank Road

Grasmere

NORTHERN APPROACHES

As the map shows and the diagrams endeavour to
simplify, there is a cobweb of paths deviating hither
and thither all over the fell - *they no not Loughrigg who
have not traced them all* - and in the service of this guide
I can count myself in their number, they are for the
explorer pure and simple to lose themselves for an
hour or two, the one bugbear.... rank bracken!

22

22   GRASMERE

22

ASCENT *from Rydal, White Moss and the Redbank Road*

Quite the majority of casual walkers stroll from White Moss GR350065
where lovely paths lead to Loughrigg Terrace and Loughrigg Cavern, and
the gentle wood-fringed delights of both Rydal Water and Grasmere. It is
a mercy that the tree canopy dulls the traffic noise. Redbank Road offers
access to Grasmere lake-shore, woods and direct climbs to the summit.

However, the more complete and intimate approaches to Loughrigg
begin from Rydal, either from the footbridge opposite the Rothay Glen
Hotel (Badger Bar), or from the small Pelter Bridge car park GR366059.
The back road going west from the car park leads by Steps End into a
bridle-lane, the quarry extraction track for Loughrigg Cavern, paths lead
on beyond the Cavern to Loughrigg Terrace or by the shore of Rydal
Water. **6** Take the footpath signposted left after the entrance to Cote
How and before the pair of cottages. Ascend the bank to a gate, now
with a wall right and handsome views to Nab Scar and Rydale. In high
summer the bracken is commensu-
rately high too, but a path exists
running on by a hand-gate and
when the wall ends traversing the
damp slope to join a path now
heading south, a spur path left
gaining the cairn on top of Lanty
Scar (Lanty being pet-name
derived from '*Lancelot*'). Continue
south over a saddle to reach the
'Piccadilly Circus' path inter-

Loughrigg Cavern

change, go right, climbing above Black Mire onto the ridge proper bound for the summit. **7** Take the lane beyond Steps End and, short of the Cavern, ascend the valley to link up with route **6** where it traverses from the wall-end, before the Lanty Scar spur. **8** On reaching Loughrigg Cavern, give the interior the benefit of a visit, using the stepping stones. Then head up the bank from the left-hand (east) side of the cave entrance. A path winds up the edge of the ridge, to become less that certain as damp hollows are encountered. Either keep south to, eventually join up with the main path from Black Mire, or be intrepid, find your own way westward, through the confusion of irregular and fragmented paths that will take you to the top.

9 From White Moss car park follow the compacted path to the foot-bridge. Paths on either side lead upstream to Grasmere lake-shore and ultimately Redbank Road. Cross the bridge and head up into the wood ahead reaching a hand-gate. Go right, now embarking upon Loughrigg's most treasured possession - the Terrace, not a row of industrial housing - quite the reverse, a wonderful path traversing the fellside. Seats en route allow for a prolonged admiration of a stunning composition, with Grasmere seen as a great lake in a bowl of fine fells. **10** Short of the gate

View from the Grasmere cairn

Focused view from the summit over Dunmail Raise to Skiddaw

into woodland, join the staircase path left, much effort has been employed to give durability to this popular climb. Mount to a ragged cairn, often called the 'Grasmere cairn' for its the prime viewpoint qualities, continue to the summit knoll set back from the brink. This route can be reached from the Redbank Road. Unavoidably, approaches from the village of Grasmere are obliged to follow this narrow, windy road, cars become the hazard for walkers in summer months, a plague on all your cars! A permissive path dips off the road left from a hand-gate and steps just beyond Lea Cottage, this leads down to the lake shore then wends delightfully through to open woodland. One may switch back right, up to the lodge there switch again left in front of the lodge on the cobbled track (avoiding the road altogether). Still within the wood, rise to a gate into a lane, go the few paces left to the gate thence directly onto Loughrigg Terrace, and the flight of steps to the top. There are two further lines of ascent, paths less-travelled, but equally effectatious. **11** South of the road fork, at the top of Redbank Road, opposite the High Close Arboretum GR 341053 a path leaves the road (no sign), winds up an open section of slope to a hand-gate. Continue up, latterly with the wall to the right, then on to the open fellside climbing to join the main north-west path to the top. **12** Further south down the minor road, a footpath is signed at a stile beside a cottage, contour slipping through coniferous woodland via stiles to a cairn short of a gate. Bear immediately left climbing with a gill, direct to the top. As a special treat, walkers may forget the summit altogether and entertain a circular tour, a useful option for those 'rare' times when the fell is enveloped in cloud.

Boathouse at the foot of Rydal Water

Starting from the Pelter Bridge car park, walk south along the Under Loughrigg road branching off right, with the path via hand-gates entering Fox Ghyll. Join the bridle-path from Ambleside crossing under Ivy Crag, with Great Langdale displayed ahead. Descend to Tarn Foot Cottage, go right, through the gate, onto the fenced drive above Loughrigg Tarn. Either follow the path off right after the The How or continue directly to the road. Rise to Redbank top road junction, taking the path in an avenue, signed right, leading down to Loughrigg Terrace. Keep right to visit either Loughrigg Cavern, or the Rydal Water shore en route to Pelter Bridge. A grand tour of just under five miles, with surprisingly little ascent.

Evening cloud gathering impressively, as seen from the southern end of the summit ridge

Wansfell Pike

Ambleside

The Summit

A fine stone-built Ordnance Survey column takes pride of place on a rock plinth. Two other contesting tops to the NE and S fail to claim summit status by a matter of a few feet. The view makes this a place of special attraction, one almost expects a topograph. Never mind, this guide provides this missing ingredient for your express and exclusive delectation.

Safe Descents

There this craggy ground due S from the summit, and much muddled outcropping elsewhere. The advice is to stick to the worn paths, they are reliable. The nearest road being due west. For Grasmere, White Moss and Rydal follow the NW path down to the W end of Loughrigg Terrace. For Ambleside the journey is that much longer heading SE along the ridge dipping beyond Ivy Crag to join the bridleway E, via Pinerigg.

Ridge Route to...

SILVER HOW   DESCENT 750 ft   ASCENT 950 ft   2.6 miles

Follow the NW path down to the E end of Loughrigg Terrace. Go left through the gate, keep right at the first fork soon joining the Redbank Road. Go right, and first left at the footpath sign, but go up the three immediate steps onto a footpath that curves left into the Huntingstile Gap, via a hand-gate. Join the ridge path proper climbing onto Dow Bank. Follow the switch-back course over Spedding Crag till a more significant step in the ridge occurs. Take the rising line by a large cairn, angling right for the scarp-top summit.

PANORAMA from Todd Crag

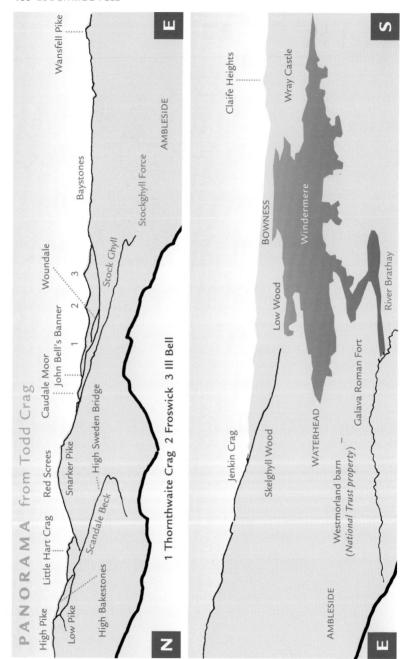

N

High Pike — Little Hart Crag — Red Screes — Snarker Pike — Caudale Moor — John Bell's Banner — Woundale — Baystones — Wansfell Pike **E**

Low Pike

High Bakestones

Scandale Beck — High Sweden Bridge

Stock Ghyll

Stockghyll Force

AMBLESIDE

1 2 3

1 Thornthwaite Crag   2 Froswick   3 Ill Bell

E

AMBLESIDE

Westmorland barn
(National Trust property)

Galava Roman Fort

River Brathay

WATERHEAD

Skelghyll Wood

Jenkin Crag

Low Wood

BOWNESS

Windermere

Wray Castle

Claife Heights **S**

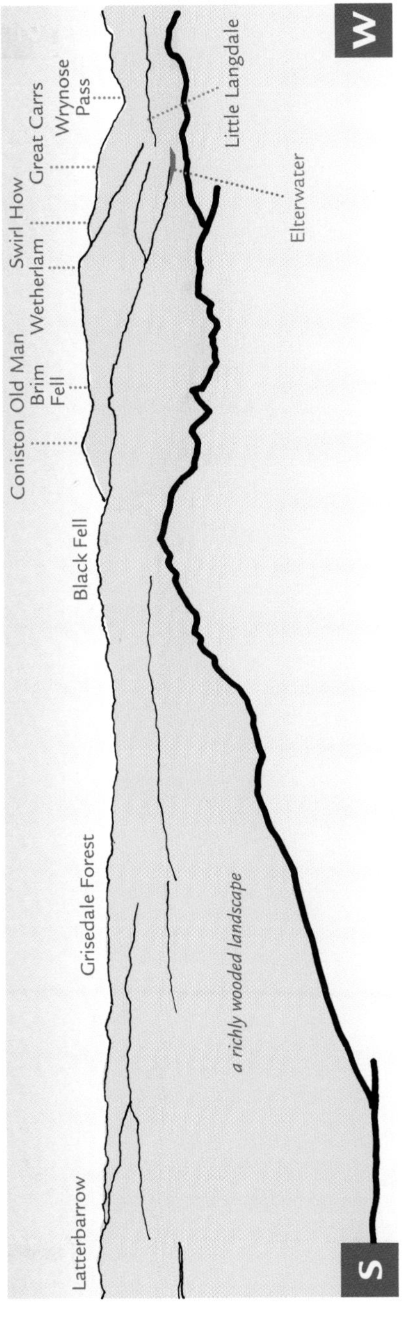

W

Great Carrs
Swirl How
Coniston Old Man
Wetherlam
Brim Fell
Wrynose Pass
Little Langdale
Elterwater
Black Fell
Gri. sedale Forest
Latterbarrow
a richly wooded landscape

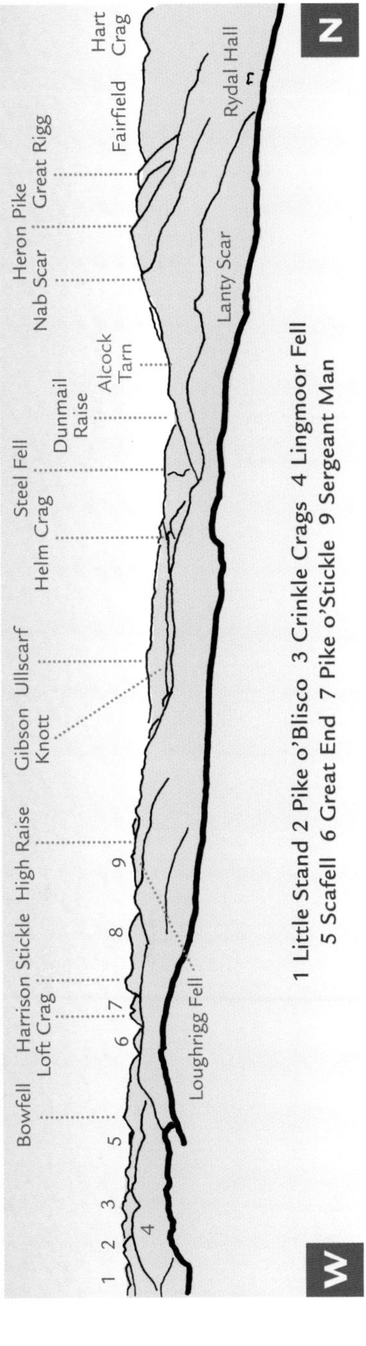

S

N

Hart Crag
Fairfield
Great Rigg
Heron Pike
Nab Scar
Rydal Hall
Lanty Scar
Alcock Tarn
Steel Fell
Dunmail Raise
Helm Crag
Gibson Knott
Ullscarf
High Raise
Harrison Stickle
Bowfell
Loft Crag
Loughrigg Fell

1 Little Stand 2 Pike o'Blisco 3 Crinkle Crags 4 Lingmoor Fell
5 Scafell 6 Great End 7 Pike o'Stickle 9 Sergeant Man

W

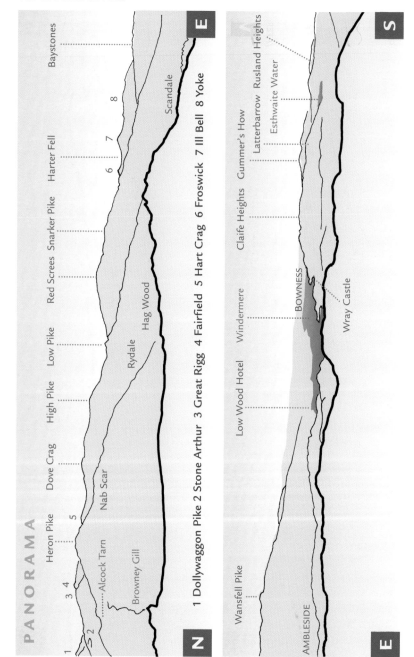

PANORAMA

N

E

Baystones — Harter Fell — Snarker Pike — Red Screes — Low Pike — High Pike — Dove Crag — Heron Pike

Scandale

8 — 7 — 6 — 5

Rydale — Hag Wood

Nab Scar

Alcock Tarn — Browney Gill

3 4 — 1 — 2

1 Dollywaggon Pike 2 Stone Arthur 3 Great Rigg 4 Fairfield 5 Hart Crag 6 Froswick 7 Ill Bell 8 Yoke

E

S

Wansfell Pike — Low Wood Hotel — Windermere — Claife Heights — Gummer's How — Latterbarrow — Rusland Heights

Esthwaite Water

BOWNESS

Wray Castle

AMBLESIDE

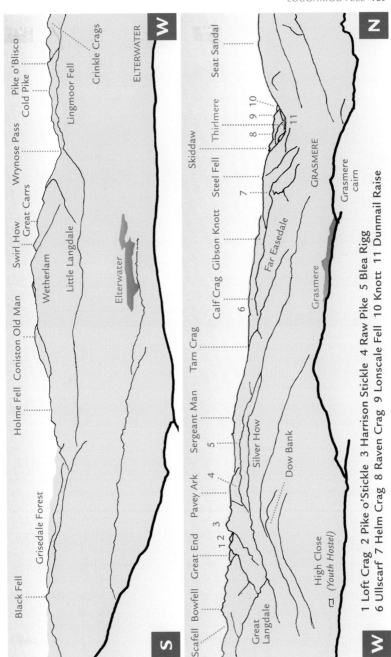

S

W

Black Fell
Griesdale Forest
Holme Fell Coniston Old Man
Wetherlam
Little Langdale
Elterwater
Swirl How
Great Carrs
Wrynose Pass
Lingmoor Fell
Pike o'Blisco
Cold Pike
Crinkle Crags
ELTERWATER

W

N

Scafell Bowfell Great End Pavey Ark
1 2 3
4
5
Sergeant Man
Tarn Crag
Calf Crag Gibson Knott
Steel Fell Thirlmere
8 9 10
11
Skiddaw
Seat Sandal

Silver How
Dow Bank
Far Easedale
6
7
Great Langdale
High Close
(Youth Hostel)
Grasmere
GRASMERE
Grasmere cairn

1 Loft Crag 2 Pike o'Stickle 3 Harrison Stickle 4 Raw Pike 5 Blea Rigg
6 Ullscarf 7 Helm Crag 8 Raven Crag 9 Lonscale Fell 10 Knott 11 Dunmail Raise

PAVEY ARK

Almost every day, whatever the season, rain or shine, of all the paths on the Langdale Pikes someone at least makes the effort to climb Stickle Ghyll. From the NDG the dark brooding brow of Pavey Ark can just be seen peering over the corrie-lip at the top of the gill.

In summer endless processions wend up the much-strengthened path to behold, awe-struck, the mighty walls across the steely waters of the tarn (*see above*). Many visitors are content just to look at the fearful buttresses. Others, with measured confidence, orbit the tarn, ascend the scree to tackle the rock-ladder of Jack's Rake. Hands and feet in action all the way, on the firmest of rock, with remarkably few moments of real exposure to daunt. It is a uniquely wonderful opportunity for the average fell-walker to experience the thrill of a classic Lakeland cliff. But it becomes more serious with wind and rain and in winter conditions it reverts to the sole preserve of mountaineers, equipped with ropes.

Easy Gully is not quite as simple as the name would imply. Loose scree leads to a chaos of large chock-stones at the top and delicate manoeuvres not in the arsenal of every walker. The North Rake provides the one direct ascent for the fell-walker, climbing from Bright Beck, path erosion is advanced so careful footing is required.

The term Ark suggests a place of refuge or shelter, while 'Pavia' appears to be an otherwise lost personal-name.

697 metres   2,288 feet

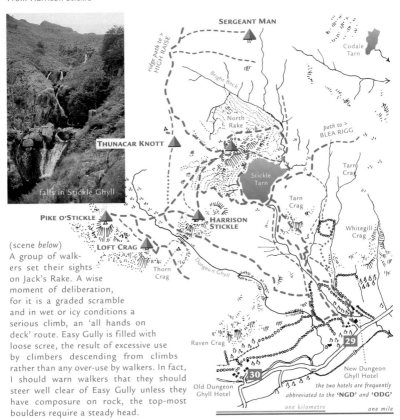

falls in Stickle Ghyll

(scene *below*)
A group of walkers set their sights on Jack's Rake. A wise moment of deliberation, for it is a graded scramble and in wet or icy conditions a serious climb, an 'all hands on deck' route. Easy Gully is filled with loose scree, the result of excessive use by climbers descending from climbs rather than any over-use by walkers. In fact, I should warn walkers that they should steer well clear of Easy Gully unless they have composure on rock, the top-most boulders require a steady head.

the two hotels are frequently abbreviated to the **'NGD'** *and* **'ODG'**

one kilometre   *one mile*

ASCENT
from New Dungeon Ghyll

APPROACHES

Either go directly up the bridle-path from the hotel or ascend from Stickle Ghyll car park information shelter. The paths meet up by the fenced gap.
1 The Pike How route leads off left from the fence gap, rising to a hand-gate turn right, passing a seat to a stile. Keep the wall right, do not ford Dungeon Ghyll. The well-marked path bears left mounting the steep slope in steady stages, much of it re-engineered to cope with the inevitable heavy foot traffic. Many walkers use this as their return leg after the ascent via Stickle Ghyll, though they would be better resorting to the Mark Gate path off Loft Crag, it has the best base. Climbing up to the saddle behind Pike How, make the move right to stand on top, it is a splendid viewpoint for Great Langdale. While the main path angles WNW a useful lesser path leads along the rim of the slope on a right-hand curve to reach the Stickle Tarn dam. This route gives a fine perspective view across the gulf of Stickle Ghyll to Tarn Crag. **2** Go straight up the paved rock path beside the tree-shaded section of Stickle Ghyll. Cross the footbridge rising to a stile. Keep to the right-hand side of the valley, the paths to the west are in a poor state, so give them a miss. Stepping through a fold, wind up the rigg between small fenced conifer plantings, to a fine four-part waterfall. At this point there are three options, either continue up the gill negotiating a rock-step, rising to a ford, to complete the climb directly upon Stickle Tarn dam. **3** Ascend the well-made stone stair which zig-zags to a higher level before angling left onto a shelf beneath Tarn Crag. **4** A green continuation goes further up the fell from where the stone-stair effectively ends. Keeping to the right of the Tarn Crag outcrops with a

Stickle Tarn

From Sergeant Man, backed by the Coniston Fells

roofless shelter left and isolated walled enclosure right. Cross over the shoulder to reach Stickle Tarn at its eastern end. **5** A far more pleasant and less well-known alternative line begins directly after leaving the NDG. Cross the footbridge located half-right after the initial gate. The path runs up behind Millbeck Farm enters an outgang lane via a hand-gate, thereafter rising from the wall onto the bracken rigg. Avoid outcropping by slanting left. Either contour onto the main zig-zagging path or climb, with tenuous initial evidence of a path in the bracken, on finding the green path skirt the right-hand shoulder of a knoll above a steep gill. Subsequently traversing the walled enclosure diagonally to a narrow wall-gap and join up with the upper section of the old shepherds' path. This passes walled boulders and slips over a saddle depression to meet the path running along the eastern shore of the tarn from the outflow.

Ahead, the massive eastern face of Pavey Ark in all its glory smiling down upon the cool dark waters of the tarn. There are three popular lines of ascent for the fell-walker from the dam - left, right and centre! **6** Go left on the obvious path, which has received some restorative paving, although more is needed. Work up the loose slope to the right of the buttresses of Harrison Stickle. Go right on meeting the higher contouring path, venturing onto the distinctively coarse-rocked ridge, clambering through the crag-shielding wall onto the summit. **7** The North Rake: Go right from the dam along the shore path to follow, then ford, Bright Beck and mount the prominent gully or rake up the east ridge. This is North Rake. All too often used as a line of descent, it has

Looking out from the chockstones at the top of Easy Gully

inevitably become badly eroded, the day being not far off when the sterling energies of path-makers will be directed at stabilising this trail too. Gaining the ridge-top, the path swings round by the broken wall, passing a pooled hollow to gain the summit, as from the north-west.

8 Jack's Rake, which, with the tiny climb onto Helm Crag summit outcrop, marks the zenith of fell-walking endeavour in the Central Fells. Paths approach from either side of the tarn. That by the west shore is the old-time favourite, climbing the scree slope from the north-west edge of the tarn via a prominent memorial cairn inscribed 'S.W.S. 1900'. The eastern approach crossing possibly the looser scree, but by keeping up right, early on, and by a deft slight of foot, one may avoid almost all of the scree! The two approaches converge at the very centre of the cliff-base. A word of advice about seductive Easy Gully angling up to the

right. At its foot an awkward rock-lip, where scree shoots, this proves to be indicative of the one greater challenge at the top. For, while in the main part the gully is straightforward and provides stunning views back over the tarn to the Coniston Fells, the gully concludes in a manner ill-suited to the faint-hearted - the author fortuitously met

Easy Gully

Double-page montage of Jack's Rake
see even 'Skye' the dog can do it without getting collie-wobbles!

Looking down first section

Looking up to ash tree

upper terrace

Stickle Tarn from the ash tree

The gun rock squeeze

Stickle Tarn from the top

Summer evening looking east on the approach from Harrison Stickle

up with descending rock-climbers who took pity on him, lifted his day-sack and watchfully guided him up the few delicate steps that clinch the climb. So don't go this way unless you are happy on rock. Jack's Rake, on the other hand, for all it requires a confident approach, is hands-on walking, if you can climb a step-ladder then you have the basic technique for this climb, for all it appears to take the cliff 'by the scruff of its neck'. In the preparation of this guide the author made two ascents, then wished he had the time to do it again (and again). There are five distinct stages to the climb, it would be an over-elaboration to call them pitches, as the groove takes several lateral 'breathers', via an ash tree and a patch of thistles, and feature a squeeze behind a fallen splinter of rock The Gun, and concludes above Great Gully, dipping momentarily, then scrambling up rock slabs to the wall-end above a projecting rock. The instinct to climb, so well developed by now, that one naturally finds a scrambly way to the top, brushing aside all notion of linking to the ridge path.

The Summit

All trace of a cairn has been lost, and to be frank the bare rock top requires no such monument to idle industry. The rocks themselves are fascinating igneous exposures displaying intricately confused patterns. There is one large perched erratic boulder just to the south and a few pools on the north and west enhancing the rock garden effect. The view is not 'the best a man can get' in these parts, but the imminence of an immense cliff under one's feet brings its own sense of tingling drama.

Safe Descents

North Rake, whilst loose in parts, is a secure line of retreat. Head slightly W of N from the top, passing through the wall, the well defined path curves right into the Rake, bound for Stickle Tarn's east shore. Though don't 'bound', a steady stride will be kinder on the trail!

Ridge Routes to...

HARRISON STICKLE   DESCENT 40ft   ASCENT 100 ft   0.5 miles

In view from the outset. The consistent path runs just under the edge, avoids the ridge-top rock tors, links with the path climbing from the south shore of Stickle Tarn, rising with two paths mounting either from the east or north. There is scope for good sport in following the ridge-top all the way. Though there is no continuous path, the final grassy rise to the summit is quite trouble free.

THUNACAR KNOTT   DESCENT 30ft   ASCENT 100ft   0.25 miles

A clear path leads off W, curving NW aiming for the depression at the head of Bright Beck. Take an early deviation left, with no trace of a path, attaining the summit cairn short of the pool.

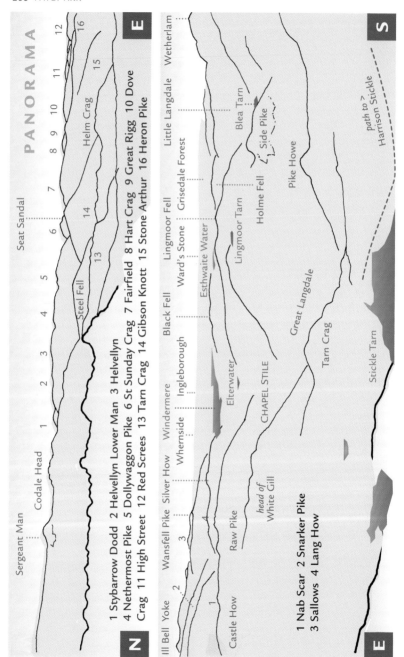

PANORAMA

N

E

Sergeant Man · Codale Head · Seat Sandal · Helm Crag

1 · 2 · 3 · 4 · 5 · 6 · 7 · 8 · 9 · 10 · 11 · 12

13 · 14 · 15 · 16

Steel Fell

1 Stybarrow Dodd 2 Helvellyn Lower Man 3 Helvellyn
4 Nethermost Pike 5 Dollywaggon Pike 6 St Sunday Crag 7 Fairfield 8 Hart Crag 9 Great Rigg 10 Dove
Crag 11 High Street 12 Red Screes 13 Tarn Crag 14 Gibson Knott 15 Stone Arthur 16 Heron Pike

E

S

Ill Bell · Yoke · Wansfell Pike · Silver How · Windermere · Black Fell · Lingmoor Fell · Little Langdale · Wetherlam

Castle How · Whernside · Ingleborough · Ward's Stone · Grisedale Forest

Raw Pike · Esthwaite Water · Lingmoor Tarn · Holme Fell · Blea Tarn

head of White Gill · Elterwater · CHAPEL STILE · Great Langdale · Pike Howe · Side Pike

Tarn Crag · Stickle Tarn

path to > Harrison Stickle

1 Nab Scar 2 Snarker Pike
3 Sallows 4 Lang How

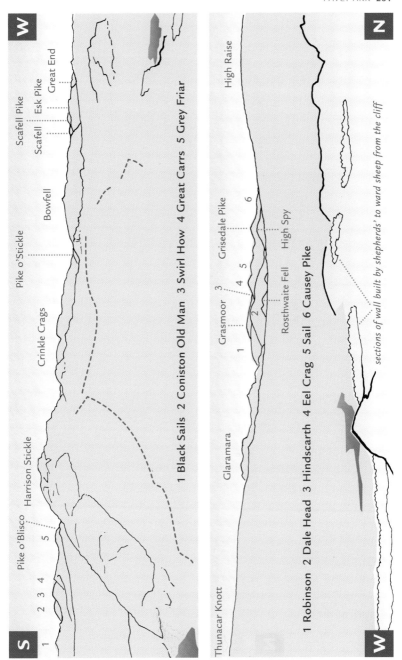

W

Scafell Pike
Scafell
Esk Pike
Great End

Pike o'Stickle

Bowfell

Crinkle Crags

Harrison Stickle

Pike o'Blisco

5

1 2 3 4

S

1 Black Sails 2 Coniston Old Man 3 Swirl How 4 Great Carrs 5 Grey Friar

N

High Raise

Grisedale Pike

High Spy

6

Grasmoor

Rosthwaite Fell

3

4 5

1

2

Glaramara

Thunacar Knott

W

1 Robinson 2 Dale Head 3 Hindscarth 4 Eel Crag 5 Sail 6 Causey Pike

sections of wall built by shepherds' to ward sheep from the cliff

PIKE O'STICKLE

The fell-name is a contraction from '*the Pike of Harrison Stickle*';
where pike is '*peak*' and stickle is '*steep*'. The stack-like structure
indicative of an extra specially hard igneous rock, a quality that drew the
attention of early industrialists - tool-makers in stone. These neolithic
tool-makers operated some four to six thousand years ago, from what is
now known as South Scree. They fashioned axes, about the length of a
spread hand, were roughed on site, wrapped in leather, slung over the
shoulder and carried to nearby polishing shops. The valley track they
followed featured a wayside shrine where stylised blessings were
hammered, probably with poorer specimen axes themselves. The
fashioning of such a high-status, culturally important, stone harvest

708 metres   2,323 feet

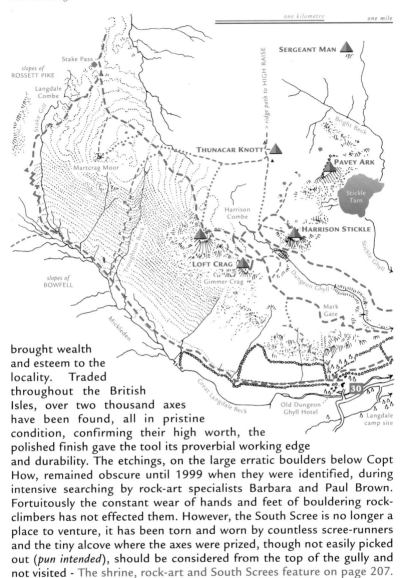

brought wealth
and esteem to the
locality.   Traded
throughout the British
Isles, over two thousand axes
have been found, all in pristine
condition, confirming their high worth, the
polished finish gave the tool its proverbial working edge
and durability. The etchings, on the large erratic boulders below Copt
How, remained obscure until 1999 when they were identified, during
intensive searching by rock-art specialists Barbara and Paul Brown.
Fortuitously the constant wear of hands and feet of bouldering rock-
climbers has not effected them. However, the South Scree is no longer a
place to venture, it has been torn and worn by countless scree-runners
and the tiny alcove where the axes were prized, though not easily picked
out (*pun intended*), should be considered from the top of the gully and
not visited - The shrine, rock-art and South Screes feature on page 207.

The Pike both backs the familiar view of the Langdale Pikes from Great
Langdale and cheekily pokes up to tease on an otherwise quite feature-
free skyline in views from the north, on the Borrowdale flank of the
range. As the object of a climb it so often is taken at the tail-end of a
tour of the Pikes, though it can worthily be ascended in its own right.

From Thunacar Knott, Crinkle Crags forms the backdrop

ASCENT *from Mickleden*

During the ascent of Troughton Beck

1 Start from the National Trust pay & display car park at the Old Dungeon Ghyll Hotel. Pass up behind the hotel to the kissing-gate, follow the valley track, via a further kissing-gate where the broad lane opens into Mickleden. Stride along the floor of this grand mountain arena with Gimmer Crag and Pike o'Stickle eye-catching features up to the right, while Pike o'Blisco, The Band, Bowfell and Rossett Pike rise to the left and ahead. The well-graded track aiding mountain rescue vehicles to approach the foot of Rossett Gill. Pass under Pike o'Stickle, glancing up at the ribbon of unstable scree spilling from the south gully. Neither ascent nor descent by this line should be considered, it is a strait in a dire state. Seek Troughton Beck, the tumbling, stony watercourse (frequently dry in summer) issuing from the open ravine high up the fell, spanned by stone flags. Ascend on the west side skirting the flood boulders, a well used and maintained path soon comes into view. Wind up the bracken slope, climbing well above the gill it provides suitably handsome views, all the excuse a walker needs for the occasional breather on the steady ascent. The moor brink attained, follow the beck on a less distinct path, until a natural fording point enables one to sweep half-left to a cairn to join the popular path from the Stake Pass. Go right,

APPROACHES

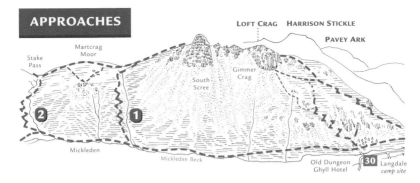

LOFT CRAG   HARRISON STICKLE
PAVEY ARK
Martcrag Moor
Stake Pass
Gimmer Crag
South Scree
Mickleden
Mickleden Beck
Old Dungeon Ghyll Hotel
30
Langdale camp site

the path duly curving right avails itself of the boulders to cross a particularly peaty patch (*see page 206*), climbing easily to the brow to be confronted by the the final rocky stage of Pike o'Stickle. The ultimate point is not gained without the hands being brought into action. Several scrambly paths lead to the top.

2 Via Stake Pass. A few paces on from Troughton Beck notice the poignant plaque to Jim Dearden, installed by his "best mate", one feels an immediate empathy with fellow fell-folk. Continue to the simple foot-bridge crossing Stake Beck, a stone indicates left to Rossett Gill and right for Stake Pass. Bear right, from the sheepfold the old pass winds up the slope

Mickleden from Stake Gill

away from the beck, then coming closer to it again higher up, from where Pike o'Stickle looks strikingly solitary. The view down Mickleden is memorable, while across the dale head admire the high buttresses of Bowfell. Fording the beck the path winds along the moraine on the eastern side of Langdale Combe, the former site of a tarn. Fifty yards short of the

cairn marking the top of the pass, reach a path junction, with a path leading left bound for Rossett Pike. Go right, mounting the oft wet slope on a strong path skirting several marshes en route to the cairn on the main slope, encountered from the Troughton Beck ascent. An attractive loop can be entertained wandering south to

Summit of Stake Pass

Erosion is a matter of concern, not rebuke. We all tend to follow routes of long custom, many paths are the only natural way through a rough mountain environment, sometimes they are lines of desire or simple bee-lines, sometimes the sheer fun of the fells gets the better of us and we leap and chase when a steadier progress would be better for the ground we tread. Peat often can be saved by placing a few large boulders as stepping stones, as below on the path up from Stake Pass. Other situations require more drastic action, as with South Scree, in view above from Mickleden, which we should now consider out-of-bounds.

South Scree

Copt How erratic rock-art and (*right*) the axe-makers 'wayside shrine' in its setting

(*above*) Summit of Martcrag Moor
(*left*) Pike o'Stickle reflected in one of the pools on the plateau

the rocky summit of Martcrag Moor, no finer place exists to study the craggy face of Bowfell. A crude shelter has been created by walkers in need of a wild country bivouac among the large boulders, while several pools adorn the plateau giving scope for camera play towards Pike o'Stickle (*as above*). The name derives from '*the lair of pine marten*' a shy species that still finds a tenuous haven in Cumbria.

The classic profile from Loft Crag with Great Gable as a distant backdrop

The Summit

A cairn rests aloft the airy location, with plenty of space for a small party to sit at ease. This is one of the treasured places in the Central Fells, living up to the great expectations. The gulf of Mickleden gives scale to Bowfell, and Pike o'Blisco. But the most exciting subject is near neighbour Loft Crag, buttressed by Gimmer Crag.

Safe Descents

Your first move must be N to the foot of the stack, and you will have judged, during your scrambling ascent, that this cannot be undertaken speedily. For Langdale follow the prominent path E down into Harrison Combe, and for Borrowdale take the clear path NW leading down to the top of the Stake Pass, going right with the bridle-path descending beside Stake Beck into Langstrath.

Ridge Routes to...

LOFT CRAG   DESCENT 200 ft   ASCENT 60 ft   1.3 miles

Descend N off the stack, then follow the obvious ridge SE, not the obvious path, which drifts down into Harrison Combe.

THUNACAR KNOTT   DESCENT 180 ft   ASCENT 230 ft   0.4 miles

From the foot of the stack head N (no path), off the line of the path to Stake Pass. Traverse the spongy depression to link up with the narrow path, running up the slope W to E, bound for the summit.

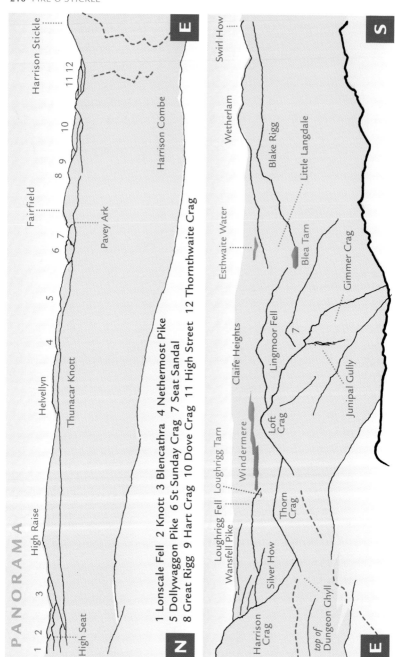

PANORAMA

N

High Seat · High Raise · Thunacar Knott · Helvellyn · Fairfield · Pavey Ark · Harrison Combe · Harrison Stickle

1 Lonscale Fell 2 Knott 3 Blencathra 4 Nethermost Pike
5 Dollywaggon Pike 6 St Sunday Crag 7 Seat Sandal
8 Great Rigg 9 Hart Crag 10 Dove Crag 11 High Street 12 Thornthwaite Crag

E

S

Wansfell Pike · Loughrigg Fell · Loughrigg Tarn · Windermere · Claife Heights · Esthwaite Water · Wetherlam · Swirl How

Harrison Crag · Silver How · Thorn Crag · Loft Crag · Lingmoor Fell · Blake Rigg · Little Langdale · Blea Tarn · Gimmer Crag · Junipal Gully

top of Dungeon Ghyll

E

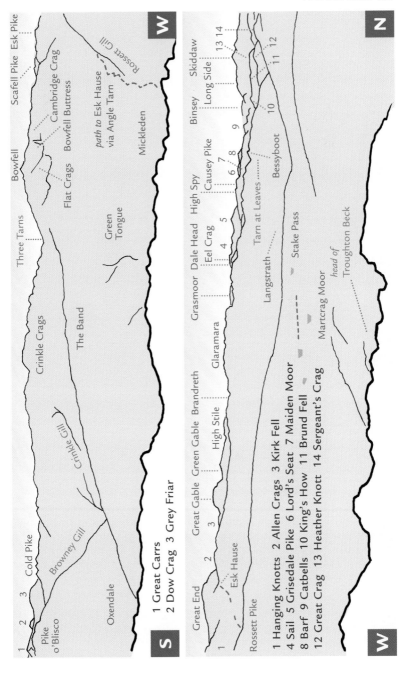

W

Scafell Pike Esk Pike

Bowfell

Cambridge Crag
Bowfell Buttress

Flat Crags

*path to Esk Hause
via Angle Tarn*

Rossett Gill

Three Tarns

Crinkle Crags

Green
Tongue

The Band

Mickleden

S

Pike
o'Blisco

Cold Pike

1 2 3

Crinkle Gill

Browney Gill

Oxendale

1 Great Carrs
2 Dow Crag 3 Grey Friar

N

Grasmoor Dale Head High Spy Binsey   Skiddaw

Eel Crag   Causey Pike   Long Side

Glaramara

Langstrath

Tarn at Leaves

Bessyboot

Stake Pass

Martcrag Moor

head of
Troughton Beck

13 14

11 12

10

9

6 7 8

4 5

Great End Great Gable Green Gable Brandreth

Esk Hause

High Stile

Rossett Pike

1 2 3

1 Hanging Knotts 2 Allen Crags 3 Kirk Fell
4 Sail 5 Grisedale Pike 6 Lord's Seat 7 Maiden Moor
8 Barf 9 Catbells 10 King's How 11 Brund Fell
12 Great Crag 13 Heather Knott 14 Sergeant's Crag

W

RAVEN CRAG

Above all else mountains beget water. Inevitably engineers will seek to draw from the resource for a swelling populous. Those that care for the wilderness must always fight with ardour to stifle dams at birth - John Muir setting the first precedent in Yosemite. In the nineteenth century the two sections of Leathes Water, linked by a midriff bridge, lay in broadened Wythburn Dale amid green pastures and beechwood, one has but faded black and white images to hint at a lost beauty. It fell prey to the needs of Manchester, a great dam constructed and foreign conifers swept up the surrounding fellsides.

One hundred years on, seeking redeeming qualities, one may admit a certain charm in peeping towards the Helvellyn range from the Armboth road, but progress towards the introduction of a greater diversity of deciduous trees along the lakeside margins must continue to be a priority. Travellers, crossing the dam road between lapping depths and fringing trees, will have their attention firmly arrested by Raven Crag at the lakes-end, the great buttressed bluff for all its smothering of trees commands avid attention. This bulwark ridge denied water engineers the considerable drainage of High Seat and Bleaberry Fell by hemming in Shoulthwaite Gill. The summit of Raven Crag is not a viewpoint, being consumed by trees, but the brink of the cliff most certainly is. Tucked under its eastern slope is a rocky hillock, Castle Crag, complete with Iron Age ramparts and, due north, a bare-topped

463 metres   1,519 feet

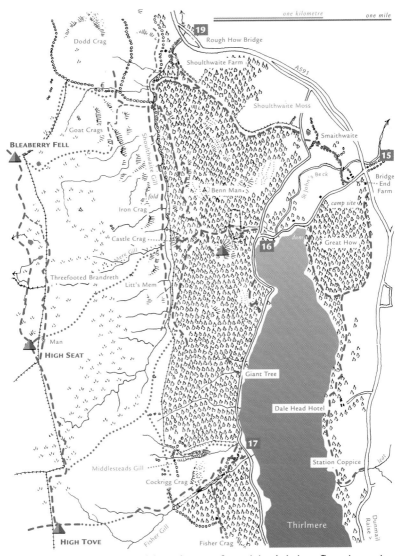

crest called Benn Man. Although not often visited, it is a fine viewpoint for the forbidding crags across Shoulthwaite Gill and Raven Crag itself (*see title view above left*). The coniferous slope between Middlesteads Gill and Shoulthwaite Farm come within the domain of Raven Crag, and offer a mixture of ascents and gradients. These woods are famous for the population of red squirrels, recent bad news has brought a community watch campaign on unwelcome sightings of grey squirrels.

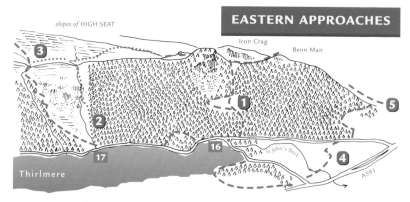

slopes of HIGH SEAT

EASTERN APPROACHES

Iron Crag

Benn Man

St John's Beck

Thirlmere

A591

ASCENT *from Thirlmere dam and Armboth*

1 The hot route to the top. The steepest, shortest and most popular path leads off from the small car park at the road junction west of the dam. Go right, then after some 100 yards left, at the hand-gate into the mature plantation. The path rises to a forest track, either cross, via the tall kissing-gate or go left, sweeping round the fenced enclosure, thus getting a close-up view of Raven Crag from below - often followed during the descent on a there & back outing. The direct route winds up through the young plantation in the deer-excluding enclosure to the top kissing-gate. Crossing the forest track once more, continue resolutely to the top of the plantation emerging onto a broad forestry track at the key point for unlocking Raven Crag. Waymarking directs left, on a made-path winding up through the conifers, and over the crown of the bluff, to steps onto the heathery crag brink.

2 Middlesteads Gill is a sneaky, distant side-door approach, ideal for creating a bigger circular outing exclusive to the Raven Crag ridge. Leave the Armboth lakeside car park following the road north (right) passing through the kissing-gate at the first bend at the beginning of the Watendlath path. Ignore the inviting path over the 'sma'brig', **3** while one may ascend the footpath rising above Fisher Gill and follow the wall right at the top, the more inviting line climbs directly from the road beside the right-hand forest fence. **2** It is steep going, hugging the fence to help avoid the bracken. As the slope

Watson's Dodd   Stybarrow Dodd

Brown Crag

Middlesteads Gill

From Thirlmere Dam

scoops, angle half-left onto the arete overlooking the impressive Middlesteads Gill ravine, enhanced by natural tree growth. Keep to the rim of the gill latterly angle right to slip round the right-hand end of the fell-bounding wall where it almost abuts the forest fence. Bear up right by the gill and fence, at next corner angle up the slope to top the length of ascending wall, gaining the low ridge. Advance beyond a cairn on a descending line to the gate entering into the forestry. Follow the main track left, with continued fine views down the Shoulthwaite Gill valley towards the Glenderaterra Gap. Arriving at the broad turning area you can be tempted left to follow the made-path to Castle Crag, or right, upon the similarly prepared trail to Raven Crag, and by continuing also consider branching half-right, just before the track begins to descend on a narrow path leading through the pines to the top of Benn Man (see summit details). **4** All three viewpoints can be included in a 7.3 mile grand tour that would continue north with the forest track and sweep round in the valley by Shoulthwaite Moss, Smaithwaite and orbit Great How to the dam, all on firm, easily graded, paths (see map).

ASCENT *from Rough How Bridge*

If, having perhaps viewed the fearsome crag during the crossing of Thirlmere dam, you are disinclined to the direct climb, then take heart it does not have to be a slog, there is another way if not 'NatWest', then naturally south! For all we may find conifers a mixed blessing, the provision of access tracks brings collateral benefits and the track rising from Shoulthwaite to the north is as sweet a route to the top as could be devised. **5** From the lay-by cross the busy A591 into the lane leading to, and through, Shoulthwaite Farm, entering Thirlmere Forest at a kissing-gate. Either follow the level bridle-path ahead to the track and turn acutely right or branch off immediately following the impromptu path. With the tall deer fence close right, leading directly up to the track, go right. Ignore the option to exit the woodland via the tall kissing-gate and bridge. Although it must be said the Shoulthwaite Gill valley path has its own unique quality as a line of ascent, back-tracking, literally, from the gate entry to the forestry GR 299181, there are two earlier ladder-stiles that give access, the first climbs pathless among the tangle of trees beside a gill from beneath Castle Crag and the second links direct onto the track a little further south. The main forest track is signposted 'Raven Crag, Fort and Viewpoint' and leads, via a sweeping zig-zag, under Sipping Crag and a later bend to the turning area on the saddle.

The Summit

The NWW signboards are correct, the brink of Raven Crag IS a viewpoint, the whole of Thirlmere reservoir can be seen backed by the high rolling skyline of the Helvellyn range, with tantalising glimpses south, over Dunmail Raise and north, to Skiddaw and Blencathra. To complete the view-spotting process one needs to move around to evade the trees, an activity hampered by deep heather and the knowledge that the cliff is all too imminent. Though this is not the summit of the bluff, there is a cairn to be found among the ragged trees behind the viewpoint to that. A cairn does mark the viewpoint itself. Close by the remains of a wall from the days when sheep needed to be discouraged from risking their necks grazing too close to the edge. The only thing eaten now are sandwiches, for this is the ideal picnic place, nicely distanced from the car-wedded tourists consuming ice cream at Station Coppice. What lies behind a name, well Thirlmere meant *'lake of the giant'* and Dollywaggon Pike meant *'peak of the elevated giant'*, so was there a time when monsters were thought to inhabit these wild hills; well, some monster certainly did construction a reservoir! There are two other special viewpoints in

the vicinity, well meriting a visit. Castle Crag, replicating Legburthwaite's more famous Iron Age site, way-marked from the track at the saddle. A made-path, with duck-boarding, leads to a low rampart embracing a rocky knoll, a narrow path via the rampart circling clockwise over the bluff (rock step), re-trace the approach to continue. Benn Man (or The Benn) the

Castle Crag, from the southern rampart

second high point on the ridge to the north is reached from the track just before it shapes to descend. Bear right on a narrow path through the pines and larches climbing the heather and bilberry hillock for a superb summit prospect, back to Raven Crag (*see title*) and westward to the crags lining Shoulthwaite Gill, most notably Iron Crag, again.

Safe Descents

All routes of ascent can comfortably be reversed.

Ridge Routes to...

HIGH SEAT   DESCENT 200 ft   ASCENT 480 ft   1.3 miles

The outcrop is so isolated on a spur ridge of High Tove, that one might be forgiven for thinking that no-one would wish make such a connection.

However, experience has shown that some visitors to Raven Crag do in fact wish to extend their wanderings up onto the main ridge, their target top High Seat. Leave the summit backtracking to the forest track, go left for half-a-mile to exit at the hand-gate. Ford the headstream of Shoulthwaite Gill, take a pathless ascending line due W to the ridge fence stile just beyond the skyline outcrop knot of the Man.

Cairn above the brink of Raven Crag

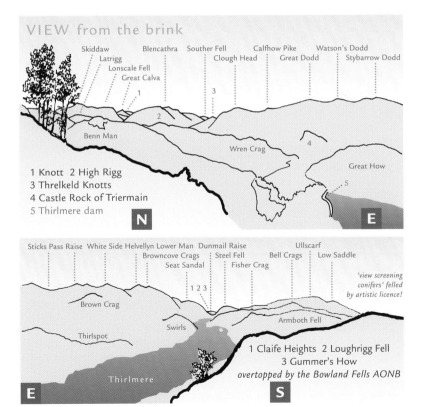

VIEW from the brink

Skiddaw   Blencathra   Souther Fell   Calfhow Pike   Watson's Dodd
Latrigg   Clough Head   Great Dodd   Stybarrow Dodd
Lonscale Fell
Great Calva
1   3
2
Benn Man
Wren Crag   4
Great How
1 Knott 2 High Rigg   5
3 Threlkeld Knotts
4 Castle Rock of Triermain
5 Thirlmere dam   **N**   **E**

Sticks Pass Raise White Side Helvellyn Lower Man Dunmail Raise   Ullscarf
                   Browncove Crags   Steel Fell   Bell Crags   Low Saddle
                   Seat Sandal   Fisher Crag
                                                        *'view screening
                                                        conifers' felled
                                                        by artistic licence!*
                              1 2 3
Brown Crag
                          Swirls   Armboth Fell
Thirlspot
                                        1 Claife Heights 2 Loughrigg Fell
                                                3 Gummer's How
E   Thirlmere   **S**   *overtopped by the Bowland Fells AONB*

SERGEANT MAN

Just as Pavey Ark is the most startling component of Thunacar Knott, so the unusual stack-like summit of Sergeant Man belongs to the basic plateau structure of High Raise. It marks the umbilical ridge connection with Easedale from where it makes a superb objective for a fell-walk, the knobby top of Codale Head appearing to be the summit for much of the journey. Its waters drain into Wythburn, Easedale and Great Langdale.

Among the delightful lexicon of fell-names, this one has an enigmatic ring. But the prosaic truth is, like Sergeant's Crag, that it reflects fifteenth century land ownership tagged onto the older Celtic term Man, for a landmark 'cairn'.

For all its distance from a main valley base, one may climb it exclusively via Stickle Ghyll and Bright Beck (*aspect of the view above*) or, having indulged in the drama of Whitecrag Gill, from Great Langdale. From Grasmere one may climb onto the ridge via Silver How and Blea Rigg or trek up Easedale via Belles Knott or even Far Easedale, approaching from the top of Codale Head. No route is dull. How could they be with such marvellous surroundings?

736 metres   2,414 feet

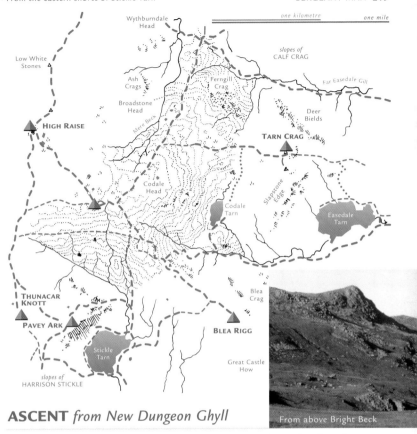

one kilometre   one mile

Wythburndale
Head

Low White
Stones

slopes of
CALF CRAG

Ash
Crags

Ferngill
Crag

Far Easedale Gill

Broadstone
Head

Mere Beck

Deer
Bields

HIGH RAISE

TARN CRAG

Codale
Head

Slapstone Edge

Codale
Tarn

Easedale
Tarn

Blea
Crag

THUNACAR
KNOTT

PAVEY ARK

BLEA RIGG

Stickle
Tarn

Great Castle
How

slopes of
HARRISON STICKLE

From above Bright Beck

ASCENT *from New Dungeon Ghyll*

A cluster of routes inevitably present themselves from this hugely popular walking base in Great Langdale. The diagram shows the primary
lines, though only one can be considered exclusive to this one destination. **1** The direct route, climbs Stickle Ghyll to the Stickle Tarn dam and
follows the east shore path. **2** There is a fork as the first feeder gill enters
the tarn, the right-hand path, well cairned, curves round a marsh rising
easily north-eastward onto the Blea Rigg ridge, this is the steadier line of
approach. **1** The direct route however, accompanies Bright Beck, do not
ford, with Sergeant Man clearly in view ahead (*see title*). Coming level
with the steeply rising east ridge of Pavey Ark, a tangible path trends up
a narrow defile due north beside a tributary gill, the path becoming less
convincing higher up as the route naturally merges with the ridge rising
to the summit. As the ridge is gained a lower path may be spotted, traversing below the fell-top from the great slab to the head of Bright Beck,
One presumes it came into being as a hasty short-cut to avoid Sergeant
Man. **3** The Whitecrag Gill route described in BLEA RIGG pages

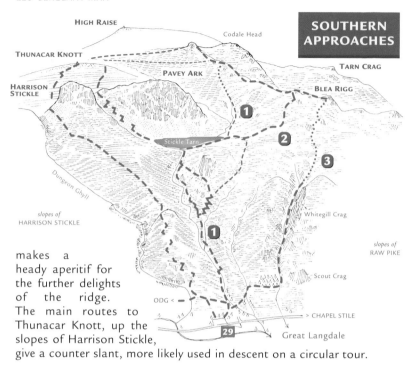

HIGH RAISE

Codale Head

**SOUTHERN
APPROACHES**

THUNACAR KNOTT

PAVEY ARK

TARN CRAG

HARRISON
STICKLE

BLEA RIGG

Stickle Tarn

1

2

3

Dungeon Ghyll

slopes of
HARRISON STICKLE

Whitegill Crag

slopes of
RAW PIKE

1

Scout Crag

ODG <

CHAPEL STILE

29

Great Langdale

makes a heady aperitif for the further delights of the ridge. The main routes to Thunacar Knott, up the slopes of Harrison Stickle, give a counter slant, more likely used in descent on a circular tour.

ASCENT *from Grasmere*

Natural routes lead up the ridges of Blea Rigg and Tarn Crag (see the respective fell chapters), though the two dale approaches are excellent alternatives. **4** The popular path to Easedale Tarn leaves the Easedale Road via the footbridge opposite Oak How (*teas*), traversing meadows via gates. Much of the way paved. The path winds up beside Sour Milk Gill, which is far from a sour sight, the excited waters churning down frenzied falls. The approach to the tarn is currently receiving the finishing touches to complete the paved parade, a walk which has long attracted visitors for all the drabness of its immediate surroundings.

Codale Tarn

Belles Knott

Conical drumlins on either side of Easedale Tarn emphasise the glacial origins of this bleak amphitheatre. The conical top of Tarn Crag looms close right, while Blea Crag forms the southern sidewall. The old path continues along the southern side of the tarn and it's main feeder gill, with several essentially stepped sections beside steep cascades. Up to the right the arresting Belles Knott flatters as a peak to climb (scramblers only), once above the falls the Knott soon shows itself to be a sham. A side path bears right, fording the gill, to visit the hanging waters of Codale Tarn with its tiny outflow and picturesque isle set beneath the great slope of Codale

Belles Knott

Head. Any ascent from here is best accomplished by keeping north beyond a ruined sheepfold to join the Tarn Crag ridge path, going west, to the rising ridge en route for Codale Head. Otherwise, keep with the main path which zig-zags up to a ridge-top path interchange west of Blea Rigg. Turn right and mount the rocky ridge north-west for the very first

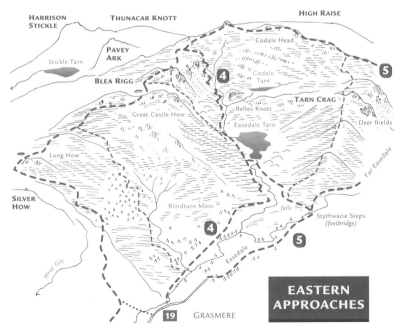

HARRISON STICKLE

THUNACAR KNOTT

HIGH RAISE

Codale Head

PAVEY ARK

Stickle Tarn

Codale Tarn

BLEA RIGG

4

5

TARN CRAG

Great Castle How

Belles Knott

Deer Bields

Easedale Tarn

Lang How

Far Easedale

SILVER HOW

Blindtarn Moss

falls

Stythwaite Steps (footbridge)

4

5

Easedale

Wray Gill

EASTERN APPROACHES

19 GRASMERE

Codale Head from the summit

glimpse of the fell-top. Two early path options re-unite at the giant slab, a solitary path continuing to ford the outflow of a marsh, climbing the distinctive summit knoll beyond.

5 The old pony path up Far Easedale provides an enjoyable alternative, signposted 'Greenup Edge' from the Easedale road-end. Proceed via the Stythwaite Steps footbridge to the saddle at the very top of the dale. Follow the metal stakes of the old county boundary fence left over Broadstone Head on to Codale Head, only now does the summit come into view.

Harrison Stickle and Pavey Ark from the ridge below the summit

The Summit

Not quite the bold stack of Pike o'Stickle, rather a kid-brother of similarly resilient rock. Fell-walkers instinctively love this high place, for all that the bare outcrop has but a bedraggled cairn as monument to the many thousands of appreciative visitations. Note the old Ordnance Survey bench-mark on the very top, dating from the survey of 1860, almost obscured by wear.

Safe Descents

Being the lynch-pin off High Raise for Great Langdale and Grasmere, the clear path leading SE down the ridge is a reliable guide in doubtful conditions.

Ridge Routes to...

BLEA RIGG   DESCENT 680 ft   ASCENT 50 ft   1.3 miles

The ridge path descending SE is well marked and supported with cairns. The slope eases at a meeting of paths which marks the transition to the broader ridge of Blea Rigg. Weaving by a rock pool, skirting three distinct rock knolls, reach the summit, distinguished by its tiny cairn perched on a chunky rock.

HIGH RAISE   DESCENT 25 ft   ASCENT 100 ft   0.5 miles

Head NW passing pools in crossing the open plateau. Missing the old fence corner by even larger pools to reach the jumble of rocks, wind-shelter and Ordnance Survey pillar at the summit.

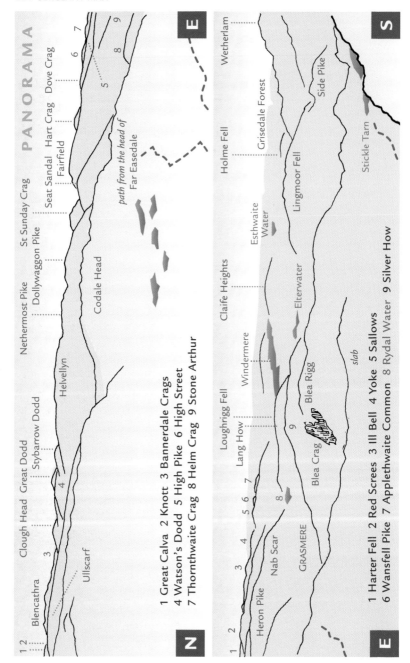

PANORAMA

E

Blencathra 1 2 — Clough Head Great Dodd Stybarrow Dodd — Nethermost Pike St Sunday Crag — Seat Sandal Hart Crag Dove Crag

Dollywaggon Pike — Fairfield

Ullscarf 3 4

Helvellyn

Codale Head

5

6 7

8 9

path from the head of Far Easedale

N

1 Great Calva 2 Knott 3 Bannerdale Crags
4 Watson's Dodd 5 High Pike 6 High Street
7 Thornthwaite Crag 8 Helm Crag 9 Stone Arthur

S

Holme Fell — Claife Heights — Wetherlam

Grisedale Forest

Esthwaite Water

Lingmoor Fell

Side Pike

Stickle Tarn

Loughrigg Fell — Lang How — Windermere — Elterwater

Heron Pike Nab Scar

GRASMERE

2 3 4 5 6 7 8

9

Blea Crag Blea Rigg

slab

E

1 Harter Fell 2 Red Screes 3 Ill Bell 4 Yoke 5 Sallows
6 Wansfell Pike 7 Applethwaite Common 8 Rydal Water 9 Silver How

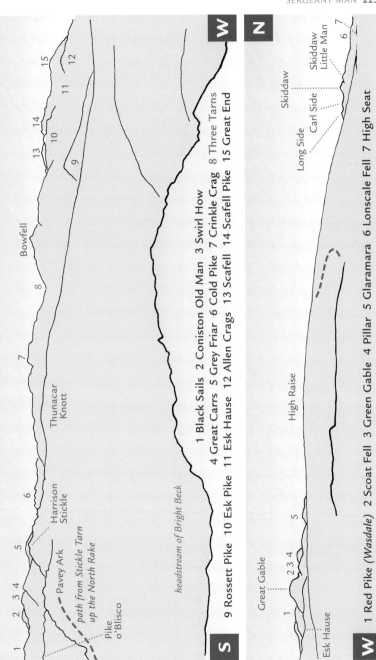

W

N

S

W

1 Black Sails 2 Coniston Old Man 3 Swirl How
4 Great Carrs 5 Grey Friar 6 Cold Pike 7 Crinkle Crag 8 Three Tarns
9 Rossett Pike 10 Esk Pike 11 Esk Hause 12 Allen Crags 13 Scafell 14 Scafell Pike 15 Great End

1 Red Pike (*Wasdale*) 2 Scoat Fell 3 Green Gable 4 Pillar 5 Glaramara 6 Lonscale Fell 7 High Seat

SERGEANT'S CRAG

Aloof, High Raise may need no massive crag to lend it distinction but, as is the way with proud ground, it falls away to reveal finer pelmets at a lower elevation. So, as the northern extension ridge dips and tapers crags abound. A set of minor outcrops lead to one solid mass draped over the ridge like a horseman's leather jacket with one great pleat gully and several bold slab pockets. Fortuitously it has a neighbour, Eagle Crag, from which, and to which, it can be compared and admired. There is no hint of twinning, the character of each is distinct.

The fell may now be the focus of climbers' attention, notably the slabs part-way up the broken face, but in recent centuries it has been mined and quarried, though the untrained eye would find it difficult to detect the residual spoil of such activity. Conventionally walkers approach the fell-top following the ridge wall having first tackled Eagle Crag. An alternative line, bereft of bracken and crags, can be found climbing from the footbridge at the foot of Stake Beck. Its one and only merit: the majestic view back across Langstrath to Rosthwaite Cam and Glaramara.

In appearance Langstrath looks like a Scottish glen with the company of mountains on every hand. Early references show the name as Langstrode, which meant 'the long marsh', though the valley floor is not particularly damp and clearly not really a 'strath' either! That most walkers know it in haste from the transience of the *Cumbria Way* does it less than justice. It is a place to amble as well as stride, relished best

574 metres   1,883 feet

on the circuit of the dale floor paths from Stonethwaite, switching on the Tray Dub footbridge below Stake Beck taking time to inspect each cascade, dub and pot.

It would appear the fell-name derives from a William Sargyante referred to in 1602, he probably gave his name to Sergeant Man too.

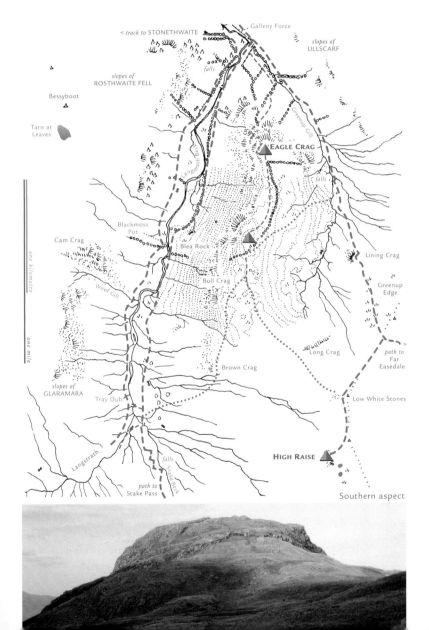

Southern aspect

From the head of Willygrass Gill, with Eagle Crag left itself overtopped by High Raise

ASCENT *from Stonethwaite*

Roadside lay-by parking is preferable to cluttering the hamlet. **1** Follow the direct ascent of EAGLE CRAG pages 68 & 69 and the subsequent ridge. Amazingly the state of the path suggests only a comparatively few undertake this initially steep, latterly intricate, but utterly exhilarating route. **2** To avoid encounters with campers and their vehicles, cross Stonethwaite Bridge, as with the former route, then cross the footbridge at the confluence of Greenup Gill with Langstrath Beck to embark on the bridle-path up Langstrath. **3** Follow the lane through the hamlet (noting the Peathouse tea-room and Langstrath Hotel for end-of-walk refreshment). The gated track passes above the popular camping meadow, latterly passing Alisongrass Hoghouse (camping barn). As the beck comes closer listen to the roar of Galleny Force down in the tree cover left. The track bends right, via a gate to accompany the clear cascading waters of Langstrath Beck, through a gate to a footbridge. **4** Either cross the footbridge to follow the bridle-path to the gate at Blackmoss Pot, by so doing coming under the slopes of Heron and Sergeant's Crags, and close to the striking Gash Rock sporting a plume of heather, otherwise known as Blea Rock. Blackmoss Pot is a tight water rock channel, deserving a moment's appreciative look, for the next mile of bridle-path pursued to the footbridge at the foot of Stake Beck is quite uneventful, although there is no denying the magical feel of this deep mountain valley. Alternatively, follow the west side footpath climbing over the ladder-stile at Blackmoss, at this point look up to the left to possibly spot climbers scaling Sergeant Crag Slabs. Below and above Blackmoss Pot the beck takes a wide shingled meandering course, with the craggy slopes of

View from Sergeant's Crag Gully

Rosthwaite Fell and Glaramara high to the right. Swan and Tray Dubs offer fine moments to draw close to the lively beck. 'Dub' suggests sheep washing pools, the term deriving from the British 'dubh' meaning *dark, or shadowed place* frequently applied to this purpose. Cross Tray Dub footbridge, ascend directly. **5** Cross the bridle-path before the Stake Beck footbridge, ascend the initially damp slope avoiding crags and most of the bracken that dogs much of the eastern fellside, climbing to the skyline. Crossing the brow of Brown Crag spy the summit of Sergeant's Crag overtopping intermediate outcrops. The westward view of Glaramara and Rosthwaite Cam gives one cause for frequent pauses en route to the ridge-top path. From the wall-stile the summit is easily achieved.

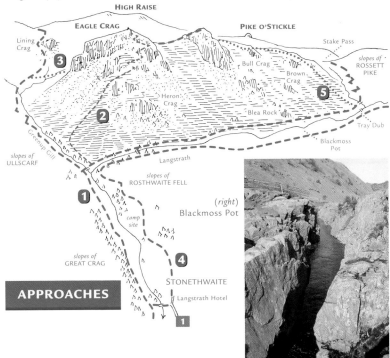

APPROACHES

(right) Blackmoss Pot

Glaramara and
Rosthwaite Cam

The Summit

The imposition of a wall, effectively isolating the upper dome of the fell, has served to restrict grazing and support a better flora than occurs in the poor acid grassland beyond. A small cairn rests upon a modest outcrop, with little hint of the impending precipice to the west to deflect attention from the fine view across and to the head of Langstrath. With a little time one may investigate down the slope to the north then west, where a grass ramp leads to the top of Sergeant's Crag Gully, one may also peer down the steep, broken face towards the climbers' Slabs and Blea Rock; impressive rock and valley scenery worth seeking out.

Safe Descents

In dubious weather, by far the best option is to cross the stile in the wall immediately south from the summit, and head NE to join the bridle-path below Lining Crag leading down Greenup Gill for Stonethwaite.

Ridge Routes to...

EAGLE CRAG   DESCENT 200ft
ASCENT 30ft   0.5 miles

Navigation just could not be simpler, head NNE from the summit on the one path with the ridge wall coming close right to a stile at the wall corner giving access to the neighbouring top.

HIGH RAISE   DESCENT 30ft
ASCENT 640ft   1.5 miles

Go S crossing the wall-stile, a narrow path weaves through a long marshy saddle. Rising onto drier ground, with less evidence of a path, at the same time losing all sense of a ridge. Keep right of Long Crag to reach the skyline at Low White Stones, go S to the summit.

Blea Rock backed by Sergeant's Crag

Langstrath Beck

PANORAMA

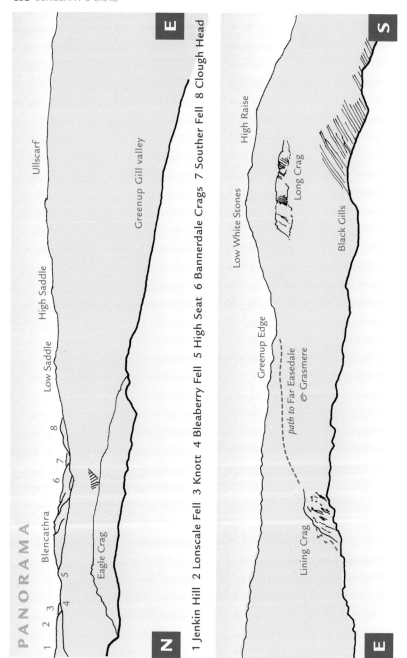

1 Jenkin Hill 2 Lonscale Fell 3 Knott 4 Bleaberry Fell 5 High Seat 6 Bannerdale Crags 7 Souther Fell 8 Clough Head

E

Ullscarf

High Saddle

Low Saddle

Blencathra

Greenup Gill valley

Eagle Crag

N

S

High Raise

Low White Stones

Long Crag

Black Gills

Greenup Edge

path to Far Easedale
& Grasmere

Lining Crag

E

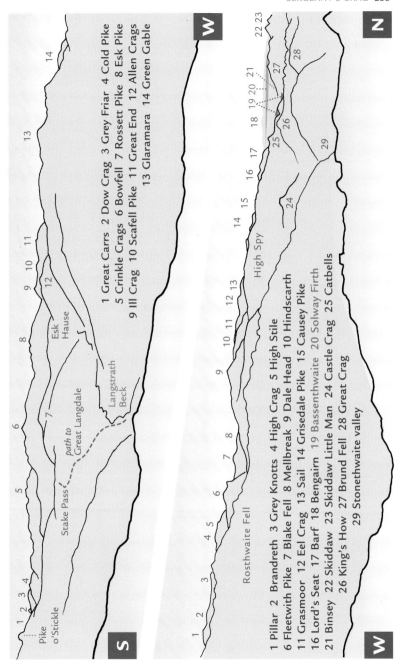

S · **W**

14 13 11 10 9 12 8 Esk Hause 7 Langstrath Beck 6 path to Great Langdale 5 Stake Pass 4 3 2 1 Pike o'Stickle

1 Great Carrs 2 Dow Crag 3 Grey Friar 4 Cold Pike
5 Crinkle Crags 6 Bowfell 7 Rossett Pike 8 Esk Pike
9 Ill Crag 10 Scafell Pike 11 Great End 12 Allen Crags
13 Glaramara 14 Green Gable

N · **W**

22 23 27 28 19 20 21 18 25 26 17 16 15 14 High Spy 13 12 11 10 24 29 9 8 7 6 5 4 Roshwaite Fell 3 2 1

1 Pillar 2 Brandreth 3 Grey Knotts 4 High Crag 5 High Stile
6 Fleetwith Pike 7 Blake Fell 8 Mellbreak 9 Dale Head 10 Hindscarth
11 Grasmoor 12 Eel Crag 13 Sail 14 Grisedale Pike 15 Causey Pike
16 Lord's Seat 17 Barf 18 Bengairn 19 Bassenthwaite 20 Solway Firth
21 Binsey 22 Skiddaw 23 Skiddaw Little Man 24 Castle Crag 25 Catbells
26 King's How 27 Brund Fell 28 Great Crag
29 Stonethwaite valley

SILVER HOW

It is said that, in certain lights, the screes of Silver How give off an argent hue which may explain its name. Whether or not this is so, it certainly has an elegant profile which melds into the Grasmere scene so sweetly that many walkers, quite wisely assume it a peak they must climb to really know the famous literary vale.

Whilst forming a backdrop to sylvan views across the lake (*see above*), it beguiles to deceive for it is nothing more than the scarp-end of a broad ridge, it subsequently gathers up height over two further knolls to Swinescar Hause, whence the terrain becomes altogether rougher. From the top of the Redbank Road, by High Close, a rolling bowling ridge advances in a north-westerly direction over Dow Bank and Spedding Crag to where Meg's Gill slices into the fell. The ridge smartly rises and extends its girth; the top of the fell lying at the northern tip of this prominent craggy escarpment.

Many ridge walkers pay no heed to the summit, avoiding the northern deviation, preferring to stride on above Meg' Gill intent on Blea Rigg, yet the summit merits a deliberative visit. The ridge to Castle How is a grand scenic parade with numerous undulations to intrigue the wanderer, though many of the paths are little better than sheep trods. Routes to the top are plentiful, all are worthy and made the more so by the scenic virtues of the ultimate point. There are four prime routes from Grasmere and three out of Great Langdale, much mixing and matching can be achieved to vary a circular tour.

395 metres   1,296 feet

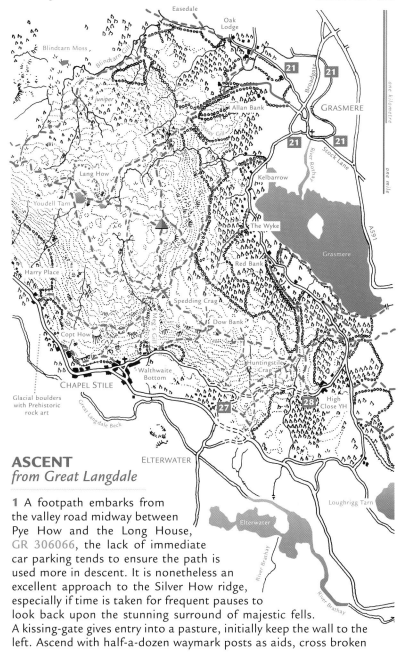

ASCENT
from Great Langdale

1 A footpath embarks from
the valley road midway between
Pye How and the Long House,
GR 306066, the lack of immediate
car parking tends to ensure the path is
used more in descent. It is nonetheless an
excellent approach to the Silver How ridge,
especially if time is taken for frequent pauses to
look back upon the stunning surround of majestic fells.
A kissing-gate gives entry into a pasture, initially keep the wall to the
left. Ascend with half-a-dozen waymark posts as aids, cross broken

From Stone Arthur

intermediate walls, much mature scrub colonises the enclosures. A ladder-stile crosses the intake wall at the top, the path, at first stony, becomes a pleasant turf trail, beyond the solitary, gill-shading holly. Wind steadily to the ridge-top at Swinescar Hause, joining the ridge path head right (south-east). Before Youdell Tarn take the opportunity to include Lang How some 62 feet higher than Silver How, scant trace of a path leads up onto its grassy ridge, a cairn giving reason to pause before winding down the southern slope to rejoin the ridge path, traverse the headstream of Wreay Gill direct to the summit.

Chapel Stile has no public parking facility (please respect residents parking).

Rock climbers honing their skills on the Copt How buttress make opportunist use of the brief widening of the road at Thrang Close GR 315057, this is the one chink in the village armoury but only for the odd car! Walkers should either employ the 'Langdale Rambler' bus or use the National Trust Walthwaite Bottom car park stroll into the community via the minor road or beside Great Langdale Beck from Elterwater Bridge.

In Meg's Gill, a stunning re-entrant ravine, the village has an irresistible climb, aided by various paths conveniently converging in its upper section. There are six points from which one may leave the road to climb onto the Silver How ridge between Meg's Gill and Huntingstile Gap. The first four routes focus on Meg's Gill itself. **2** A matter of 100 yards east of Harry Place Farm, opposite a roadside barn, a footpath is discreetly signposted. The path climbs the bank to a stile in a wall-linking fence, ascending with the wall right, join a green track going right. Crossing the saddle behind Copt How, which meant '*the look-out hillock*', it was, and is not an easy top to get onto for a watching brief! The path traverses the rough slopes taking one notable rocky step up during its approach to Meg's Gill. This top path can be joined from three other paths ascending from the village. **3** One begins from the aforementioned verge where a footpath is signed from a gate leading to a stile and an awkward descent through the old Thrang Quarry. Just before entering a lane - another access from the village street west of Holy Trinity Church - bear up left between quarry retaining walls to mount the rigg with a gill left. The path forks, both meet the Copt How path, however the right-hand path is the better option. **4** A further path leaves the road east of the church before Walthwaite Lodge. Climb the bank, with the wall right, on a narrow path through the bracken. Rounding the wall on the brow, ascend on the upper west side of the Meg's Gill ravine, rising to meet the top path.

From the Rothay vale to the north-east

Now continue up the gill to a high ford, contour with a fine view down and across to a waterfall below the ford. Finally rise onto the ridge, precisely where the Silver How escarpment imposes itself on the lesser ridge from High Close. **5** Other paths from the road include the route onto Spedding Crag/Dow Bank saddle beginning east of Speddy Cottage, pass through a hand-gate and ascend with a wall right. Up to the left see Raven Crag, a popular evening haunt for climbers. Rise to a turning point where the path switches left leading straight up to the saddle. **6** From GR 328054, on the minor road running east from the village, a turf path bears off half-left for 150 yards, then turns directly uphill through the bracken. A strong sheep path (footpath) may be followed left, contouring to the turning point on the path up from Speddy Cottage, or one may

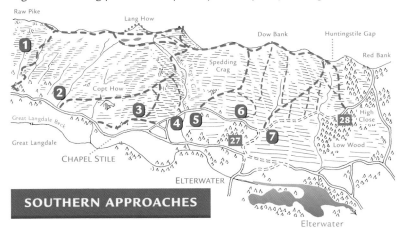

SOUTHERN APPROACHES

Langdale Pikes beyond Youdell Tarn

simply keep going up to the cairn on Dow Crag. **7** From the open common above the Walthwaite Bottom car park several paths leave the road for the Huntingstile Gap. The first, in particular, being the primary route, departs some few yards right of the steep road junction GR 332052. An early branch left climbs onto the Dow Bank ridge, while the main thrust of the path takes a steady line passing an electricity compound to reach the deep gap. Ostensibly this is a route over to Grasmere, latterly descending as a cobbled lane to the Redbank Road at Lea Cottage.

ASCENT *from Grasmere*

Redbank Road car park. Choose from three popular paths, a rough invention and a surreptitious approach. **8** From the middle of Grasmere village, at the junction of Broadgate with Langdale Road, take the no-through-road leading north-west. Enter the parkland environs of Allan Bank. Keep right on the approach drive to reach the cottages, enter a narrow gated lane. This point can be reached from Easedale Road, via Goody Bridge Cottages where a footpath leads over stepping stones, via hand-gates, up a pasture to cross a drive rising to a fence-stile into the lane above the cottages. The lane duly emerges at a kissing-gate onto the open fell. The path climbs initially with a wall close left rising through juniper. Watch for the path forking left to a ford of Weay Gill, this is the

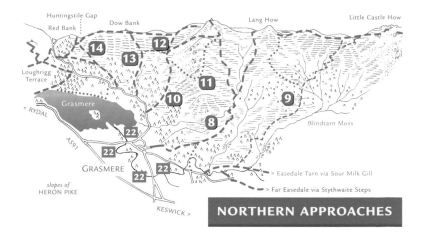

NORTHERN APPROACHES

direct line to the fell summit, while the right path wanders onto the ridge under Lang How. **9** Via Blindtarn Moss, the name probably derived from its hidden nature. Follow Easedale Road, cross Easedale Beck via the footbridge at Oak Lodge. Advance along the roughly cobbled path soon running with a wall to the left and beck right. After the restored New Bridge watch for the yellow waymark on the gate left guiding, via a meadow, to a metal gate and through light woodland to join, at another a gate, the track leading to a pair of holiday cottages. Pass on by the white railings to a wooden gate in the field corner. Continue with the wall left, jostling with the gill in ascending to a waymark post directing right, below a gate with private notice affixed. Dense bracken is replaced by juniper at the open hollow of Blindtarn Moss. The path forks take the more minor left-hand path. After a small ford the indistinct path continues up the wet slope through juniper and rushes. The fell eases and a sheep path materialises drawing up onto skyline and the ridge path. Turn left, pass three tarns beneath Lang How. A fine viewpoint for the Langdale Pikes Youdell Tarn, the larger pool encroached by reed has the least open water. The other two have tiny isles and are host to bog bean. At the third tarn take the right-hand fork path bound for Silver How, now clearly in view ahead.

Approaches from Redbank Road, a busy thoroughfare in summer colonised by a walkers and cars in almost equal proportion, to the annoyance of both! **10** From the entrance to Redbank Road car park go left with the road. At the drive entrance to Kelbarrow, opposite the Faeryland boat hire/tearoom, go right, up the walled lane. Ascend via two kissing-gates, now under the rough slope of the fell, the path keeps

From the path above Kelbarrow

the intake wall close left. **11** Should you relish a spot of rough stuff walking, you may consider branching right as the path first levels. A sheep path contours across the scree and bracken slope, becoming less definite as you come high above the open pasture section of the approach. Climb to the skyline well before the craggy ravine of Wray Gill, follow the scarp top, there is no path. The views of the lake and over the village to Great Rigg and Fairfield are exceptional. **12** Otherwise continue to the wall corner, either ascend the eroded gully direct to the summit or continue via two fords, to the ridge-top path interchange. Turn right, mounting via a large cairn, keep right, along the scarp brow to the summit. **13** As a more sylvan option, though with hampered views, continue with Redbank Road to turn right, into the drive leading to The Wyke. The fenced drive passes between stately oaks. At a gill crossing, with the house in view, turn right, slipping over the higher bridge and, via the remains of a metal kissing-gate, embark upon a path which rises as a stony trail through light birch wood to reach a wall-stile and hand-gate onto the fell. Either continue through the scrub and bracken onto Dow Bank, or go right, with the wall right, via marshy patches, to the curving wall corner and ascend the gully direct. **14** Another path leaves the Redbank Road further up opposite Lea Cottage, initially rising as a drive to Huntingstile House, this becomes a cobbled lane to a hand-gate rising to the Huntingstile Gap. A metal gate, immediately left of the hand-gate, provides access to a lovely woodland parade, re-joining Redbank Road opposite the path to Loughrigg Terrace. At this point a path steps off the road, and goes up three immediate steps to curve round, via a hand-gate into the Gap. To complete the suite, impromptu paths leave the open road west of High Close Youth Hostel, again gathering in the Gap in readiness to mount the Dow Bank ridge.

The Summit

Lang How

A tumbled wreck of a cairn sits on the bare top surveying the luxuriant strath of Grasmere vale. The all-round view is most rewarding. Visitors can train their eyes both at the detail within the vale, of village, meadow, woods and lake, and to the lovely surround of higher fells. So whilst is is not the highest point upon the near mass of fell, Lang How (*see above*) having that status, it is the natural viewpoint. A place to gaze at ease and compose worthy words to eloquently express the enchanting scene, as in Victorian times, the esteemed local wordsmith William Wordsworth was want to do. Be sure he too sat here too!

Safe Descents

The eastern slope of the fell is lined with crags, so all descents need to begin from the depression some 100 yards WSW from the cairn. The path leading N, fording Wray Gill, bound for Allan Bank, being the best in poor visibility. S find assurance in the ridge path leading south-east reaching the unenclosed Elterwater to High Close road off Dow Bank.

Ridge Routes

Meg's Gill

BLEA RIGG

DESCENT 150ft   ASCENT 680 ft   2 miles

The path leads off north-west passing below Lang How, superior to Silver How by 62 feet. Pass two pools hosting bog bean and over the brow a much larger tarn, reed encroachment is so advanced that it has the least open water of the three, yet many a camera must have been directed at this view of the Langdale Pikes. The path weaves easily along the ridge until the marshy hollow of Swinescar Hause, the line of least resistance trends diagonally across the slope by a curious low shelter to traverse Castle How. Fellwanderers may choose to head up from the sheepfold (pathless) to reach to top of Raw Pike (no cairn) and the southern top of Great Castle How, with its fine view of Blea Rigg ahead. These routes reunite at the quartz stones and pass pools en route the summit.

Crinkle Crags headwall of Oxendale, from the vicinity of Swinescar Hause

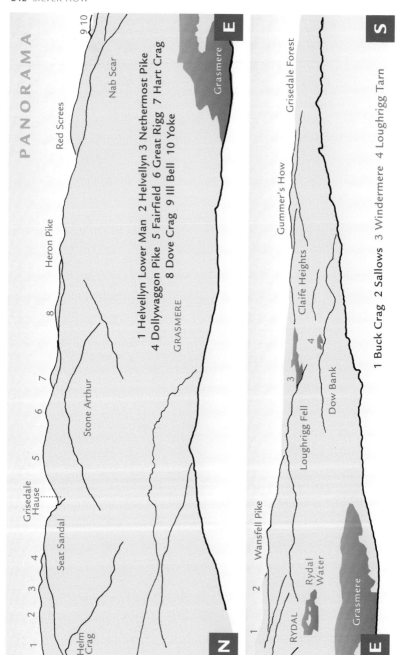

PANORAMA

N

Helm Crag — 1 2 3 4 Seat Sandal — Griesdale Hause — 5 6 7 8 Stone Arthur — Heron Pike — Red Screes — Nab Scar — 9 10 — **E**

GRASMERE

1 Helvellyn Lower Man 2 Helvellyn 3 Nethermost Pike
4 Dollywaggon Pike 5 Fairfield 6 Great Rigg 7 Hart Crag
8 Dove Crag 9 Ill Bell 10 Yoke

Grasmere

E

RYDAL — 1 2 Wansfell Pike — Rydal Water — Grasmere — Loughrigg Fell — 3 Dow Bank — 4 Claife Heights — Gummer's How — Grisedale Forest — **S**

1 Buck Crag 2 Sallows 3 Windermere 4 Loughrigg Tarn

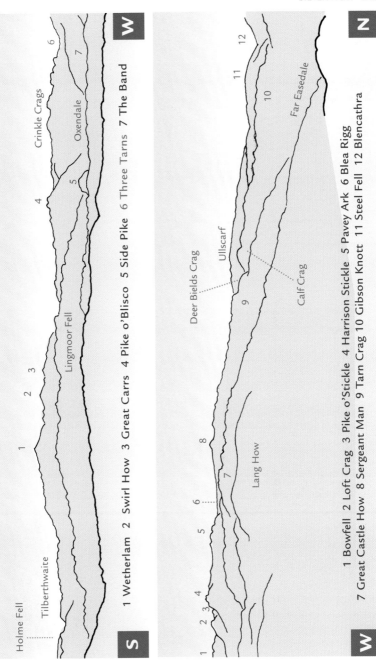

W

Crinkle Crags

Oxendale

Lingmoor Fell

Holme Fell

Tilberthwaite

1 Wetherlam 2 Swirl How 3 Great Carrs 4 Pike o'Blisco 5 Side Pike 6 Three Tarns 7 The Band

S

N

Far Easedale

Deer Bields Crag

Ullscarf

Calf Crag

Lang How

1 Bowfell 2 Loft Crag 3 Pike o'Stickle 4 Harrison Stickle 5 Pavey Ark 6 Blea Rigg
7 Great Castle How 8 Sergeant Man 9 Tarn Crag 10 Gibson Knott 11 Steel Fell 12 Blencathra

W

STEEL FELL

A triangle of sturdy fell defined by Greenburn, Wythburn and Dunmail Raise. Less frequently considered as a direct objective from Grasmere yet, when undertaken from Town End, as the first part of a Greenburn horseshoe, it really shows off its metal.

It is a lovely little fell to climb, the proximity to the A951 making it something of a steal too! The fell-name does not relate in any way to either ore or any allied alloy it is actually a variant of shieling, *'fell of the summer steading'*, after the stamp of Steel Rigg on Hadrian's Wall.

Overbearing Dunmail Raise, and set upon the Lakeland watershed, its situation lends it quite some distinction as a viewpoint, certainly the massive bulk of Helvellyn is fully appreciated. Being so distantly connected to Calf Crag lends the fell a certain stand-alone quality, which may cause it to be considered a single after-noon's objective. However, circular tours can easily be contrived, based upon either Wythburn Dale or Dunmail Raise.

From Helvellyn Screes

553 metres   1,814 feet

ASCENT *from Grasmere*

1 Lay-by parking at Mill Bridge (*bus stop above Town Head*). Follow the road down to Low Mill Bridge crossing the Rothay, turn right and directly after Ghyll Foot

continued below...

Originally West Head was called Steel End, when both farms existed they each had 100 acres of valley pasture, but when the holdings were amalgamated, the former was pulled down the name taken by the surviving part.

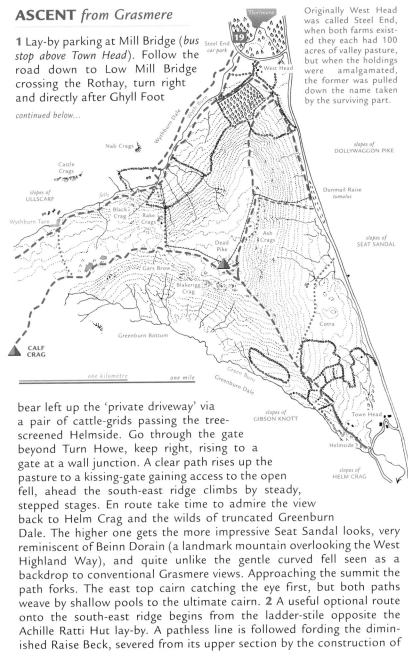

bear left up the 'private driveway' via a pair of cattle-grids passing the tree-screened Helmside. Go through the gate beyond Turn Howe, keep right, rising to a gate at a wall junction. A clear path rises up the pasture to a kissing-gate gaining access to the open fell, ahead the south-east ridge climbs by steady, stepped stages. En route take time to admire the view back to Helm Crag and the wilds of truncated Greenburn Dale. The higher one gets the more impressive Seat Sandal looks, very reminiscent of Beinn Dorain (a landmark mountain overlooking the West Highland Way), and quite unlike the gentle curved fell seen as a backdrop to conventional Grasmere views. Approaching the summit the path forks. The east top cairn catching the eye first, but both paths weave by shallow pools to the ultimate cairn. **2** A useful optional route onto the south-east ridge begins from the ladder-stile opposite the Achille Ratti Hut lay-by. A pathless line is followed fording the diminished Raise Beck, severed from its upper section by the construction of

Dead Pike

Ash Crags

Blakerigg Crag

3

Dunmail Raise

slopes of SEAT SANDAL

20

Achille Ratti Climbing Club hut

slopes of CALF CRAG

1

2

A591

Cotra

Greenburn Dale

Town Head

SOUTHERN APPROACHES

slopes of HELM CRAG

Ghyll Foot

21

the Thirlmere Reservoir, thereby diverting the head-stream into the reservoir. Cross the Cotra moraine keeping right, encountering bracken on the rise, contour above the enclosure wall to the skyline ridge.

ASCENT *from Dunmail Raise*

3 Girder your loins and steel yourself for this one. There is actually nothing out of the ordinary about this quick climb (you don't have to imbibe 'Irn Bru' aforehand!). Use either the generous lay-by GR 330111, or draw off the highway on the north-bound dual-carriageway adjacent to the ladder-stile GR 327117. Climb the pasture slope drifting towards the gill and boundary fence. As a finger of scree reaches down, slip over the gill and, keeping the fence tight right, climb the steep final section. The brow arrives to sooth the sweated brow. Take a breather, gaze over the gulf of Dunmail Raise into the impressive ravine of Raise Beck, sliced into the Helvellyn massif as if struck by a massive lumber-jack's axe. Either follow the sheep trod along the edge of Ash Crags or, keep to the ridge path closer to the fence leading to the summit at the fence corner, as a precaution on those frequent gusty days.

ASCENT *from Wythburn*

Two, at a pinch three, routes can be contemplated from this northern base. **4** The principal route being the north ridge. Leave the Steel End car park turning left. Follow the road to the entrance to West Head Farm. A sign directs right at the beginning of the old bridle path to Dunmail Raise. Formerly this was Steel End Farm but for viability the old West Head Farm land was incorporated into the one holding giving 100 acres of in-take pasture. The former West Head Farm site has been cleared, Stenkin barn being the only surviving element. Pass up by the cottages and subsequent farmhouse a short lane leading to a gate. Ignore the obvious gravel track right, instead keep the wall close right along a green track. Pass through a gate then leave the bridle-way. Head up the bank coming above the plantation to reach a hand-gate where a

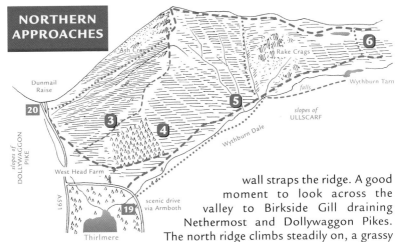

NORTHERN APPROACHES

wall straps the ridge. A good moment to look across the valley to Birkside Gill draining Nethermost and Dollywaggon Pikes. The north ridge climbs steadily on, a grassy plod only relieved by pauses to look back down the length of Thirlmere. The grassy ridge relents to a gentler gradient on the broadening upper ridge, leading by a metal stake on a knoll, to a stile in the right-angle of the boundary fence. From here the fence makes the awful drop directly to Dunmail Raise, making this edge is a fine spot to gaze down on the ancient cairn in the pass, as well as up the facing Raise Beck to Cofa Pike and Fairfield. Continue either along the brink of Ash Crags with the sheep track or, closer to the fence the easy final quarter-of-a-mile to the summit, prudently, when a strong wind funnels through the Dunmail gap (occasionally the roar of military trainer jets add to the noise).

Two ascents can be considered out of upper Wythburn Dale. From the Steel End car park go left the few yards to a kissing-gate or continue over the bridge a further few yards to a hand-gate and steps leading down into the meadow. The two paths advance in harmony either side of the fenced Wythburn Beck, via gates, ladder-stiles or stiles to re-unite at a wooden footbridge. **5** The first option will appeal to people a little less concerned about ease of travel and more intent on getting to the top. Ascend beside wall and fence adjacent to the minor gill due south. As a means of gaining the ridge, it is practical, safe, but oh so steep! **6** More serenely, continue on the dale path climbing above the southern bank of

Wythburn Beck. There are two fine waterslide cascades, which are all the more exciting when a strong wind surges spray back. Pass the twin portal moraines anciently breached, draining the former Wythburn Dale Tarn.

Greenburn Dale from Blakerigg Crag

Water nonetheless does tend to linger, it must love the place, as I suspect will you. Above, Castle Crag's overhanging buttress catches the eye. Pass the sinuous vestige tarn, branch off the clear path climbing pathless left onto the ridge. Skirt right, around the two large plateau top tarns, to join the ridge path leading unerringly east for one mile to the summit.

Dunmail Raise from Ash Crags

The Summit

Otherwise known curiously as Dead Pike, no cause for dread for this is a cracking viewpoint, its principal cairn resting on a small plinth of reddish rock beside remains of the old metal county boundary fence. 100 yards due east, at a slightly lower elevation, a second cairn sits at the angle of the old metal fence. A more recent wooden fence switches upon the summit taking a cleaner line north to the point some four-fifths of a mile distant, where the pre-1974 Cumberland/Westmorland boundary fence plummets east to Dunmail Raise. The all-round view is inspiring. Grand is the huge whaleback western aspect of the Helvellyn range; charming, the long view up Thirlmere to Blencathra; elsewhere see the Coniston Fells in a tight huddle and the massive bulk of fell at the core of the Central Fells rising to High Raise and, much nearer, the broad mass of Ullscarf, enhanced when shafts of sunlight play on the near buttresses of Nab and Castle Crags.

Safe Descents

The north and south ridges are benign enough.

Ridge Route to...

CALF CRAG   DESCENT 295 feet   ASCENT 225 feet   1.4 miles

Walk W beside the fence with the occasional marshy hollow to straddle. Dipping, as the fence departs N, several knolls are avoided en route to a large marsh containing two innominate tarns. Thereafter the path is less well defined, losing company with the intermittent metal boundary stake, as it sweeps SE over damp ground at the head of Greenburn Dale rising to prominent knoll top of Calf Crag.

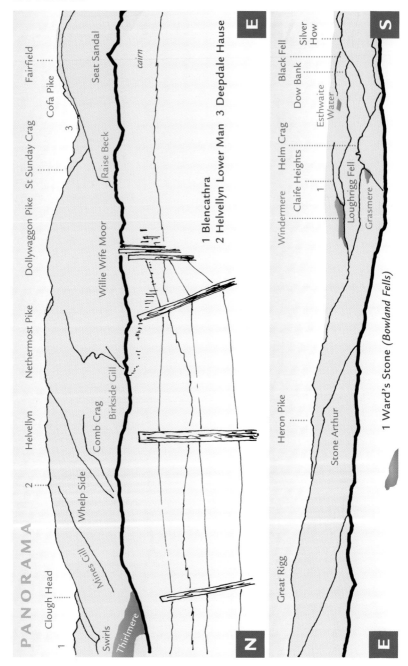

PANORAMA

E

Fairfield
Cofa Pike
St Sunday Crag
Dollywaggon Pike
Nethermost Pike
Helvellyn
Clough Head
Swirls

Seat Sandal
3
Raise Beck
cairn
Willie Wife Moor
Comb Crag
Birkside Gill
Whelp Side
Mines Gill
Thirlmere
2
1

1 Blencathra
2 Helvellyn Lower Man 3 Deepdale Hause

N

S

Black Fell
Silver How
Dow Bank
Esthwaite Water
Helm Crag
Claife Heights
Windermere
Heron Pike
Great Rigg

Loughrigg Fell
Grasmere
Stone Arthur
1

1 Ward's Stone (Bowland Fells)

E

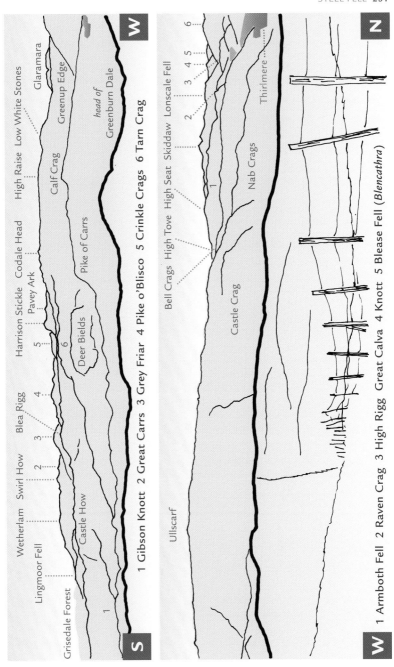

W

Glaramara — Greenup Edge — Calf Crag — Low White Stones — High Raise — Codale Head — Harrison Stickle — Pavey Ark — Blea Rigg — Swirl How — Wetherlam — Lingmoor Fell — Grisedale Forest

head of Greenburn Dale — Pike of Carrs — Deer Bields — Castle How

S

1 Gibson Knott 2 Great Carrs 3 Grey Friar 4 Pike o'Blisco 5 Crinkle Crags 6 Tarn Crag

N

Thirlmere — Lonscale Fell — Skiddaw — High Seat — High Tove — Bell Crags

Nab Crags — Castle Crag — Ullscarf

W

1 Armboth Fell 2 Raven Crag 3 High Rigg Great Calva 4 Knott 5 Blease Fell (*Blencathra*)

TARN CRAG

Codale Head the 'cold dalehead' of Easedale, throws down ridges to embrace two chill-watered upland sheets, Codale and Easedale Tarns. With Blea Rigg casting shadows from its southern brink, Tarn Crag basks in the sun to the north (*see above and below*), in turn casting cool shade into Far Easedale. The tiny upper tarn has a certain charm, which to be frank, that is absent from the lower lake, for all that the earlier tourists made it a place of special resort. What is witnessed is a post-glacial landscape of moraine and barren slopes, bracken is everywhere, paler strips betraying the course of rills spilling from the stony fellsides. From the outflow, where Sour Milk Gill begins its eventful journey, the domed top gives the fell identity with the tarn, hence its name.

The fell can be conveniently climbed via the spine of its east ridge or from either flank, via the tarn, or more eventfully from directly under Deer Bields Crag additionally. A more circuitous route via Codale Tarn, gives prominence to the pencil-point of Belles Knott. For all the shadows the fell is best seen from high on Calf Crag, with Deer Bields and Ferngill Crags adding a rugged grandeur to Far Easedale. There are no ascents worthy of normal discourse in these upper reaches, though one may climb from the saddle at the head of the dale and join the ridge from Broadstone Head.

From the outflow of Easedale Tarn

485 metres   1,591 feet

ASCENT *from Grasmere*

1 Follow Easedale Road via Goody Bridge to cross the footbridge opposite Oak Lodge. A path leads via a hand-gate across a meadow coming close to Easedale Beck with a wall close left. Ignore the inviting New Bridge right, unless using the footpath to avoid the last stretch of road to Easedale House, en route for the Far Easedale bridle-way. From a gate cross Blindtarn Gill bridge, ignore the track to Brimmer Head Farm right, keep forward across open pasture, via a gateway to enter a paved lane at a kissing-gate. The lane opens climbing alongside, and above, the white waters of the aptly named Sour Milk Gill. Ford the gill to gain the prominent rising ridge of Tarn Crag. When the beck is in spate continue to the outflow of the tarn, follow a path skirting damp ground, heading back downstream on the north side. By either means take the first strike onto the rising ridge of Tarn Crag, bracken is the challenge, not enough fell-walkers come this way to beat it back. Climb faithful to the ridge-top by a rock tor above Greathead Crag, aiming for the ultimate skyline notch, turn right to reach the small summit cairn on the prominent and well-defended headland. **2** Another option is to fight through the bracken on the north side of the tarn through the moraine from its outflow, to climb an old shepherd's trod on an indistinct zig-zag onto the high ridge left of Greathead Crag. **3** If seeking to develop a circular tour with the sole intent of Tarn Crag, then there is wisdom in bringing Codale Tarn into the equation. Continue with the main path from the outflow, running along the south side of the tarn to join the main feeder gill below Blea Crag; the path has been greatly improved, in parts a stone staircase rising with the

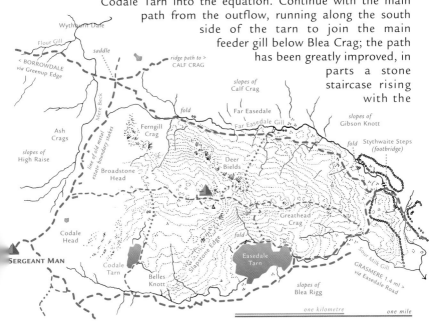

Dinosaur of Deer Bields

cascades, a scene enhanced by the spire-like presence of Belles Knott. A minor path forks right above the cascades, fords the gill, climbing over the west shoulder of Belles Knott to reach Codale Tarn, a place of quiet retreat. The quaint rocky isle may tempt a few to try their luck at reaching without wetting their socks! Pass the tiny outflow, climb the damp northern slope by a ruin sheepfold to join the ridge path, going right to the summit.

4 With equal alacrity the fell can be approached from Far Easedale, on the bridle-path made all the more popular as part of Wainwright's 'A Coast to Coast Walk'; that route naturally taking advantage of the Helm Crag – Gibson Knott ridge, as a choice variation to the wild shadowy depths of the dale. From the road-end at Easedale House follow the public bridle-way signs guiding 'Far Easedale, Borrowdale', this advances to the Stythwaite Steps footbridge. The name indicates a former 'steep clearing' perhaps in some way reflected in the walled enclosures up to the right on the slopes of Gibson Knott. Cross the footbridge and either follow the path up by the wall, noting the massive boulder capped with a luxuriant heather growth to the left, onto the ridge-end, linking to the

From Blea Crag

Sour Milk Gill

route from Sour Milk Gill. Alternatively, continue right, on the clear path running up Far Easedale. Passing on by the naturally drained site of a tarn overlooked by Pike of Carrs. Try branching from the path in a search for the least bracken in the vicinity of a gill, an apparent grass strip gives the illusion of an easy way, keep eyes focused on the towering cliff of Deer Bields. There is no path but the going is basically trouble-free, if tangly and wet. Near the base of the crag is a group of mighty boulders, the bottom one, a particularly fine specimen, has the demeanour of a dinosaur (*see above*)! Boulder hop, there is precious little scree, then either clamber straight onto the ridge or keep up right above the crag. Prolong contact with the eastern rim of the fell before finally being forced to drift left to join the ridge path rising up through the notch to the ultimate point.

The Summit

The craggy top-knot is a thoroughly delightful place to visit, from the small cairn enjoy a lovely view back towards the green strath Grasmere, only lacking is Easedale Tarn itself. This deficiency speedily remedied by going south, back across the ridge path in the notch, some 100 yards, to stand beside a significantly larger and strategically placed cairn commanding a bird's eye-view down upon the glistening waters. The summit ridge, running westwards, deserves to be relished for its own sake; the pools and rocks a wild garden to explore.

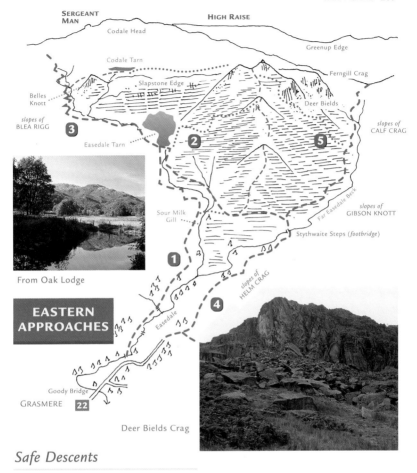

SERGEANT
MAN

HIGH RAISE

Codale Head

Greenup Edge

Codale Tarn

Ferngill Crag

Slapstone Edge

Belles
Knott

Deer Bields

slopes of
BLEA RIGG

3

slopes of
CALF CRAG

Easedale Tarn

2

5

From Oak Lodge

Sour Milk
Gill

slopes of
GIBSON KNOTT

Far Easedale Beck

Stythwaite Steps (*footbridge*)

1

slopes of
HELM CRAG

**EASTERN
APPROACHES**

4

Easedale

Goody Bridge

GRASMERE **22**

Deer Bields Crag

Safe Descents

Stick to the ridge due E, at the foot, either go right for the Stythwaite Steps footbridge or right to ford Sour Milk Gill.

Ridge Route to...

SERGEANT MAN DESCENT 20 ft   ASCENT 840 ft   1.2 miles

A narrow ridge path weaves west along the marshy top amid glaciated rock outcropping, as the slope steepens watch not to catch your feet in peat holes caused by surface wash-out. The path ascends beside a gill to reach a cigar-shaped pool adorned with bog bean then links up with the ridge path ascending Broadstone Head from the saddle at the top of Far Easedale. Follow the old county boundary fence metal stakes left to Codale Head, rounding a marsh to the summit stake.

PANORAMA

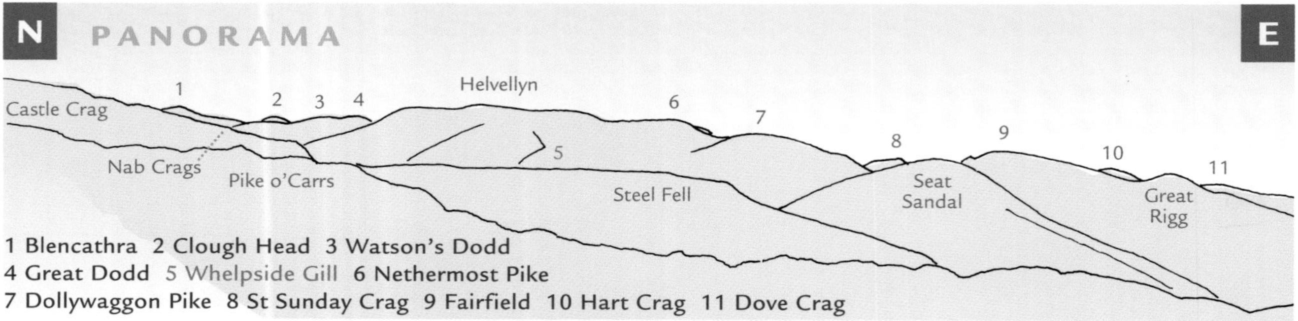
N
E
Helvellyn
Castle Crag
1
2
3
4
6
7
8
9
10
11
5
Nab Crags
Pike o'Carrs
Steel Fell
Seat Sandal
Great Rigg

1 Blencathra 2 Clough Head 3 Watson's Dodd 4 Great Dodd 5 Whelpside Gill 6 Nethermost Pike 7 Dollywaggon Pike 8 St Sunday Crag 9 Fairfield 10 Hart Crag 11 Dove Crag

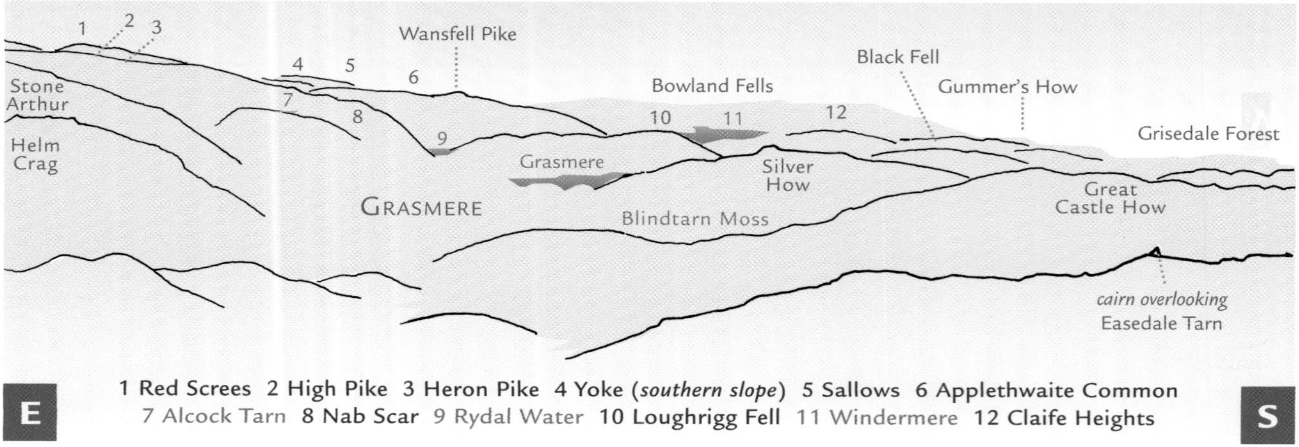
E
S
1
2
3
Wansfell Pike
Black Fell
Gummer's How
Stone Arthur
4
5
6
7
8
9
10
11
12
Bowland Fells
Grisedale Forest
Helm Crag
Grasmere
Silver How
GRASMERE
Blindtarn Moss
Great Castle How
cairn overlooking
Easedale Tarn

1 Red Screes 2 High Pike 3 Heron Pike 4 Yoke (*southern slope*) 5 Sallows 6 Applethwaite Common 7 Alcock Tarn 8 Nab Scar 9 Rydal Water 10 Loughrigg Fell 11 Windermere 12 Claife Heights

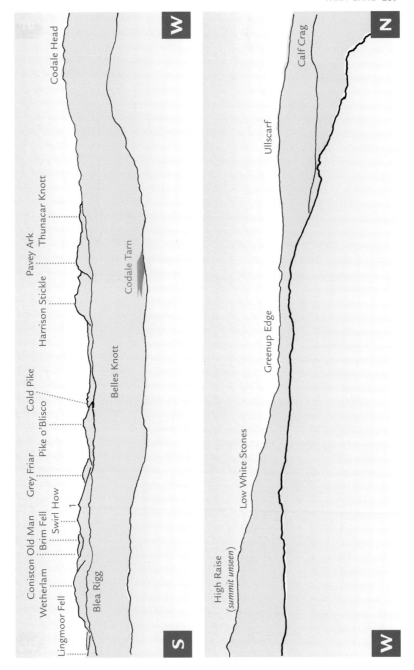

W

Codale Head

Thunacar Knott
Pavey Ark
Harrison Stickle
Cold Pike
Pike o'Blisco
Grey Friar
Swirl How
Brim Fell
Coniston Old Man
Wetherlam
Lingmoor Fell

Codale Tarn

Belles Knott

Blea Rigg

S

N

Calf Crag

Ullscarf

Greenup Edge

Low White Stones

High Raise
(*summit unseen*)

W

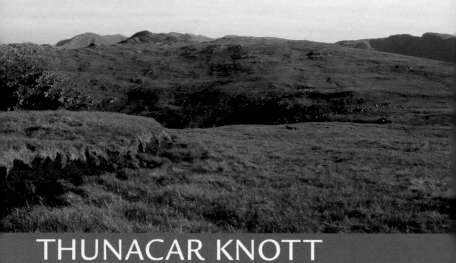

THUNACAR KNOTT

The Old Norse terms thunr 'thin' and karr 'man' suggest that this fell derives its name from the nickname of some early Scandinavian shepherd, who was a particularly lanky character.

Harrison Stickle

summit cairn

Above the handsome face of Pavey Ark the fell is the natural crown, but hived-off, it is a beret bereft. A gentle final swelling abraded with vertically fractured rock clitter and a shallow pool. Even the summit fails to be a convincing moment. Authoritive writers have frequently cited the 'lower' north top as the summit (*see above*), such is the uncertainty. Most fell-walkers hasten on to High Raise, Sergeant Man or the Pikes, brushing over the eastern shoulder little caring, nor aware that a separate fell is at hand. It has barely a watercourse to call its own, nor other feature to stand it apart. Nought but the great sky above, a panorama of fells that would be the envy to many a lesser compatriot height... and yes, the raging fury of the elements.

723 metres   2,372 feet

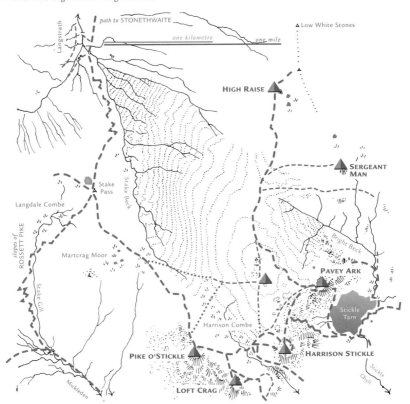

ASCENT *from Great Langdale*

HIGH RAISE
SERGEANT MAN
Codale Head

HARRISON STICKLE
PAVEY ARK

Stickle Tarn

Dungeon Ghyll

ODG <

29

Great Langdale

Consult the routes to HARRISON STICKLE on pages 111,112, either by **1** Pike How or **2** Stickle Ghyll completing the ascent, via the ridge or the narrow trod rising due north out of Harrison Combe.

ASCENT *from Langstrath*

The long march from Rosthwaite (4.5 *miles*) or Stonethwaite up Langstrath via the Stake Pass is normally undertaken as an integral part of the *Cumbria Way*. Most walkers being content to slip over Langdale Combe into upper Mickleden, with fabulous scenery every step of the way. But 'red-blooded' sorts with energy to burn, will think nothing of knocking off the Pikes, with Thunacar Knott taken en route to Harrison Stickle. Alternatively, it may be considered as part of a great circular

SOUTHERN APPROACHES

intent with High Raise, returning via Greenup Edge. **3** For the early stages consult SERGEANT'S CRAG page 228. From the cairn at the top of the pass a strong path branches south onto the peaty ridge of Martcrag Moor, traversing some pretty horrid ground before the slope steepens. Coming close to a gill branch half-left (ESE) from the main path to Pike o'Stickle, rising up the grassy fell, skirt the rocky rim to reach the summit cairn.

The Summit

There are two tops, each with cairns to north and south of a shallow hollow filled with a pool. The southern cairn is 'the' summit whatever the quirks of tradition may try to claim, in my book the top of a fell is the summit! The panorama is the meat and matter of this place, there is a lot to see, but qualitively at its best to the west.

Vertically fissured plateau bed-rock

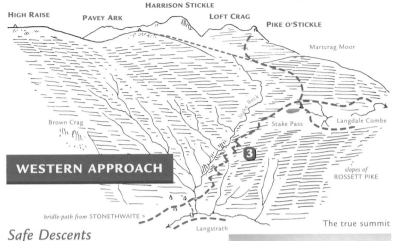

HIGH RAISE PAVEY ARK HARRISON STICKLE LOFT CRAG PIKE O'STICKLE Martcrag Moor

Stake Beck

Brown Crag Stake Pass Langdale Combe

WESTERN APPROACH **3** slopes of ROSSETT PIKE

bridle-path from STONETHWAITE > Langstrath The true summit

Safe Descents

A narrow trod leads due south into Harrison Combe, joins the path directly below Harrison Crag above the upper Dungeon Ghyll gorge. It runs perilously along the rim of the ravine, so care is needed here. An alternative option would be to cross the large stepping stones and make for the Thorn Crag col joining Mark Gate, a very well secured path leaving Loft Crag. Both routes reach down to the New Dungeon Ghyll.

Ridge Routes to...

HARRISON STICKLE   DESCENT 150 ft ASCENT 190 ft   0.6 miles

Head S largely over a grassy terrain latterly swerving to the right of a rock tor.

HIGH RAISE   DESCENT 150 ft ASCENT 280 ft   1 mile

At last a chance to lengthen the stride, one might be walking the Wessex Downs, but for the scenery! Go north, drifting down to join the ridge path from Pavey Ark, cross the depression at the head of Bright Beck. Beyond, the path has been re-aligned to reduce wear on a fragile soil along the gentle rise to the summit.

SERGEANT MAN   DESCENT 150 ft ASCENT 200 ft   1 mile

Follow suit with the High Raise path, only take the second path angling half-right. As the ground begins to rise after the depression contour to the summit knot. The first path leads through an outcrop and traverses the slope well below Sergeant Man, a kind of speedy short-cut for anyone racing to Grasmere. Shame on them!

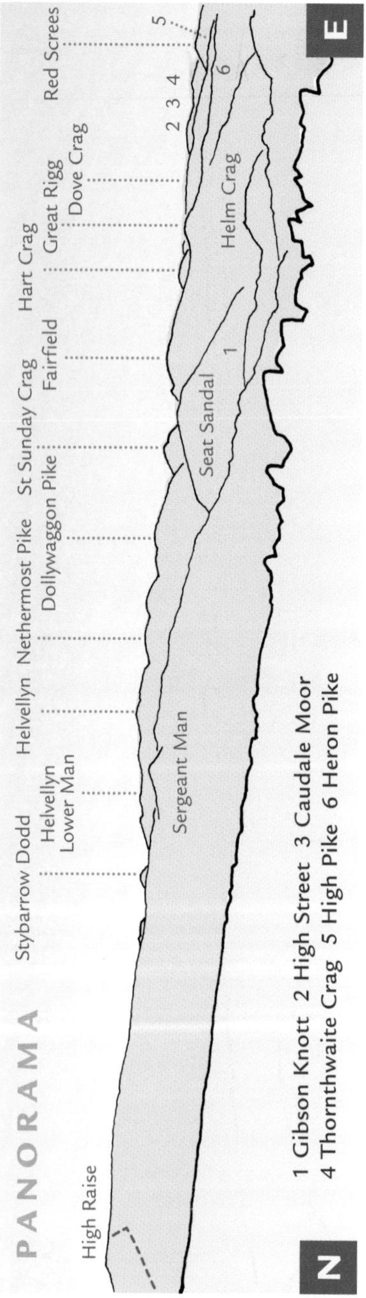

PANORAMA

High Raise

Stybarrow Dodd

Helvellyn
Lower Man

Helvellyn

Nethermost Pike

St Sunday Crag
Dollywaggon Pike

Hart Crag
Fairfield

Great Rigg
Dove Crag

Red Screes

5

2 3 4

6

Sergeant Man

Seat Sandal

1

Helm Crag

N

E

1 Gibson Knott 2 High Street 3 Caudale Moor
4 Thornthwaite Crag 5 High Pike 6 Heron Pike

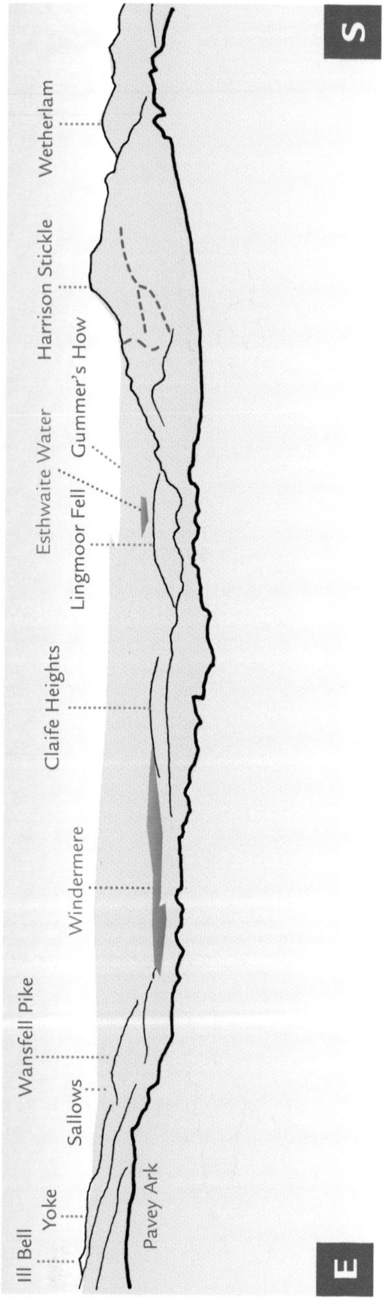

Ill Bell

Yoke

Sallows

Wansfell Pike

Windermere

Claife Heights

Lingmoor Fell

Esthwaite Water

Harrison Stickle

Gummer's How

Wetherlam

Pavey Ark

E

S

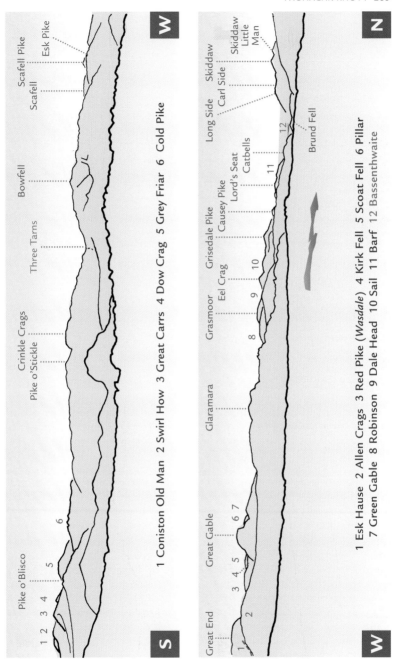

S

W

Pike o'Blisco · Crinkle Crags · Pike o'Stickle · Three Tarns · Bowfell · Scafell · Scafell Pike · Esk Pike

1 2 3 4 · 5 · 6

1 Coniston Old Man 2 Swirl How 3 Great Carrs 4 Dow Crag 5 Grey Friar 6 Cold Pike

W

N

Great End · Great Gable · Glaramara · Grasmoor · Eel Crag · Griesdale Pike · Causey Pike · Lord's Seat · Catbells · Long Side · Carl Side · Skiddaw · Skiddaw Little Man

1 · 2 · 3 4 5 · 6 7 · 8 · 9 · 10 · 11 · 12 · Brund Fell

1 Esk Hause 2 Allen Crags 3 Red Pike (*Wasdale*) 4 Kirk Fell 5 Scoat Fell 6 Pillar 7 Green Gable 8 Robinson 9 Dale Head 10 Sail 11 Barf 12 Bassenthwaite

ULLSCARF

Ⓞne seldom hears the praises of Ullscarf. For all the comparative tameness of the upper plateau, in harmony with High Raise, it really is a splendid place to stride, the summit, and several lateral points including Low Saddle, Standing, Tarn and Nab Crags are all quite exceptional viewpoints in their own right.

The higher ground fails to live up to its brave front of crags, those that form a stern defence to Wythburndale especially giving observers the illusion of a seriously craggy height. A cursory knowledge of the drainage of the fell is crucial to knowing where you are, a wrong turn can leave you a long way from your intended valley base. Ullscarf is not a fell to trammel with in misty conditions, the whole point of its pivotal situation being lost, as may the hapless wanderer be too, especially on the eastern slopes where the terrain is confusing even under crystal clear conditions!

The fell is defined to the south by damp Wythburn Dale and, the altogether sunnier, Greenup Gill being divided from the natural northern extension to the range by an old bridlepath which runs over a wet depression below Standing Crag. This annexing of Bell Crags does not concur with former guides, though the logic is without flaw. To the north-west, that part of the fell known to Watendlath folk as Coldbarrow Fell, descends in an uncluttered fashion to Green Comb and Great Crag either side of Dock Tarn.

726 metres   2,382 feet

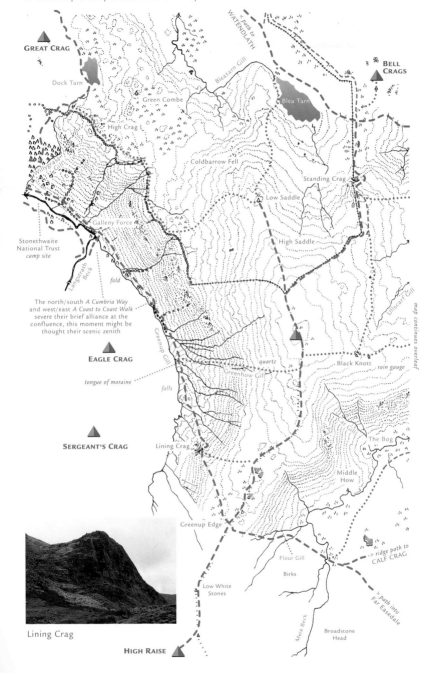

GREAT CRAG

Dock Tarn

Green Combe

High Crag

< *path to*
WATENDLATH

Bleatarn Gill

Blea Tarn

BELL CRAGS

Coldbarrow Fell

Standing Crag

Low Saddle

High Saddle

Wythnat Gill

Galleny Force

Stonethwaite
National Trust
camp site

Langstrath Beck

fold

The north/south *A Cumbria Way*
and west/east *A Coast to Coast Walk*
sever their brief alliance at the
confluence, this moment might be
thought their scenic zenith

Greenup Gill

EAGLE CRAG

tongue of moraine

falls

quartz

Greenhow Gill

Black Knott

rain gauge

Ullscarf Gill

map continues overleaf

SERGEANT'S CRAG

Lining Crag

The Bog

Middle
How

Greenup Edge

Flour Gill

Birks

> *ridge path to*
CALF CRAG

Low White
Stones

Mere Beck

Broadstone
Head

> *path into*
Far Easedale

Lining Crag

HIGH RAISE

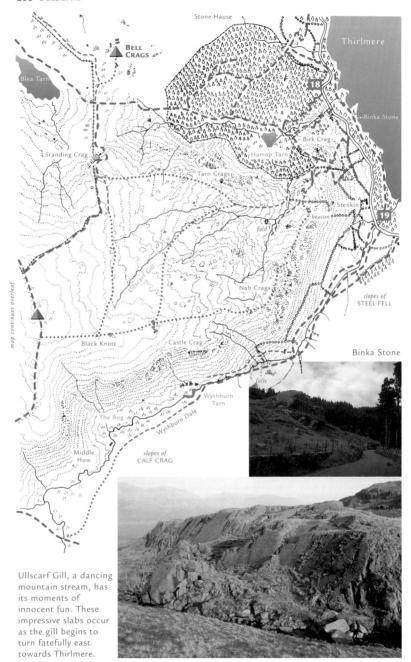

Thirlmere

Stone Hause

BELL CRAGS

Blea Tarn

Standing Crag

Binka Stone

Birk Crag

Harrop Tarn

Tarn Crags

Stenkin

beacon

fold

Nab Crags

slopes of
STEEL FELL

map continues overleaf

Ullscarf Gill

Black Knott

Castle Crag

Binka Stone

falls

Wythburn Tarn

The Bog

Wythburn Dale

Middle How

slopes of
CALF CRAG

Ullscarf Gill, a dancing
mountain stream, has
its moments of
innocent fun. These
impressive slabs occur
as the gill begins to
turn fatefully east
towards Thirlmere.

ASCENT *from Stonethwaite*

1 From the three-way signpost beside the telephone kiosk, leave the hamlet by the lane left as to 'Greenup Edge'. Cross Stonethwaite Bridge, momentarily pausing to gaze into the the turquoise waters of Stonethwaite Beck and lend on the pipe railings to look upstream to the shapely profile of Eagle Crag, which maintains a strong presence during this valley approach. After the gate meet the bridle-path from Rosthwaite, turn right and through the next gate enter a lane on a rough track with continues via several further gates. Across the beck upon the strath meadow the camping field is seldom empty, such is the perennial allure of the Stonethwaite valley as a base for fell adventurers. Proceed beyond the footbridge above the Langstrath Beck/Greenup Gill confluence. Keep ahead up the Greenup Beck valley. At the hand-gate notice the overhanging crag high left along the rim of the valley, where peregrine falcons have been known to nest. The path receives periodic remedial repair to cope with the heavy boot traffic. **2** Gird your loins for a simple, yet energetic, pull up the steep fellside. After fording Greenhow Gill the path bears onto the right-hand side of the first tongue of moraine. Abandon the bridle-path bearing up onto this rigg left and climb beside Greenhow Gill, keep to the west side ascend steeply onto the brow. The slope begins to ease enabling one to enjoy the handsome views back to Pounsey Crag. Keep beside the dwindling gill coming up by a line of quartz outcropping. Cross peaty exposures to join the ridge path, go left with little remaining ascent to the summit. **3** Normal people, choose normal routes, and without a second thought will continue with the pony path through the moraine, crossing the dry tarn site, to ascend the gully to the left of Lining Crag, a spot of hands-on walking one might say! At the top, the way ahead is in sore need of a sabbatical, the multitude of cross-ridge walkers having churned so much of the path down to bare peat. In order to minimise the transformation of Greenup Edge

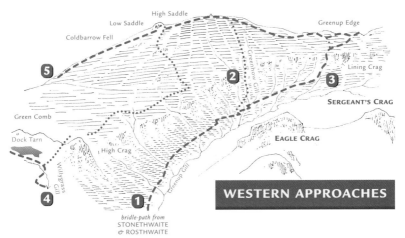

Low Saddle · High Saddle · Greenup Edge · Coldbarrow Fell · Greenhow Gill · Lining Crag · **5** · **2** · **3** · Green Comb · **SERGEANT'S CRAG** · Dock Tarn · High Crag · **EAGLE CRAG** · Willygrass Gill · Greenup Gill · **4** · **1** · **WESTERN APPROACHES**

bridle-path from
STONETHWAITE
& ROSTHWAITE

Old path above the former West Head Farm

to 'brown-up', play your part in its reprieve by diverting due east onto the ridge. There is little or no evidence of a path but the going is so much sweeter. The broad ridge is awash with pools, keep left to miss the worst of the spongy ground. Traversing to the ridge path, mount northward to the summit, with the occasional stake stump from the old metal estate fence as guides.

4 A special route, ideal for anyone looking for an unusual ascent, (possibly using the Greenup Gill path for a circular return,) ventures onto the northern rim of the valley bound for Low Saddle. Follow the approach to GREAT CRAG page 101, via Lingy End. After crossing the stile ascend until a wall is seen riding up to the right, ford gill, outflow of Dock Tarn, climbing with the wall to the right over the shoulder of High Crag. Delight in the view beyond over the meeting of the Greenup Gill and Langstrath valleys, with Eagle and Sergeant's Crags centre-stage and the long view to Bowfell at the head of Langstrath, quite unforgettable. The route traverses rough ground to come alongside the wall protecting the edge. The wall has the scenic impact of some heroic stone frontier march, rising and falling in these stirring mountain surroundings. Keep alongside the wall until a gill re-entrant breaks the steady progress, angle up the rough slopes to the cairn on Low Saddle, a viewpoint that provides the best survey of the northern sector of the Central Fells. Follow the ridge up to High Saddle, join the fence crossing a stile at the top, heading south to the summit.

Ridge-top stake

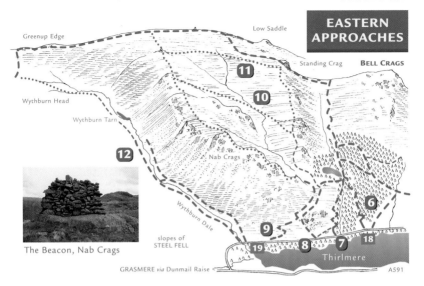

Greenup Edge
Low Saddle
Standing Crag **BELL CRAGS**
Wythburn Head
Wythburn Tarn
Nab Crags
11
10
12
Wythburn Dale
6
slopes of STEEL FELL
9
19 **8** **7** **18**
Thirlmere
The Beacon, Nab Crags
GRASMERE *via* Dunmail Raise
A591

ASCENT *from Watendlath*

5 One wonders how many visitors to this gorgeous little community have stood on the packhorse bridge, looked across the tarn and known they were looking straight at Ullscarf, even the farmer calls it Coldbarrow Fell! This is an efficient start-point consult BELL CRAGS page 29 following route **9**. Ford precisely at the outflow of Blea Tarn, follow the western shore, nipping up onto the ridge at the first bay, there is nothing to impede, nor anything to encourage speed! Climb steadily to crest Low Saddle.

ASCENT *from Dobgill and Steel End*

Eastern approaches are so different, is this the same mountain? When viewed across Thirlmere, through the trees from the speeding main road the near eastern skyline is so craggy that it suggests great tidings for the explorer. The early stages of all approaches measure up to this perception, but Ullscarf is no alpine peak and the backing slopes soon falter into mediocre moorland. What am I saying? This is Lakeland. Given the sunshine and the day, even these barren slopes have their beauty, the words of a besotted devotee, well perhaps! **6** From Dob Gill a made-path climbs directly to the outflow of Harrop Tarn. **7** A further path begins from the road south of Dobgill Bridge, rising via hand-gates to cross the forest fence by a ladder-stile and subsequent duckboarding to the footbridge below the outflow. The main forest track leads west, as it forks on two occasions keep up left, rising as a path to the double

Harrop Tarn from Tarn Crag

kissing-gate exiting the conifers. The bridle-path mounts the slope to the broad depression traversed by a fence, Do not go through the hand-gate, instead, turn left, following the fence by a pool to the base of Standing Crag. Bear up left, via an easy gully, clambering to the top to re-join the fence. Take the opportunity to appropriate 'stand' at the brink of the cliff to gaze at the fine view north. Follow the fence up to the acute corner, walking free of the fence left, to attain the summit cairn.

8 Start from a roadside gate GR 318138, south of the glacially smoothed outcrop known as the Binka Stone, so called from its likeness to 'a door-step'. Angle diagonally left across the slope beneath Birk Crag, a groove leading through the juniper to a rising wall. At the top either venture to the cairn on top of the crag and a smart descent to Harrop Tarn via a tall hand-gate or cross the adjacent stile and follow the plantation fence to ford Ullscarf Gill. Bear left on a green path that curves up onto the ridge above a cluster of sheepfolds, becoming lost as a tangible path. Continue onto the rising ridge to gain the edge of Tarn Crag, a fine viewpoint for Bell Crags (see that fell's title) and overlooking the plantations surrounding Harrop Tarn. Hold to the edge, stepping down a rock band or two, crossing marshy ground to reach the ridge fence above Standing Crag.

9 Best begun from the Steel End car park. Follow the road right to go through the yard and gates at Stenkin (barn). Follow the wall to the site of the original West Head Farm, almost all trace of this farmstead has been removed. Its economic footings lost when the reservoir stole its

North from the acute fence corner

valley pasture, it seems somehow unseemly that the name was borrowed by the one farm that remained, which had held the topographically appropriate name of Steel End. Bear up left by the fence to a hand-gate in the fell bounding wall. A continuing path of ancient purpose winds up the rough fellside, coming close to the rising wall shielding Birk Crag, this path is more obscure in the damp ground. Continue to a wall gap; the shepherd's path progresses as to sheepfolds within Ullscarf Gill. However, immediately through the wall, bear up left to the prominent cairn, known as The Beacon. The short length of wall set up as The Beacon is a replacement for a finer structure thrown down over fifty years ago, vandalism is not new! The continuing ridge, rising above Nab Crags, gives ample scope for the inventive fell-wanderer. There is no path, which seems strange when minded how bold the ridge appears when viewed from the Armboth road-end at the A591. Pass a curious ruin in the shelter of the first step of the ridge, thereafter, make what progress appeals in order to culminate upon a modest cairn directly overlooking the footbridge far below in jaws of Wythburn Dale. The ridge now turns west and it is less easy to keep to the scenic edge. A deep re-entrant gill may tempt the more intrepid fellsman to ascend from the depths of Wythburn Dale, but such a notion comes with a health warning! The ridge rises progressively to a cluster of pools above Castle Crag. **10** This point can be reached less impressively it has to be said, from route **9** by

following Ullscarf Gill, via a slabby ravine, curving south towards the brink. **11** An old shepherds' traverse can be attempted from Standing Crag, formerly marked by a string of cairns bee-lining to Black Knott, now only one cairn remains across the pretty torrid headstream terrain. Black Knott is an oasis on the ridge. Head west to meet up with the ridge path, walking free north to the summit.

The Summit

Walkers cross the summit and think little of the event, heaping greatest praise on Low Saddle as the panoramic high point of their visit. There are broad acres of acid grassland declining into the peaty wastes of Ullscarf Gill to the east, coarser slopes spill quickly westward to Greenup and Bleatarn Gills. The stumps of the old estate fence may cause some visitors to stumble, but far better that, than to ruin the fell-top with an actual fence. Sadly, henceforward up the spine of the range to Bleaberry Fell and a little beyond, a stockproof fence has been re-instated.

Standing Crag

Safe Descents

Well, the fence has one merit, but only one mind. In mist the fence, that has its acute corner some 350 yards north of the summit cairn, is a sure guide. Follow it right, to the top of Standing Crag, the path veers right to work down a gully to its base, then on beside the continuing fence to a hand-gate in the damp depression. From here join the old bridle-path linking Watendlath left (through the gate) and Thirlmere (Dob Gill). For anyone 'mistified' with Borrowdale as their destination, cross the stile at the acute corner, go left hugging the fence down to the wall running along the edge above the Greenup Gill valley. Follow this wall right to reach Dock Tarn and the path down through the woods by Lingy End.

Ridge Routes to...

BELL CRAGS   DESCENT 660 ft   ASCENT 125 ft   1.9 miles

Head north to the acute corner of the fence, go right following the fence to the top of Standing Crag. Bear down right to the crag base, the fence resumes, follow this beyond the pools and ridge-top hand-gate, skirting marshy ground to bear half-right onto the short summit ridge.

HIGH RAISE   DESCENT 390 ft   ASCENT 510 ft   2.5 miles

Go south, a definite path with the old metal fence stakes as guides giving confidence, until dipping to an area of large pools that give cause to watch one's footing, a right-hand bias ensures driest boots. Cross the Greenup Edge depression, climbing SSW via Low White Stones to the OS pillar and wind-shelter marking this the roof of the range.

Low Saddle looking to Ullscarf

PANORAMA

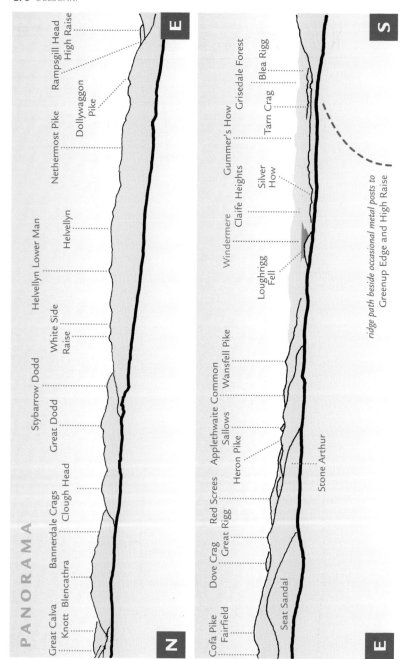

E

Rampsgill Head
High Raise
Dollywagon Pike
Nethermost Pike
Helvellyn Lower Man
Helvellyn
White Side
Raise
Stybarrow Dodd
Great Dodd
Clough Head
Bannerdale Crags
Great Calva
Knott Blencathra

N

S

Griesdale Forest
Blea Rigg
Tarn Crag
Gummer's How
Claife Heights
Silver How
Windermere
Loughrigg Fell

Wansfell Pike
Applethwaite Common
Sallows
Heron Pike
Red Screes
Dove Crag
Great Rigg
Cofa Pike
Fairfield
Seat Sandal
Stone Arthur

ridge path beside occasional metal posts to
Greenup Edge and High Raise

E

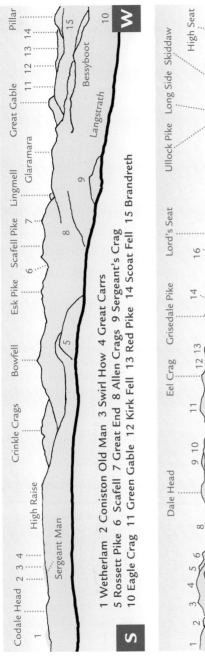

Codale Head 2 3 4 — High Raise — Sergeant Man — Crinkle Crags — Bowfell — Esk Pike — Scafell Pike — Lingmell — Glaramara — Great Gable — Pillar — Bessyboot — Langstrath

S — **W**

1 Wetherlam 2 Coniston Old Man 3 Swirl How 4 Great Carrs
5 Rossett Pike 6 Scafell 7 Great End 8 Allen Crags 9 Sergeant's Crag
10 Eagle Crag 11 Green Gable 12 Kirk Fell 13 Red Pike 14 Scoat Fell 15 Brandreth

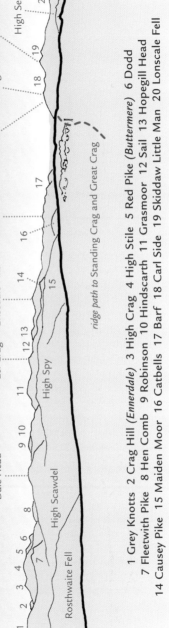

Rosthwaite Fell — High Scawdel — Dale Head — High Spy — Eel Crag — Grisedale Pike — Lord's Seat — Ullock Pike — Long Side Skiddaw — High Seat

ridge path to Standing Crag and Great Crag

W — **N**

1 Grey Knotts 2 Crag Hill (*Ennerdale*) 3 High Crag 4 High Stile 5 Red Pike (*Buttermere*) 6 Dodd
7 Fleetwith Pike 8 Hen Comb 9 Robinson 10 Hindscarth 11 Grasmoor 12 Sail 13 Hopegill Head
14 Causey Pike 15 Maiden Moor 16 Catbells 17 Barf 18 Carl Side 19 Skiddaw Little Man 20 Lonscale Fell

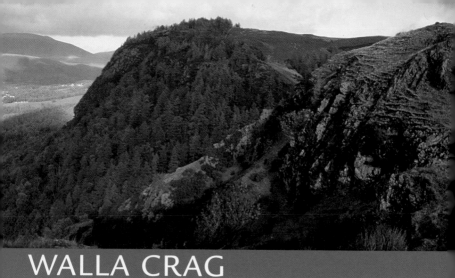

WALLA CRAG

Travellers venturing south from Keswick along the Borrowdale Road get their first taste of the rocky dramas ahead when they see, rising above the green canopy of Great Wood, the massive 'wall of crag' appropriately called Walla Crag.

Strictly the fell is the north-west shoulder of Bleaberry Fell, separated from the higher ground by a wide upland hollow drained by Brockle Beck. To the south the short incursion of Cat Gill separates the fell from Falcon Crag, which has no pretensions for separate fell status, despite that, of the two cliffs, it is a major two-tiered sporting venue for rock-climbers.

There is no doubting the individualistic qualities of this imposing façade so luxuriantly wreathed in trees. At its centre the outcrop is riven by Lady's Rake a damp vegetated gully, do not be tempted to even try to ascend this rotten hollow, even climbers give it a miss!

Down the decades the summit has been a prime objective for evening strolls from Keswick. As a viewpoint it is unrivalled for its views across to the Keswick vale, and blessed too with a lovely view over Derwentwater. While the bold escarpment suggests a difficult climb, it can be out-flanked to give the gentlest of climbs, not that steeper lines need be resisted, including a secretive under-cliff trod which can be awkward in damp conditions when tree roots are slick.

Castlehead Wood backed by Keswick

379 metres   1,243 feet

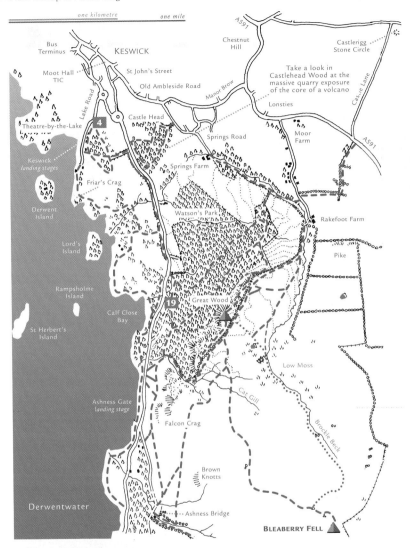

one kilometre   one mile

Bus
Terminus
KESWICK

Chestnut
Hill

Castlerigg
Stone Circle

Moot Hall
TIC

St John's Street

Old Ambleside Road

Manor Brow

Take a look in
Castlehead Wood at the
massive quarry exposure
of the core of a volcano

Castle Lane

A591

Theatre-by-the-Lake

Castle Head

Lonsties

Springs Road

Moor
Farm

A591

Keswick
landing stages

Springs Farm

Friar's Crag

Watson's Park

Rakefoot Farm

Derwent
Island

Lord's
Island

Pike

Rampsholme
Island

Great Wood

Calf Close
Bay

St Herbert's
Island

Low Moss

Car Gill

Ashness Gate
landing stage

Falcon Crag

Brockle Beck

Derwentwater

Brown
Knotts

Ashness Bridge

BLEABERRY FELL

ASCENT *from Keswick*

1 Start from the Moot Hall in Market Square at the centre of Keswick.
Head south-east following the pavement of St Johns Street becoming the
Old Ambleside Road after Castlehead Close, to turn right into Springs
Road (note there is no scope for car parking in this vicinity). Pass by
Springs Farm via a gate into Springs Wood ascend beside the gill on
a popular path in close harmony with the beck, switching right to run

alongside pasture fencing. After the Great Wood path merges pass through a kissing-gate soon to dip into the dell and cross a footbridge, rising to meet the minor road at steps and a hand-gate. Go right, the road forks at Rakefoot Farm, go right signed 'Wallacrag'. Cross the footbridge rising with a wall right to a stile, ascending with the wall right, and either go through the first hand-gate winding up within the scarp edge enclosure or continue to the top crossing a stile to the summit cairn.

ASCENT *from Great Wood*

2 A lovely lakeside approach from the Lake Road car park, via Friar's Crag, Ings Wood and Calfclose Bay make the ideal presage to the climb. Three contrasting and delightfully sylvan routes lead to the top from the National Trust car park. **3** Cat Gill. Head south, passing above the former car park area. Ignore the forest track that swings left, keep forward upon the footpath leading to the footbridge spanning Cat Gill. Do not cross, instead, ascend the cobbled path rising steeply beside the cacophony of the ravine via two hand-gates. Pass through a kissing-gate then via a zig-zag stepped section to another kissing-gate. Following up the steps by the wall the slope eases. Either continue with the wall left or cross the stile to complete the ascent within the tree-fringed scarp enclosure. Take one notable early 'spur opportunity' to wander left for a special view over Derwentwater. Continue to pass/reach and cross a stile in the wall, now above the inaccessible gully of Lady's Rake, advance on on a popular path to the open summit.

4 The undoubted beauties of Great Wood well merit a more leisurely line along the forest tracks. Either head north, switching right as the gate to the valley road comes into view, gently rising, ignore the track left into the Watson's Park section of the wood,

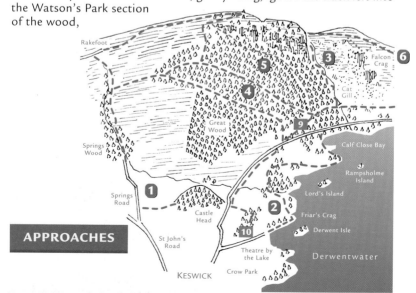

the track swings right and merges with the footpath from Springs Wood and promptly bears off up the bank with a small gill right. This point can be reached more directly by advancing south from the car park, only this time swing left climbing steadily with the forest track. Where the track levels and shapes to descend cross a small gill. Bear up sharp right. Ford the gill below the enclosure fence corner continuing now up the right bank. Emerge from the woodland, keep the fence right until the slope eases onto heathery ground with superb views of Skiddaw and Blencathra the rich reward. Either go through the hand-gate in the wall to complete the ascent, principally in the pasture, or keep up the escarpment edge attractively garnished with heather. A matter of yards beyond the hand-gate notice the small balcony viewpoint. This is not only a fine moment to pause and survey a sumptuous prospect towards Keswick, but it marks the top of the sub-edge or undercliff path. **5** The undercliff path, and very much the third way requiring a degree of confidence as there is some awkward footing. At the point where the forestry track sweeps left, spot an unwaymarked narrow path rising directly up through the conifers. This climbs and winds assiduously towards the foot of the crag directly beneath Lady's Rake. It duly drifts left seeking ledges and tight tree passages consistent but never more than a thin trod. Keep directly below the escarpment outcropping. Towards the end of the traverse after a gill, one particular ledge at a dry gully, may be found troublesome in damp conditions. Emerging at the aforementioned balcony go right to climb the attractive escarpment edge.

ASCENT
from Ashness Bridge

Few visitors miss the opportunity to admire and photograph the famous view from above the bridge. What the majority fail to realise is, that this is but one component of a suite of four stunning viewpoints of this prospect of Skiddaw. To draw the composition together one should embark on a circular expedition, best begun from this the first formal car park up the Watendlath road GR 269196. **6** Advance north re-crossing the bridge. One may follow the footpath contouring ahead to a hand-gate in the down wall subsequently forking half-right up the bracken slope.

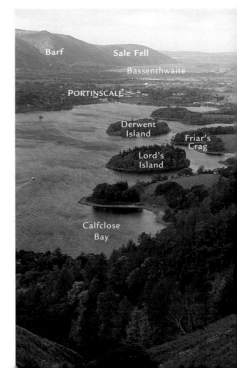

Barf   Sale Fell
Bassenthwaite
PORTINSCALE
Derwent Island
Friar's Crag
Lord's Island
Calfclose Bay

Overlooking Cat Gill

The path climbing, less than comfortably in places, up to a stile in a modern fence to join the higher path in a wet patch devoid of bracken. Alternatively, bear up directly from the bridge, cross the fence stile beside the old fold ascending, to where a path bears off left up the bracken slope, to a hand-gate in the wall. This point can also be attained from the lower path, after passing through the hand-gate, rise directly with the wall right, though bracken does tend to diminish ones enthusiasm, to reach an adjacent hand-gate in the fence. The prominent path climbs steadily to easier ground. Watch for a side path, half-left, which can be followed down the grassy spur to the cairn on the top of Falcon Crag. This is the second notable viewpoint of the tour, providing a superb prospect over Great Wood framed by Walla Crag and Derwentwater. Climb back up to the path to traverse above the steep re-entrant of Cat Gill, ford the gill en route to the stile into the Walla Crag escarpment enclosure. The summit of Walla Crag provides the third viewpoint. To reach the fourth, continue down the northern scarp, through the heather, to the small balcony at the top of the undercliff path, this provides the most pleasing view of Skiddaw and Blencathra. Head on down the edge path to reach the forest track turning left, re-tracing route **2** to meet the lower footpath. Bear left to cross the Cat Gill footbridge and traverse the undulating path below Falcon Crag, at one point slipping through a gorse tunnel. The crag is famed for its climbs and, appropriately, resident peregrines.

The summit cairn backed by Clough Head and Great Dodd

The Summit

Nature has provided the fell a bald crown of naked rock, to the west the ground falls precipitously. Heather enlivens the near ground, interlaced with native trees lining the edge to north and south. Hence this is a momentous belvedere from which to admire the perennially attractive fell surround of Derwentwater. The summit cairn is set back from this

Glenderaterra
Valley

Blease Fell

Castlerigg Stone Circle

Hall's
Fell

Scales
Fell

Souther
Fell

Doddick
Fell

THRELKELD

Blencathra from the balcony

brink. Beyond the wall the fell merges into sheep pasture. In recent years the fell's height has been re-assessed, three metres being added to its height, ruining the neat simplicity from its former imperial figures. All visitors are drawn to the rocky western edge for the best views – confirming the fullest reign and visitor inclination the panorama is taken from this spot. Standing on the fell witness the stark division between the sleeker lines of the Skiddaw slates, as expressed by the North-Western Fells across the lake, and the igneous rocks of the Borrowdale Volcanic group gathering in force to the south, culminating upon Scafell Pike.

Safe Descents

For Great Wood car park, Cat Gill and the paths that swing down from the north are fine but avoid the undercliff path. The easiest option of all is to head for Rakefoot Farm on the green tracks across the open pasture NE and descend the sheltered Spring Wood path.

Ridge Route

BLEABERRY FELL   DESCENT 175 feet   ASCENT 850 feet   1.2 miles

Head S, cross the wall-stile following the Ashness Bridge path. After some 200 yards bear half-left SSE at a cairn, onto the path crossing the upper Cat Gill ford. The line becomes clearer after traversing the damp ground, rise to glance by a sheepfold to the E of a knoll, skirt the peaty hollow before climbing the steep and severely eroded NW prow to a viewpoint cairn. Continue via a further large cairn to the summit wind-shelter cairn.

PANORAMA

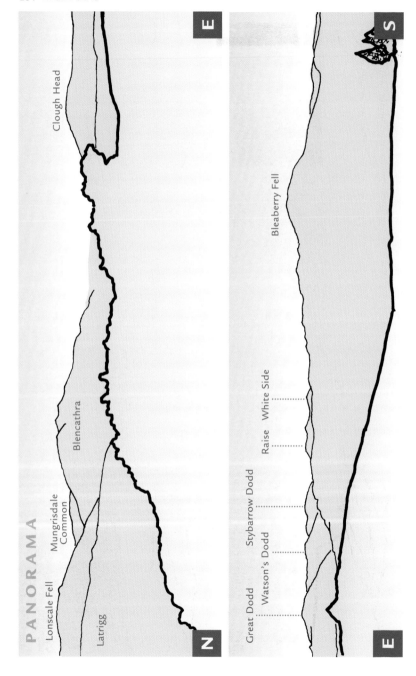

N

E

Lonscale Fell

Mungrisdale Common

Latrigg

Blencathra

Clough Head

E

S

Great Dodd

Watson's Dodd

Stybarrow Dodd

Raise   White Side

Bleaberry Fell

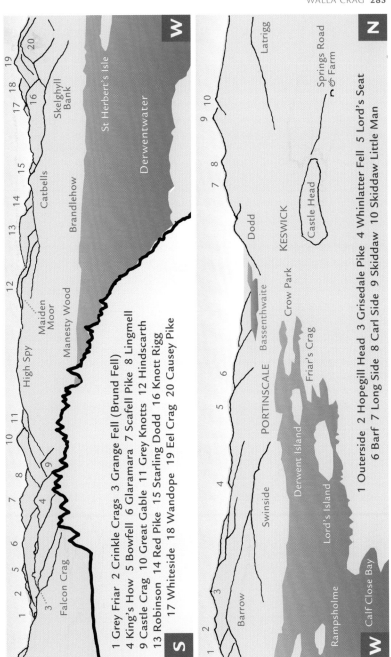

W

1 Grey Friar 2 Crinkle Crags 3 Grange Fell (Brund Fell)
4 King's How 5 Bowfell 6 Glaramara 7 Scafell Pike 8 Lingmell
9 Castle Crag 10 Great Gable 11 Grey Knotts 12 Hindscarth
13 Robinson 14 Red Pike 15 Starling Dodd 16 Knott Rigg
17 Whiteside 18 Wandope 19 Eel Crag 20 Causey Pike

S

Falcon Crag

High Spy

Maiden Moor

Manesty Wood

Brandlehow

Catbells

Skelghyll Bank

St Herbert's Isle

Derwentwater

N

1 Outerside 2 Hopegill Head 3 Grisedale Pike 4 Whinlatter Fell 5 Lord's Seat
6 Barf 7 Long Side 8 Carl Side 9 Skiddaw 10 Skiddaw Little Man

Latrigg

Springs Road & Farm

Castle Head

KESWICK

Dodd

Bassenthwaite

Crow Park

PORTINSCALE

Friar's Crag

Swinside

Derwent Island

Lord's Island

Barrow

Rampsholme

Calf Close Bay

W

A Precious Place

We know that the fells are ostensibly farmed country in a different guise, though our perceptions might well be of a grazing land for an army of sheep! For all the trauma that Foot & Mouth wrought in 2001, their number is still too great to sustain a properly balanced fell habitat, one that nature would ordain given half a chance. Many walkers will share with sheep a detest of bracken, wet or dry. The wild fire encroachment of this rank weed high up the fells, is due to the almost total loss the native woodland, to which it once was a natural open aspect understorey, forfeit to the excesses of sheep grazing. Hence the merits in the 'Flora of the Fells Project', launched in Spring 2003 to co-ordinate action in recreating some measure of bio-diversity to the mountain environment. This important project is being co-ordinated by the Friends' of the Lake District with English Nature, The National Trust and others.

For the casual visitor and fell-walking enthusiast perhaps no other organisation more surely represents their values and interests than the Friends' of the Lake District, for seventy years the ever-vigilant guardians of the whole Cumbrian landscape. My suggestion, affirm your affinity... join and lend them your much valued support - *website*: www.fld.org.uk.

Many readers will be delighted to learn of the recent formation of The Wainwright Society. Initiated through Kendal Museum where AW spent most Thursdays in his retirement, captioning and cataloguing in his inimitable meticulous hand. Contact the membership secretary via: membership@wainwright.org.uk. Alfred Wainwright represented the richly coloured tapestry of Lakeland in black and white, his guides were works of art, full of wit and clarity. He knew only too well that the landscape deserved the greater palette and expression wielded by the painter and photographer. Hence in making this series I have sought to marry a personal love of pen & ink, personally nurtured by AW, with a delight in colour photography. Yet for all the hues and tones my rainbow may bring, the master-class of his '*Pictorial Guides*' will endure as classics.

The Stonethwaite valley